Developing Active Adult Retirement Communities

PRINCIPAL AUTHOR
Diane R. Suchman

CONTRIBUTING AUTHORS
William E. Becker
Kathleen B. Cecilian
Wayne S. Hyatt
Gregg T. Logan
William R. Parks

 ULI

Urban Land Institute

About ULI—the Urban Land Institute

ULI—the Urban Land Institute is a nonprofit education and research institute that is supported and directed by its members. Its mission is to provide responsible leadership in the use of land in order to enhance the total environment.

ULI sponsors education programs and forums to encourage an open international exchange of ideas and sharing of experiences; initiates research that anticipates emerging land use trends and issues and proposes creative solutions based on that research; provides advisory services; and publishes a wide variety of materials to disseminate information on land use and development. Established in 1936, the Institute today has more than 16,000 members and associates from more than 60 countries representing the entire spectrum of the land use and development disciplines.

Richard M. Rosan

President

Recommended bibliographic listing:
Suchman, Diane R., et al. *Developing Active Adult Retirement Communities.* Washington, D.C.: ULI—the Urban Land Institute, 2001.

ULI Catalog Number: D102
International Standard Book Number: 0-87420-846-7
Library of Congress Catalog Card Number: 2001086561

Cover image: ©Susan LeVan/Artville

ULI Project Staff

Rachelle L. Levitt
Senior Vice President, Policy and Practice
Publisher

Gayle Berens
Vice President, Real Estate Development
Practice

Jo Allen Gause
Senior Director, Residential Development
Project Director

Richard Haughey
Director, Multifamily Development

Diane R. Suchman
Project Director and Principal Author

Nancy H. Stewart
Director, Book Program

Eileen Hughes
Managing Editor

Sandy Chizinsky
Manuscript Editor

Betsy VanBuskirk
Art Director

Anne Masters Design, Inc.
Book Design/Layout

Meg Batdorff
Cover Design

Diann Stanley-Austin
Director, Publishing Operations

About the Authors

Diane R. Suchman is an independent writer and consultant on real estate development, specializing in housing, community development, and revitalization strategies for low-income neighborhoods. She has served as special assistant to HUD's assistant secretary for policy development and research and was previously director of housing and community development research for the Urban Land Institute. She has also worked as a real estate market analyst. The author of five books and numerous chapters, articles, and case studies, Ms. Suchman has a master's degree in planning from the University of Virginia.

William E. Becker has been a national marketing consultant and marketing executive for builders of community developments for seniors for over three decades. He and his clients have received numerous awards for their marketing campaigns. Before forming his own company, he directed strategic market planning, strategy, and sales for Leisure Technology Corporation, a public company with active adult retirement communities throughout the United States. An active author and teacher, Mr. Becker served as a professor of marketing in the Graduate Studies Department at New York University's Real Estate Institute and is a coauthor of the Urban Land Institute's *Residential Development Handbook*. He has also served as president of the Institute of Residential Marketing of the National Association of Home Builders and is a member of the Urban Land Institute's Residential Development Council—Gold Flight. He has also served as president of the Institute of Residential Marketing.

Kathleen B. Cecilian is president and owner of KC & Associates, a full-service, personalized marketing and strategic planning firm that serves the real estate industry. She specializes in master-planned residential developments—in particular, sophisticated, amenity-rich communities—and in providing services to merchant builders. Previously, Ms. Cecilian was with the Leo Burnett company, one of the world's largest advertising agencies, where she gained valuable insight into how America's brand leaders persuade consumers to purchase their products. Ms. Cecilian is a full member of the Urban Land Institute and a member of its Residential Development Council—Gold Flight. She is also a frequent lecturer on marketing trends to industry organizations.

Wayne S. Hyatt is chairman of Hyatt & Stubblefield, PC, in Atlanta, Georgia. A member of the Georgia, New York, and Texas bars, he received his B.A. and J.D. degrees from Vanderbilt University. He has practiced exclusively in the field of community association law since 1973. The first president and a board member of his condominium association, he has worked with community associations and community developers in all 50 states and several foreign countries. He is a member of the American College of Real Estate Lawyers, the Anglo-American Real Property Institute, the American Law Institute, the Urban Land Institute, and the Community Associations Institute, where he served as president. Mr. Hyatt recently served as chair of the planning committee for the highly acclaimed Communities Tomorrow Summit sponsored by the Community Associations Institute. He has taught community association law at Emory University Law School since 1983 and has written three books and numerous articles on community associations.

Gregg T. Logan is managing director of Robert Charles Lesser & Company, an international real estate advisory services firm with offices in Atlanta, Georgia. Since joining the firm in 1979, Mr. Logan has translated market, demographic, and trend data into practical solutions for clients, providing market-driven development and strategic planning advice for proposed and existing real estate developments. His market and consumer research experience encompasses both public and private sector work, nationally and internationally. He is an expert on the impact of changing demographics on future real estate demand, especially with regard to various forms of community development that target the mature market. A graduate of the University of California at Los Angeles, he has taught real estate development methods to graduate students in the city planning program at the Georgia Institute of Technology. A prolific writer and frequent speaker to industry groups, Mr. Logan is a member of the Urban Land Institute's Community Development Council and chairs the Urban Land Institute's 700-member Atlanta District Council.

William R. Parks is president of PDC, Parks Development Consulting, Inc., in Scottsdale, Arizona. After a long and rewarding career as the director of architecture at Del Webb Corporation, Mr. Parks established his own consulting firm in 1997. PDC is located in Scottsdale, Arizona, and provides lifestyle programming and qualitative analysis and design consultation to builders and developers of active adult communities. As chairman of the Design Awards Committee, Mr. Parks is active in the National Council on Seniors' Housing of the National Association of Home Builders, and he is the author of the *National Directory of Lifestyle Communities*.

Contributors

Myril Axelrod, president, Marketing Directions Associates, New Fairfield, Connecticut

Ian Buckberry, ULI Australia representative, North Tamborine, Queensland, Australia

Richard J. Diedrich, executive vice president, Diedrich/NBA, a subsidiary of Niles Bolton Associates, Atlanta, Georgia

Sue Firestone, president/chief executive officer, Sue Firestone & Associates, Santa Barbara, California

Roger Galatas, president/chief executive officer, Roger Galatas Interests, LLC, The Woodlands, Texas

Ronald Garl, president, Ronald M. Garl Golf Course Design, Inc., Lakeland, Florida

Donald Jacobs, president, JBZ Architecture + Planning, Newport Beach, California

Oliver Jerschow, planning and real estate consultant, Toronto, Canada

Ehud Mouchly, chief executive officer, READI, LLC, and REProjectCapital.com

Mary Jo Peterson, president, Mary Jo Peterson, Inc., Design Consultants, Brookfield, Connecticut

Kenneth Plonski, director, public relations and customer communication, Del Webb Corporation, Phoenix, Arizona

William B. Renner Jr., associate principal, EDSA, Fort Lauderdale, Florida

Kenneth Rohde, principal, KTGY Group, Irvine, California

Barbara G. Rosenthal, president, Rosenthal Qualitative Research, Potomac, Maryland

Mary B. Schwartz, U.S. Census Bureau, Suitland, Maryland

Daniel C. Van Epp, president, The Howard Hughes Corporation, Las Vegas, Nevada

David S. Wolff, president, Real Estate Diagnostics, Inc., Toms River, New Jersey

Advisory Committee

William E. Becker
Managing Director/President
The William E. Becker Organization
Teaneck, New Jersey

Kathleen B. Cecilian
President
KC & Associates
Flemington, New Jersey

Lawrence Comegys
President, Florida Region
Pulte Homes Corporation
Tampa, Florida

Roger Galatas
President and Chief Executive Officer
Roger Galatas Interests, LLC
The Woodlands, Texas

Anne Mariucci
Senior Vice President
Del Webb Corporation
Scottsdale, Arizona

Leslie Marks
Executive Director
National Council on Seniors' Housing,
    National Association of Home Builders
Washington, D.C.

Acknowledgments

This book would not have been possible without the participation and assistance of many individuals. Most the obviously, the authors of the chapters and feature boxes generously shared their expertise. The advisory committee gave me valuable guidance and suggestions throughout the manuscript development process. The developers of the projects featured as case studies provided not only information about their communities but insight into the industry and its direction.

Among the many people who assisted the creation of this book, I am especially indebted to Myril Axelrod, William Bone, Art Danielian, Norman Dreyfuss, Bill Feinberg, Bill Frey, George Fulton, LeRoy Hanneman, Leon Harper, Steve Hullibarger, Chrissy Jackson, David Mayhood, Barbara McDonald, Kenneth Plonski, Bill Renner, Ed Robson, Michael Rubin, Robert Sharpe, Bill Slenker, Robert Snyder, Jo Anne Stubblefield, and Daniel C. Van Epp. Many others provided valuable comments that appear as quotations throughout the volume.

The ULI production staff—especially Nancy Stewart, Sandy Chizinsky, Diann Stanley-Austin, Betsy VanBuskirk, Eileen Hughes, and Anne Masters—did an outstanding job of transforming raw text into an attractive publication. I would also like to express my appreciation to Gayle Berens, Lloyd Bookout, Joan Campbell, Karen Danielsen, Rick Davis, Jo Allen Gause, Rick Haughey, David Mulvihill, Adrienne Schmitz, and Cynthia Suchman for their advice, help, and encouragement.

To those named above and to the others who have contributed to this book, thank you.

Diane R. Suchman

Preface

As the members of the baby boom generation—who have fueled consumer purchases of all sorts of goods at every stage of their life cycle—approach retirement age, residential real estate developers are becoming keenly interested in the potential surge of demand for active adult retirement communities (AARCs). As a result, participation in this sector of the development industry has begun to expand and to become more competitive, and is expected to continue to do so.

This book was developed in response to the heightened interest and activity: it provides an overview of the AARC development business, discusses the current state of the art, identifies the lessons learned from recent experience, and describes how the business is evolving. The information is geared to the interests and needs of real estate development professionals, homebuilders, public officials, members of the financial community, providers of development services, academics, and others who have a basic understanding of and interest in the real estate development process.

For the purposes of this book, AARCs are defined as developments that are restricted or targeted to people who are 55 years or older—or, as they say in the business, "55 and better." Typically, active adult communities attract people who are aged 55 to 74 (though age-targeted communities often sell to younger buyers); those 75 and older often need or prefer living arrangements that provide more supportive services.

Communities that are age-restricted must adhere to the requirements of the federal Fair Housing Act amendments, as described in chapter 6, and exclude children as permanent residents. Those that are age-targeted are intended, through their location, project concept, development components, design, and marketing, to attract approximately the same age group, but do not—and legally cannot—exclude anyone on the basis of age. Age-targeted developments often include preretirement and second-home buyers as well as people older than 55.

Chapter 1, which provides an overview of the AARC business, includes a discussion of the various types of active adult communities and developers and the issues associated with their development. Chapter 2 describes how to assess the AARC market—including demographic, economic, and psychographic considerations and how these would apply to a specific development opportunity. Chapter 3 explores the concept of "lifestyle," which is considered the key element that motivates the market. Chapters 4, 5, and 6 highlight the most important considerations in project planning and design, the all-important marketing tools and strategies, and the legal and regulatory framework that shapes AARC development practices. Chapter 7 presents ten case studies that offer examples of the range and variety of AARC development activity today. Together, the case studies represent different product types, locations, target markets, price ranges, and the work of different types of developers. The final chapter describes how the industry is evolving in response to consumer demand, increasing and sophisticated competition, new technology, and shifts in the larger economic environment.

The information in this book is based on the professional knowledge and experience of the various authors, supplemented by recent published information and interviews with AARC developers and other industry participants. Information in the case studies was derived from site visits, interviews with project developers, and printed materials provided by the developers. All site plans and floor plans should be considered preliminary and subject to change without notice. Though the authors believe that the material in this book is timely, true, and complete, no attempt has been made to verify independently the accuracy of the information provided.

Diane R. Suchman

Table of Contents

Developing
Active Adult
Retirement
Communities

1

Introduction and Overview

Diane R. Suchman

Lured by the promise of a burgeoning market, residential developers around the country are either entering or considering participating in the active adult retirement community (AARC) business. This chapter discusses the nature and history of the AARC developments being built in the United States today, gives a brief overview of how the AARC business differs from other types of real estate development, and highlights some of the key considerations involved in developing these kinds of communities.

The AARC market differs in many ways from the market for primary family homes, especially with respect to buyers' motivation and buying style, the needs and preferences of residents, and product design. AARC communities provide residents with a distinct, adult-oriented lifestyle choice rather than simply with a place to live. And, as a rule, the lifestyle choice is more important to the consumer than the home itself. In the case of smaller communities,

Dee Why Gardens, in New South Wales, Australia, is a leasehold active adult community of attached homes.

Del Webb Corporation's Sun City Palm Desert has created a spectacular oasis in the resort community of Palm Desert, California.

providing a sense of security is paramount. In addition, communities that are age-restricted (or, as some say, age-qualified) are subject to unique and ongoing regulatory requirements. Because AARCs are targeted or restricted to people who are aged 55 or older, the community amenities, programs, and services are geared to mature adults rather than to children (as would be the case in intergenerational communities).

Although AARCs typically consist of for-sale, single-family, ranch-style homes on small lots, along with common recreational facilities and a wide range of social programs, not all AARCs fit this profile. Homes may be two-family, multifamily, or townhomes; there may be two-story models or models with basements; the development may include low-rise, mid-rise, or high-rise condominiums. The purchase arrangements may involve land-lease or other alternatives to fee-simple ownership. The defining characteristics are the age market and the lifestyle offered.

HISTORY AND SCOPE

There are few statistics on the size of the AARC business, but the following brief description of the industry's history and key players, provided by Gregg Logan, senior vice president of Robert Charles Lesser & Company, of Atlanta, Georgia, provides some insights into how it has evolved. In the 1960s, the industry was in its infancy, there were few communities, and those being built were generally large by today's standards, ranging in size from 2,800 to 26,000 units, with an average size of about 8,000 units. (Though, as William E. Becker, managing director/president of The William E. Becker Organization, in Teaneck, New Jersey, points out, a number of companies, including US Home, Lennar, and Leisure Technology Corporation, were building communities with between 1,000 and 2,500 units at that time.) Some of these communities, such as The Villages of Lady Lakes, in central Florida, are still active in the market.

The number of new AARCs declined during the real estate "depression" of the early 1970s, but the few that did get built were quite large, with as many as 17,000 units. During the 1980s, as more companies entered the market, the number of AARC developments grew substantially. The average number of units was then 4,588, ranging from a low of 903 to a high of 26,000 (at On Top of the World, in Florida). Interest in AARCs reached new levels in the 1990s, when more than 50 communities were brought to market, mostly in the second half of the decade. Average community size declined to 2,363 units, and competition heated up as the number of developers in the market continued to increase.

Del Webb pioneered the AARC development business—and, as described in the feature box on the following page, has built more than 80,000 housing units in AARCs nationwide since opening the first Sun City in 1960. The company, known for conducting thorough research on all aspects of the market for its large-scale, all-inclusive, age-restricted developments and extensive amenity offerings, is widely considered the industry's brand leader: Del Webb sets the pace for others to follow—or at least to watch very carefully.

While Del Webb sells the most homes, US Home has developed the largest number of AARCs and ranks second in number of home sales. US Home's strategy has been to develop in many locations, with a comparatively low level of investment in each community and a low break-even point—50 sales per property per year. Del Webb's strategy, in contrast, has been to develop in a few major retirement destinations, with a very high level of investment and a high break-even point—about 250 sales per community per year. Other major players include Hovnanian, Lennar Homes, Pulte Homes Corporation, Robson Communities, and UDC. A number of firms—especially family-run operations—have each developed only a single large AARC.

The strongest market is in Florida, where 38 percent of all AARC units are located. Arizona is next, with 21 percent, followed by California, with 16 percent. Nevada has 8 percent and New Jersey 4 percent. Today, many developers feel that despite significant inventory in places where older people can move to retire, even more opportunity may exist in the many other places where mature adults live now, such as Atlanta, Chicago, Los Angeles, New York, and other major cities.

Today, fueled by an expected surge in the number of potential buyers as the baby boomers reach retirement, AARC development is expanding. As outlined briefly in the accompanying feature box and discussed in detail in chapter 2, the increase in demand is likely to be significant, and retirement-community developers are gearing up to create a presence and a reputation in markets across the country.

Types of AARCs

The term *active adult retirement community* encompasses various types of communities, all of which compete for the older homebuyer. These communities can generally be differentiated on the basis of size, target market, and location.

Demographic Trends

- The population of people age 55 to 69 will grow by more than six million between 2000 and 2005.

- 55.9 million Americans were 55 or older in 1997, and that number is expected to hit 74.7 million in 2010.

- The national annual market for new active adult retirement housing is now approximately 400,000 units, and demand is estimated to rise to 700,000 by 2002.

- 45 percent of baby boomers expect to move to another home in retirement, and 23 percent say they will move out of state.

- Most production of active adult retirement housing is anticipated in the $100,000 to $250,000 range.

Source: Del Webb Corporation, *Investor Fact Sheet,* fall 1999.

History of the Del Webb Corporation

When the Del Webb Corporation opened its flagship Sun City community on January 1, 1960, it drew 100,000 visitors on its first weekend and by the end of the year had sold 1,300 homes. At buildout, Sun City was home to 46,000 residents in 26,000 homes. Sun City's focus on delivering lifestyle to an age-qualified audience became a company hallmark and, in the decades that followed, created the industry model for this new market niche.

Since its creation in 1928, the company had established a reputation for developing profitable, high-quality, large-scale commercial and residential projects. It was the prime contractor on landmarks such as Madison Square Garden and the Los Angeles County Museum of Art. During World War II, the company won the contracts for a number of military housing projects, demonstrating its ability to create communities on previously barren land. Del Webb built the first casino/hotel in Las Vegas, Bugsy Siegel's famous Flamingo Hotel, which was followed by many other resort properties. In time, Del Webb became the largest gaming operator and private employer in Nevada.

In 1961, Del Webb went public on the New York Stock Exchange, trading as WBB. The company's involvement in other residential and commercial projects continued until 1987, when Del Webb decided to divest its gaming and commercial interests and focus primarily on the development of master-planned active adult communities nationwide. In 1998, Del Webb acquired two existing active adult communities in Florida, which operated under the name of Spruce Creek Communities. By January of 2000, the company had built 13 Sun City communities and sold more than 80,000 homes. The company's revenues had grown to $1.5 billion by fiscal year 1999: three-quarters of that was from its active adult developments.

Evolution of the Active Adult Community Concept

The Sun City concept has evolved with the changing preferences of customers age 55 and older. Continuously updating consumer information is at the core of Del Webb's success. The company has what may be the housing industry's strongest commitment to making research-based decisions in all aspects of its business, obtaining demographic and psychographic data from tens of thousands of current and future prospects every year.

In the 1960s, Sun City attracted residents with simple, relatively small, and modestly priced homes. The lifestyle was fairly simple as well, with recreational activities such as shuffleboard, lawn bowling, crafts, and golf (on shorter courses with basic designs). Buoyed by the success of its first community, Del Webb quickly opened Sun City communities in Florida and southern California, but because of the demands of the company's gaming and commercial operations at the time and the fairly remote locations of the two developments, the decision was made to sell both communities in the early 1970s. By the late 1980s, Del Webb divested its gaming and commercial operations and began marketing its unique brand of master planning outside the Phoenix area, developing communities in Tucson, California, and Nevada.

Using findings from Del Webb's research arm, company officials began increasing the size of the homes and offering additional recreational amenities and club activities. During the early 1990s, the company began offering large, luxurious recreation centers in its Sun City communities. These facilities included swimming pools, walking tracks, and the latest in exercise equipment. Golf courses continued to evolve as well, becoming more demanding while remaining "playable" for golfers of all skill levels. In the final decade of the 20th century, Del Webb became a truly national company, developing new Sun City communities in Illinois, South Carolina, and Texas.

Today's Sun City communities offer much larger homes, as well as customized landscaping and interior design. The lifestyle amenities have evolved as well; Del Webb's newest communities offer a "resort living" environment. In the 1960s and 1970s, the communities offered shorter, executive golf courses. Today, serious golfers are looking for higher-quality golf courses as a setting for their new home. While today's golfers are more serious about their game, other Sun City residents are more serious about their health and the activities they are involved in. Gone are shuffleboard and other, more sedate, activities—replaced by in-line skating, *t'ai chi* classes, weight training, swimming, and jogging.

Another stage in the evolution of the company—and the industry—is represented by the development of large active adult communities outside the Sunbelt. For many years, Del Webb and others in the business focused on providing a retirement lifestyle in warmer climates, a strategy that often required residents to relocate from other states. Ironically, as wealthier retirees became more and more mobile, the company that had attracted thousands of retirees to Sunbelt states discovered through its research that most people preferred to retire within easy driving distance of their longtime family homes. That discovery prompted Del Webb's first "four-season" community, Sun City at Huntley, northwest of Chicago. Its 1999 opening was so well received that Del Webb now plans to build more such communities in the Midwest and Northeast.

Current Organization and Operations

Del Webb's corporate headquarters remain in Phoenix, where major strategic decisions are made by its executive staff in conjunction with its board of directors. Each Del Webb community has its own general manager, who directs a strong staff that is given enough autonomy to be successful while still remaining accountable at the corporate level.

In addition to its research-based decision making, the company attributes its success to the following factors:

- The creation of a multidisciplinary team that has the ability to conceive, plan, entitle, finance, build, and market communities that are the size of small cities
- A focus on delivering exactly the lifestyle demanded by customers and on high-quality, competitively priced housing

- Sophisticated programs to manage every phase of customer and prospect communication
- A well-established and growing capacity to enjoy economies of scale in nationwide purchasing and contracting
- A balanced program of entitling and controlling land and homesites in advance of immediate needs, allowing for steady expansion nationwide.

As the 21st century begins, Del Webb sees tremendous opportunities for growth. Recent studies conducted by the company show that there are two million leading-edge baby boomers who say that they are likely to move to an active adult community. Using its four decades of experience in meeting the demands of its active adult customers, Del Webb will continue to grow and evolve to fulfill the boomers' expectations.

Source: Kenneth Plonski, director, public relations and customer communication, Del Webb Corporation.

Size. AARCs can be categorized as large (more than 1,500 units), moderate-sized (300 to 1,500 units), or small (fewer than 300 units). Large communities feature more diverse offerings in their site plans, amenity packages, and choice of housing products, and they attract buyers from a larger market area. Large AARCs can be broken down further into age-restricted and non-age-restricted developments. Both types are typically amenity-rich, and are often centered around golf.

Moderate-sized communities may be age-restricted or not, and typically offer a clubhouse but no golf course within the development. Larger communities within this category may include an 18-hole "bundled" (included) golf course and country club. Small age-restricted and age-targeted communities generally offer a close-to-home product with more limited home choices (but choices, nonetheless!) and fewer, appropriately sized amenities within the gates.

One of the key issues for larger projects is the difficulty of finding sites of workable size, price, and location. For smaller projects, the key issue is often how to satisfy the increasing demand for amenities, given the number of units across which costs can be spread.

Other types of products that compete for the market of 55- to 74-year-olds include age-targeted country-club communities, second-home and preretirement communities, and resort communities. Often such communities evolve over time into age-targeted AARCs.

Because of the many players, product types, projects, and locations, it is difficult to offer an accurate statistical description of the AARC business. William Parks, of PDC, Parks Development Consulting, in Scottsdale, Arizona, recently tried to obtain some descriptive data by surveying as many AARCs as he could identify through a variety of sources. The feature box on page 10 summarizes the responses to that survey.

Golfers practice their shots at the driving range at Indian Ridge Country Club, in Palm Desert, California.

Target Market. The potential market for AARCs is diverse and controls substantial wealth. Individual households within the target age group vary considerably: they may or may not have children, may or may not be retired, may be rich or poor, athletic or sedentary. Yet, "exasperating as they are to pin down, they are nonetheless a force that will rock the housing market."[1] From a developer's standpoint, it is useful to segment this age cohort according to certain characteristics, such as the propensity to move to an AARC, age, income, marital status, and "niche status."

AARCs appeal to empty-nesters and retirees whom Myril Axelrod, president of Marketing Directions Associates, Inc., in New Fairfield, Connecticut, describes as "living in homes that have become too large and too wasteful, too difficult to maintain, too lonely as their neighbors and friends leave and are replaced by younger, less compatible neighbors." However, only a small fraction of people over age 55 change homes in any given year, and only a fraction of those move out of state. Historically, only a small percentage of those in the potential market have moved to an AARC. "The main competition," explains Norman Dreyfuss, executive vice president of The IDI Group Companies, "is the family home." Whether historical patterns will hold in the future is an open question.

Within the target span, the age of prospective buyers is an important consideration because their life experiences, especially during the time when they "came of age," can determine their values and preferences later in life. These attitudinal differences (which are discussed in chapter 2) include, for example, the tendency to seek familiarity or new experiences and the tendency to be cost-conscious or to spend more freely on luxuries.

AARCs can be tailored to a range of price levels, from affordable to extremely luxurious, with amenities designed accordingly. Income and wealth—including equity in their current

Summary of Data from the *National Directory of Lifestyle Communities*

Since 1998, PDC, Parks Development Consulting, Inc., has collected and catalogued the names and locations of more than 600 active adult retirement communities throughout the United States. In September 1999, ProMatura Group LLC surveyed the communities on the list; the *National Directory of Lifestyle Communities* contains profiles of the 353 communities that returned completed surveys. For the purposes of the directory, a lifestyle community is defined as an active, for-sale housing development that is either age-qualified to younger senior citizens or is designed for and targeted to that age group through marketing and community amenities.

Industry Overview

General profile

1. Builders

Number of active builders	152
Percent with a single community	70%
Percent with multiple communities	22%
Percent with 5 or more communities	5%
Percent with 10 or more communities	3%

2. Primary types (by product)

Communities that sell site-built housing	52%
Communities that sell manufactured housing	47%
Communities that sell lots only	2%

3. Legal restrictions

Age-qualified (55 and over)	78%
Age-targeted	22%

4. Community sizes

Small (1–300 units)	38% of communities
Median size	181 units
Median land area	43 acres
Medium (301–1,500 units)	43% of communities
Median size	566 units
Median land area	282 acres
Large (1,501 and above)	19% of communities
Median size	2,999 units
Median land area	1,600 acres
All communities	
Median size	414 units
Community size range	23–9,750 units
Median land area	163 acres
Range of land area	4–20,000 acres

5. Aggregate number of units and average absorption

Total number of housing units planned	272,652
Total number of housing units built	151,821
Annual average absorption	71 units (per community)

Geographic distribution

1. By Sunbelt

Communities located in the Sunbelt	73%
Communities located outside the Sunbelt	27%

2. By U.S. Census Bureau subregions

New England	5.9%
Middle Atlantic	8.2%
South Atlantic	49.0%
East South Central	2.3%
West South Central	2.5%
East North Central	2.3%
West North Central	1.1%
Mountain	17.8%
Pacific	10.8%

3. By major states

Florida	32%
Arizona	12%
California	8%
South Carolina	6%
North Carolina	6%
New Jersey	6%
Connecticut	5%

Characteristics of communities within the Sunbelt

1. Size

Large communities	76.6%
Medium-sized communities	74.5%
Small communities	54.7%

2. Primary type

Site-built home communities	70.1%
Manufactured-home communities	75.6%

3. Legal restrictions

Age-targeted communities	81.6%
Age-restricted communities	70.8%

Benchmarking (Industry Practices)

Amenities

Clubhouse	88.7%
Outdoor swimming pool	87.0%
Fitness center	69.8%
Arts and crafts room	62.6%
Walking trails	62.6%
Tennis courts	55.3%
Recreational vehicle storage areas	50.0%
Shuffleboard	48.8%
Ballroom with stage	45.3%
Computer center	40.9%
Golf course	39.7%
Bocce court	38.2%
Restaurant	34.6%
Community gardens	29.8%
Indoor swimming pool	22.7%

Proximities

1. Small communities

Median time/distance to a hospital	5 miles (10 minutes)
Median distance to a university	8 miles

2. Medium-sized communities

Median time/distance to a hospital	5 miles (10 minutes)
Median distance to a university	12.9 miles

3. Large communities

Median time/distance to a hospital	7.5 miles (13.5 minutes)
Median distance to a university	12 miles

Homeowners' associations

1. Community security

Communities that have security gates	45.4%
Communities that have roving patrols	45%

2. Average monthly homeowners' association fees

Small communities	$113.34
Medium-sized communities	$141.26
Large communities	$152.04

3. Ownership

Streets

Private	79.5%

Golf course

Developer	47%
Homeowners' association	23%
Public facilities district	6%
Third party	24%

Facilities

Developer	67.6%
Homeowners' association	32%
Public facilities district	0.4%

Sales centers

1. Communities with an on-site sales center — 74%

2. Types of sales offices

Freestanding	50%
In a model home	32%
In a model-home garage	9%
In the community center	8%

3. Median number of models — 5 (average, 6.18)

4. Median number of floor plans — 10 (average, 18.7)

Popular products

1. Median size of most popular plans (sq. ft.)

Detached home	1,900
Attached home	1,690
Manufactured home	1,500
Condominium	1,408

2. Median price of most popular plans

Detached home	$175,075
Attached home	$175,250
Manufactured home	$74,900
Condominium	$140,000

Source: William R. Parks, PDC, Parks Development Consulting, Inc., Scottsdale, Arizona.

The information was derived from the *National Directory of Lifestyle Communities,* copyright 1999, PDC, Parks Development Consulting, Inc. No part of this feature box may be reproduced in any form or by any means without written permission of PDC, Parks Development Consulting, Inc.

home—determine how much different groups within the market have to spend on a new home. According to the National Association of Home Builders' recent analysis of the 1997 American Housing Survey, older Americans tend to have the wherewithal to participate in the AARC market: "Active adults on average combine the high incomes of younger households with the substantial wealth of older households. Moreover, active adults have the highest proportion of households with incomes over $150,000."[2] Luxury developments, such as Indian Ridge Country Club, in Palm Desert, California, are designed to appeal to the more affluent mature buyer. At the affordable end of the AARC spectrum, manufactured-home communities, such as Clover Commons, in Pittsburgh, provide a modestly priced option for active adults.

Certain AARCs are targeted to specific niche markets—for example, according to leisure-time interests, ethnic or racial background, or affinity group. A familiar example is an AARC developed specifically to appeal to golfers; others, now underway, are targeted to other niche markets—gay and lesbian retirees, deaf retirees, former members of the military, and former academics.

Location. The level of activity and maturity of the AARC industry varies across the country. In areas such as Florida, Arizona, and southern California, AARC developments have evolved over a 40-year period, attracting "snowbirds" and retirees from coastal cities and the upper Midwest. The accompanying feature box describes the historical development of such communities in Florida. Similarly, the Ocean County area of New Jersey has a well-developed AARC industry that draws retirees from the populous New York, New Jersey, and Philadelphia metropolitan areas.

Like other housing markets, regional AARC markets have their own characteristics and preferences. For example, in New Jersey, mature buyers have tended to be more conservative and to prefer more traditional, colonial homes with large lots. In California, however, small lots are more familiar and acceptable, and buyers prefer more informal, open floor plans.

As more and more people seek retirement options that are near their children and near their former homes, and that will allow them to maintain familiar ties, developers have begun building AARCs in nontraditional locations, especially near metropolitan areas. Market saturation (which leads to higher prices, higher taxes, crowding, traffic congestion, and a scarcity of sites) in some traditional retirement destinations has also fueled the search for new locations for developing AARCs.

What constitutes proximity to a metropolitan market is still being tested. For most developers, it means a location within a metropolitan area, but often in an outlying suburb where land can be assembled and entitled more easily and at more reasonable cost. However, AARCs have also been built on suburban and urban infill sites.

Evidence of the trend toward tapping metropolitan markets is offered by the recent forays of powerhouse developers—such as Del Webb, Pulte, and US Home—into these markets. To develop AARCs in metropolitan markets, US Home has entered into partnerships with well-

A Short History of Florida's Active Adult Communities

Much of the history of active adult retirement communities (AARCs) has been written in Florida. During the past 50 years, the state grew from 2.6 million people to over 15 million, and the cohort of those 60 and over is the largest in the country.

In Florida, AARCs have their roots in simple, large-scale land development. In the 1950s, companies like General Development created retirement communities such as Cape Coral, Lehigh Acres, and Port St. Lucie on enormous tracts of land. The land was subdivided into lots (110,000 in Cape Coral) and—through aggressive marketing techniques—was sold on an installment basis. Generally, the developer provided drainage and paved access to the lots, but utilities were added later. The "communities" did not have social programs, nor were they very successful financially. But today, they have become viable retirement destinations for a later generation of retirees.

Another major community developer, Coral Ridge Properties, began developing for the retirement market in 1963, with the opening of Coral Springs—a 13,000-acre, age-targeted community west of Fort Lauderdale. Coral Springs surprised its developers by attracting more families than older people. However, its developer, Watermark Communities, Inc., is now developing 24 large-scale communities, many of which are targeted to active adults, and all of which feature resort amenities such as golf, health clubs, marinas, and beach clubs. (Westinghouse Communities bought Coral Ridge in the 1970s, and Watermark Communities bought Westinghouse Communities in the mid-1990s.)

The wealthy have long been coming to Florida to vacation or "to winter." Palm Beach and Sarasota, and enclaves such as Mountain Lake Estate, in Lake Wales (which was designed by Frederick Law Olmsted Jr.), were developed in the 1920s. Building on the image, and often the location, of these affluent winter destinations, developments such as Lost Tree, Boca West, and Johns Island began in the 1970s to sell a country-club lifestyle to the preretirement and retirement market of the "Eisenhower generation." Now, many of these communities are looking for ways to revitalize their physical amenities and social programs to attract the next generation. A number of them, including PGA National, in Palm Beach Gardens, and Bonita Bay, in Bonita Springs, began in the mid-1990s to include continuing-care facilities within their gates in order to accommodate their older residents.

In the 1970s, age-restricted active adult communities blossomed in south Florida and elsewhere. The first Century Village was opened in Palm Beach County in 1973. Three others were built in Boca Raton, Deerfield Beach, and Pembroke Pines. Each of the three features about 8,000 mid-rise condominium units on approximately one square mile of land. Each of the central clubhouses contains more than 130,000 square feet and includes a theater that accommodates 1,800 people. Through their sheer numbers, retirees at the Century Villages have become a political force to be reckoned with in their communities. Variations on the Century Village concept, including Rossmoor Leisure Village, near Fort Lauderdale, also appeared in the early 1970s, with the added amenities of golf and "theme architecture."

Country-club living became available to less affluent segments of the market during the 1980s, with the development of affordable age-restricted communities that offered "bundled golf." These communities feature narrow, short, but playable "executive" golf courses. Small detached homes and multifamily units line the fairways; the clubhouses, though modest, serve as the center of social life. Such developments have been built primarily by homebuilders, such as US Home. In addition to their more upscale offerings, major innovative land and community developers, such as Bonita Bay Properties, have included bundled golf developments as subdivisions within their larger developments.

Affordability and broad market appeal have been the keys to success in markets such as western Palm Beach County, central Florida, and northern Florida, where builders such as Lennar Homes and Oriole Homes are building age-restricted communities with clubhouses and homes priced to attract middle-income residents. An even more affordable retirement housing alternative is manufactured housing. Seeking out infill sites, developers have created manufactured-home communities for retirees in prime locations. Especially in central Florida, these age-restricted active adult communities have shed their "trailer park" image and offer amenities such as golf, clubhouses, and activity programs. The largest include thousands of fee-simple manufactured homes within the gates of a planned community.

Today, diverse adult communities are flourishing in Florida. In the late 1990s, Del Webb entered the Florida market by acquiring two amenity-rich, age-restricted Spruce Creek communities. Avatar Retirement Communities, a longtime Florida community developer, is applying the concept of new urbanism to the age-restricted active adult community. At its Poinciana development, near Orlando, Avatar has "deconstructed" the traditional large clubhouse to create a town center consisting of numerous adjoining common facilities.

Both Collier Enterprises and Bonita Bay Properties feature communities that cater to wealthy active adults in southwest Florida. Collier's Reserve, which opened in 1991, and Bonita Bay, which opened in 1985, carefully fit golf, homesites, and trail systems and other recreational amenities into land that is laced with natural waterways and wetlands. These represent the developers' creative response to state and federal regulations, as well as to the market's strong preference for natural amenities.

Future trends point to more social activities; more recreation in the form of golf and health and fitness; and an emphasis on natural features in Florida's active adult communities. Actual town centers, as pioneered by DiVosta and Company, are being programmed into many large-scale communities, and developers are revising plans for existing communities to include more communal elements, such as health clubs.

Source: William B. Renner Jr., associate principal, EDSA, Fort Lauderdale, Florida.

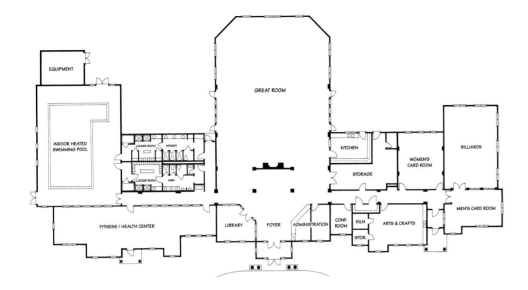

Among the offerings in the 17,000-square-foot clubhouse at The Fairways at Lake Ridge, a Kokes Family Community in Lakewood Township, Ocean County, New Jersey, is a large central great room for social and educational events.

regarded local builders who have already established the necessary contacts and organizational structure, subcontractor base, and market knowledge.

Because the pool of potential buyers is smaller and because the concept is still being tested, AARCs in nontraditional, four-season metropolitan markets tend to be smaller than those in retirement destinations, and the industry in these locations is often less mature. In some metropolitan areas, pent-up demand for AARCs has resulted in early successes—a pattern that may or may not continue as more developers enter these markets.

Regardless of whether they are drawn to a retirement destination in a different state, in an area within their state but outside their current city of residence, or in a nearby location, prospective purchasers usually decide on a location before "shopping" for a community. In other words, people self-select the location; the developer provides the product.

Within any given area, developers may choose to create AARCs as freestanding entities or within larger, master-planned communities. For those who choose the second option, there are different approaches, as described in the feature box on the following page.

Age-Restriction versus Age-Targeting

Developers interested in serving the active adult retirement market must decide whether to develop an AARC as an age-restricted or an age-targeted community. From a market standpoint, there are advantages and disadvantages to either choice, and a wise developer will include this issue in the market research.

Some older people—especially those over 65—want to be among people like themselves, who have the leisure to socialize and an interest in doing so; they also want to be where all the facilities and programs will be geared toward the interests of their age group and where they will not be bothered by the everyday annoyances children can create. Because the product is age-limited and more specifically definable, developers of age-restricted communities can deter-

The Woodlands and Summerlin:
Different Approaches to Age-Restricted Subdivisions

The large-scale master-planned communities of The Woodlands, near Houston, Texas, and Summerlin, in Las Vegas, Nevada, are similar in size and in their variety of housing products, amenities, and community facilities. Both include subdivisions of age-restricted active adult retirement housing. However, they differ markedly in when, how, and how much active adult housing was included, and their different experiences yield useful observations for developers of other master-planned communities.

The Woodlands, which opened in 1974, is located on a 26,000-acre, densely wooded site north of Houston. Developed by The Woodlands Corporation (TWC), originally a subsidiary of the Mitchell Energy & Development Corporation (which was purchased in 1977 by Crescent Real Estate Equities and Morgan-Stanley), it consists of seven residential villages, a mixed-use town center, commercial and institutional districts, an open-air performing arts pavilion, a regional mall, a hospital, a community college, a university center, and extensive open space (approximately 25 percent of the site). As of 1999, its population totaled 56,000. When the community is substantially built out in 2010, its population is expected to be approximately 150,000—including an on-site employment base of about 70,000 people.

Summerlin, located on 22,500 acres on the western edge of Las Vegas, is being developed by The Howard Hughes Corporation (since 1996, a subsidiary of the Rouse Company). The development was begun in 1988. As of the end of 1999, it had approximately 43,000 residents in approximately 17,000 homes. At completion in 2015, it is expected to include a total of 160,000 people in 60,000 homes. Summerlin will consist of approximately 30 residential villages, a mixed-use town center, three mixed-use village centers, four business parks, approximately 15 golf courses, six resort hotels, a library and performing arts center, parks and open space, public and private schools, churches, and various community facilities.

In 1988, early in the project's development, Summerlin's developer sold a 1,900-acre parcel of property to Del Webb Corporation—its first land sale. According to Daniel Van Epp, president of The Howard Hughes Corporation, in developing a large property, "you want to address every market segment." Del Webb's research had indicated that market demand for its Sun City product was strong in that location, and the land sale provided the Hughes company with an infusion of funds that made possible the early construction of Summerlin's community infrastructure and amenities.

Del Webb's predictions proved accurate; homes in Sun City Las Vegas sold quickly—even faster than anticipated. Over an 11-year period, through 1999, all 7,500 homes in Sun City Las Vegas were sold. Located on Summerlin's northern border and including an extensive range of amenities, facilities, and programs for the exclusive enjoyment of its own residents, the development is physically and socially separate from the rest of the community. Other than walking paths, there are no shared amenities or recreational facilities. As a result, the inclusion of Sun City Las Vegas in Summerlin had little effect on the planning and design of the larger community, except for the nature and sizing of retail shops and services.

The rapid pace of Sun City sales was both a blessing and a problem for the larger Summerlin community. On the one hand, it was evidence of early success; on the other hand, the community became identified with retiree housing. When the first family village opened in the early 1990s, a strong marketing program was needed to overcome the "age-restricted" image. In addition, according to Van Epp, when a large age-restricted component is included within a master-planned community, "you are also creating a political constituency that will oppose school bonds and other actions designed to benefit family villages."

As Sun City Las Vegas neared sellout, The Howard Hughes Corporation designated another parcel within Summerlin for an age-restricted community in order to continue to tap the strong, demonstrated market for age-restricted active adult housing in the area. Hughes sold a 735-acre property to Sunrise Colony Corporation, which plans to build a 2,000-unit, age-restricted development called Siena.

In The Woodlands, the approach to including housing for active adults was somewhat different. The developer first created an environment that attracted a mix of ages, but especially young families. Later, several means were used to attract grandparents and retirees: a number of features were included as the community grew that would appeal to older people—such as shopping, a hospital, and care-oriented facilities for seniors. In addition, the developer created two small neighborhoods of 70 age-restricted homes each, which share amenities with the larger community, and one larger age-restricted neighborhood of 450 units, which has its own separate recreational facilities. The larger neighborhood is adjacent to a community college that has developed special educational opportunities for seniors. The smaller age-restricted neighborhoods are located adjacent to other neighborhoods that are not age-restricted. The homeowners' associations are separate but compatible, and all contribute to the support of the community's major infrastructure.

According to Roger Galatas, president and chief executive officer of Roger Galatas Interests, LLC, and former chief executive officer of The Woodlands, providing a variety of opportunities to live within small, age-restricted environments serves the needs of older adults who "like to be near elementary schools and hear children play, but don't want tricycles in their driveways." At the same time, Galatas added, "We were able to integrate this very productive age group into the life of the larger community."

Galatas noted that largely because of the interaction between older and younger people within The Woodlands (including the fact that many extended families of grandparents, children, and grandchildren all live in the community), seniors generally support the community fees—which benefit everyone—and the school bond issues, which benefit the children of The

Woodlands. In fact, the importance of education has proved to be a unifying force among all age groups. And, according to Galatas, The Woodlands' flexible approach to building neighborhoods for both families and seniors has added substantially to the annual volume of new home sales and to the quality of life in the community.

In both Summerlin and The Woodlands, not all older people have chosen to live within age-restricted developments. Both communities estimate that approximately 15 percent of the residents of non-age-restricted developments are either retirees or older working people who are looking for a place to live now and when they retire.

Source: Conversations with Roger Galatas, president and chief executive officer, Roger Galatas Interests, LLC, The Woodlands, Texas; and Daniel C. Van Epp, president, The Howard Hughes Corporation, Las Vegas, Nevada.

mine more precisely who makes up their market and can focus their energies on serving that group. "Age-restriction," explains Michael Rubin, president of Avatar Retirement Communities, "is a rifle shot; age-targeting is more of a shotgun approach."

A larger group of prospective buyers will likely balk at the idea of age-restriction, either because they prefer to live among a more diverse group of residents or because they—or a younger spouse—think of retirement communities as "places for old people" and do not want to designate themselves as members of that category. If a community is not age-restricted, the developer can market and sell to a larger pool of buyers; however, it cannot then legally prohibit children and teenagers from residing in the community.

According to Margaret Wylde, president and chief executive officer of ProMatura Group LLC, in Oxford, Mississippi, the preference for age-restriction declines with increasing income. The results of a recent telephone survey indicate that among older people whose incomes are less than $20,000, 9.3 percent would prefer an age-restricted community; among those with incomes above $50,000, only 5.9 percent would.

The community's location may also affect the choice between age-restriction and age-targeting. Age-restricted communities within otherwise intergenerational master-planned communities can offer certain facilities for their residents' exclusive use, but within an environment of greater age diversity, perhaps including children and grandchildren. In resorts or vacation areas where second homes are popular, age-targeting allows the developer to attract somewhat younger buyers who may later decide to live in the home full-time after retirement. On the other hand, in traditional retirement destinations, where large, all-inclusive, age-restricted communities tend to be more the norm, there is demonstrable market acceptance of that choice. Age-restricted communities located near metropolitan areas that have many intergenerational neighborhoods can offer mature consumers yet another option.

If they opt for age-restriction, developers must be aware that meeting the requirements of the federal Fair Housing Act amendments will impose additional administrative burdens on the sale and operation of the community. (These requirements are detailed in chapter 6.) The choice between age-restriction and age-targeting may also be influenced by the attitudes, requirements, and regulatory environment of the governing jurisdiction.

THE AARC BUSINESS

Developers now in the AARC business range from giants like Del Webb, whose active adult communities represent about three-fourths of its total housing units; to divisions of large homebuilding companies like Pulte Homes Corporation; to large or small private independent developers; to developers of manufactured-home communities. And, according to David Mayhood, president of The Mayhood Company, in McLean, Virginia, in some locations developers of traditional housing products, such as garden apartments, are being led into the business by their increasingly older customers.

The public and private entities that develop these products are affected by the same kinds of changes that are influencing other segments of the industry—mergers and acquisitions, initial public offerings, and the need to create company and product identities, or "brands." As with other kinds of real estate development companies, "going public" involves certain tradeoffs: access to capital versus the need to satisfy investors' short-term demands. And, because an AARC developer is also the builder, firms tend to be more vertically and horizontally integrated than is typical of other kinds of homebuilders or community developers.

Tasteful and comfortable furnishings invite visitors to enjoy Christmas in the clubhouse at Heritage in the Hills, an active adult retirement community developed by US Home Corporation in the Detroit suburbs.

Robson Communities

From a developer's standpoint, the AARC business differs from the development of inter-generational communities in important ways and poses its own set of challenges, including financing and risk, economic impacts on local economies, government regulations and relationships, and market and marketing considerations, which are discussed in the sections that follow. Other issues peculiar to this business, according to Ed Robson, president of Robson Communities, Inc., in Sun Lakes, Arizona, are the growing competitive environment, the need to keep the product current in the face of a changing market, getting people to the product, the challenge of creating an exciting product on a small lot, and building the right product, since "you can't build what you like: you have to build what the customer wants."

Financing and Risk

Developers interviewed for this book agreed that the front-end costs associated with development are the greatest barrier to entry into the AARC business. Substantial amenities—enough for buyers to see and taste the lifestyle that's being offered—must be in place when the first user comes in. Because of the huge initial expense—which, depending on the size and luxuriousness of the community, could run as high as $150 million—developing AARCs involves higher risks. The major risks would be those associated with an economic downturn or an increase in interest rates.

However, financing issues depend somewhat on project size; as Rubin points out, "at the 1,00–1,500-unit level, financing isn't really a problem. At 5,000 units, the numbers become intimidating." Another consideration is whether or not the community includes a golf course. Jim Migliore, president of US Home's Special Projects Division, indicates that the economics of golf is one reason that his firm is interested in doing smaller AARC developments. "The equity investment in a large golf course development is many millions of dollars. With a small prototype, you can go in with a lower investment and a lower risk."

Whether a company is public or private also affects risk tolerance (and the expectation of returns). Robson points out that "as a private company, we can wait four to five years for returns; with public companies, it's a different imperative." Public companies must also comply with the regulations of the Securities and Exchange Commission and publish quarterly documents. "But it allows us to raise capital in the public sector when others may not be able to," adds LeRoy Hanneman Jr., president and chief executive officer of Del Webb Corporation. "We can plan better and be more flexible."

An established company can sometimes fund the upfront costs internally, through the sale of other assets, or with a line of credit secured by company assets. However, a startup developer will probably need an equity partner, because, according to Ehud Mouchly, chief executive officer of READI, LLC, and REProjectCapital.com, in Santa Monica, California, "traditional lenders will not take this kind of risk—unless the developer has an established track record and a good relationship with the bank."

Robson Communities' SaddleBrooke development is located just outside of Tucson, a traditional retirement destination that offers dramatic scenery and superb winter weather.

Because of the huge upfront costs that are typical in developing AARCs, carrying costs can be prohibitive. As Rober Eck, vice president for land development at Sun City at Huntley, notes, "There's a tension between wanting more time for project planning and the desire to minimize the time and risk exposure between the initial investment and the generation of revenue."

In addition to coping with higher hard costs, AARC developers must spend more on the community's "software." For example, during the development period, the developer must not only create the homeowners' association but cover the costs of a facilities director and social director, special events, and startup recreational activities and programs. In contrast, social programming for an intergenerational development requires less direct involvement—as well as less expense—on the developer's part.

The major risks in AARC development include oversupply, fluctuations in interest rates, and an economic downturn (which could make retirees' current homes difficult to sell). Market risk, fueled by continuously evolving consumer tastes and preferences, is another concern, especially in large, multiphase developments or in new locations where the nuances of the market have not yet been tested. What the coming baby boom market will want is an open question. "Developers are introducing communities into untested areas, adding layers of new services, and retooling home designs and features, all in the hope that they can find the perfect mixture before the leading edge of the 76 million Boomers reaches retirement age."[3] Nonetheless, because it serves a market of people who often own their homes and have prepared financially for their retirement, the AARC business is somewhat less susceptible to market fluctuations than the development of intergenerational communities.

In an intergenerational community, developers and builders need to set aside funds to provide mortgage money to sell homes if money becomes tight. In AARCs, a large percentage of buyers pay cash, so this is less of an issue. However, in order to pay cash for a new home, older buyers first have to sell their old homes, and they may have trouble doing so when the market is slow. So the developer must offer contingent sales or second mortgages.

Economic Impacts of AARCs

Especially when compared with other types of residential developments, AARCs provide local governments with economic benefits. According to the National Association of Home Builders (NAHB), under conservative assumptions, the one-year benefits of 100 single-family AARC homes in a typical city—not including ongoing participation in the local economy—include more than $10 million in local income, approximately $850,000 in local taxes, and 253 local jobs.[4] At the same time, active adults impose less of a burden on most public services than do residents of other types of developments. In addition to financial benefits, an influx of active adult residents brings human resources to the receiving community in the form of experienced, interested, and active citizens and volunteer workers.

Financing Active Adult Retirement Communities

Because of their size and upfront infrastructure requirements, large active adult retirement communities (AARCs) typically require a tremendous capital commitment over an extended period of time, often bridging more than a single business cycle. As an investment, an AARC is analogous to a "zero coupon junk bond," demonstrating little economic performance and financial return until late in the investment cycle. The long-term investment in an AARC should command extraordinary returns when compared with other investment opportunities that typically offer more consistent returns over a shorter period. However, as a rule, new large-scale AARCs will be challenging undertakings because, in addition to the front-end capital requirements, investors face significant regulatory risks and uncertainties.

Capital and Returns

Capital Markets and Land Investment

Increasing cost of infrastructure exactions and community demands (for example, for lower densities) tend to take away more of the traditional land profit, to the detriment of the investor/owner. The resulting lower and less predictable profits make AARCs less attractive to long-term capital. In addition, as developers bring AARCs into the market in the next several decades, they will be faced with several paradoxes:

1. Capital markets will be broader but there will be fewer sources of financing. Sources of capital for real estate have become numerous and diverse, and include a potpourri of sources including securitized instruments such as Commercial Mortgage-Backed Securities (CMBs), bank and non-bank debt, investment and merchant banks, opportunity funds, and others from increasingly varied domestic and offshore sources. However, AARCs lack important features needed to make them attractive to capital markets: clear return expectations, acceptable risk profiles, and predictable time horizons—dimensions that enable third party investors to evaluate the offering and monitor and trade the assets. As a result, the AARC developer is becoming a non-entity in the capital markets.

There is no consistent source of AARC financing. The size of the overall AARC market is not large enough to command widespread attention; the nature of the AARC business is not well understood; and, AARCs usually attract investors (and satisfy lenders) only when there is excess capital and few other opportunities. Each AARC is usually a "one-off" project that is a non-replicable, one-of-a-kind community that is individually financed, and there are few opportunities to spread risk by accessing secondary markets.

Traditional financing sources are no longer available. Publicly traded corporations, especially transportation and resource companies, have withdrawn to core businesses. Gone, too, are local financial institutions, such as savings and loans. Only major landowners remain and, if starting "raw" without a history of cash flow and market performance, the financing problems are formidable.

There are currently few sources of money for the independent acquisition of land and its subsequent improvement without a significant infusion of private, non-traditional "at-risk" equity. A few of the publicly held builders (e.g., Del Webb, Pulte, US Home, and others) have partially solved the problem by issuing unsecured corporate debt. As evidenced by the low multiples and the depressed prices of these companies' stock, Wall Street still does not understand the business of home building, much less AARC development. Thus even these organizations have been seeking ways of unburdening their balance sheets from corporate and secured project debt by structuring deals through private placements and other techniques of "off-balance-sheet" financing.

2. AARCs will face increasing levels of risk but offer lower rates of return. Investors expect to be compensated for perceived risk. Historically, the achieved rates of return on successful AARCs have ranged from negative to 20–25% in some unique cases. Some investors would assert that the returns have been inadequate to compensate for the perceived risks.

Traditionally, the risks have been those confined to the business plan environment, and were based on uncertainties of costs, revenues, and the absorption rate of land parcels—factors that could be measured, if not mitigated, by the skill and experience of the developer. Increasingly, however, the developer must face four new factors: Increasing upfront investment requirements, expanding expectations of risk-adjusted returns, AARCs' increased vulnerability to changes in the business cycle, and growing dimensions of entitlement risk.

3. Land is expensive but worth little. The derivation of "land residuals" from discounted cash flows has become the dominant way to determine land value. Compared to the "comparable sales" approach, this method makes possible easier quantification of future revenue streams and development costs, though it can result in a wider margin of error.

In recent past business cycles, the concept of "negative residual land values" emerged. Negative land values can occur at points in time during a project's development when estimates of future revenue streams would not justify its replacement cost. Because AARCs are long-term, front-loaded developments, their land could be valued highly at one point in the cycle but "negatively valued" at another point. This short-term view of a long-term asset will obviously affect the ability of the AARC to survive business cycles and secure financing for ongoing operations.

4. AARCs demand a lengthy commitment but capital will be impatient. The long life spans of AARCs are their major vulnerability. Largely as a result of the regulatory process, the time required from concept to final development has increased dramatically and will likely continue to increase. At the same time, capital has become more impatient. As financial markets become more efficient, investment and lending funds seek out incremental higher returns and move rapidly from one asset class to another. There will be a higher degree of separation between the

investment motivation and the AARC objectives. The AARC developer will have "hot money" partners willing to "jump ship" at the earliest opportunities for alternative, short-term returns.

AARCs and the New Economic Realities

Although windfalls from AARC development are still possible, there is little likelihood that a globally-restructured economy will embrace an investment that is so contrarian, unique, and obtuse as compared to other opportunities. To attract money, AARC developers or their financial intermediaries must package financing, describe and quantify risk in standardized terms, and anticipate policy, social, and technological changes that will affect their business.

Develop New Ways to Package Financing

Opportunities to craft local, custom ventures with landowners remain a desirable source of capital but will be limited. Thus, only rarely can an AARC be financed "from cradle to grave" by a single source. Instead, it will need to be broken into financing pieces and phases that conform to the demands and appetite of the capital market players. A succession of financing packages could be required, matched to perceived risks and anticipated investment horizons. These stand-alone financing "traunches" could be keyed to development phases, such as acquisition, predevelopment and entitlement, land development, etc.; and to development phases that represent an investment cycle of three to six years. In this context it is reasonable that AARC developers have been trying to develop ever smaller AARCs, down to 500–600 units from the 4,000–5,000-unit communities. Once the process becomes institutionalized, portfolio managers, rather than local sources or partners, could more easily invest in AARCs and trade the underlying paper.

Develop New Ways to Quantify Risk

The most difficult step will be to reach consensus on "universal" measures of risk. There are not enough AARCs in the market at any one time to obtain the benefits of risk management through portfolio diversification. Financing for a single "one-off" project demands more specificity and less generalization in an underwriting effort, and will not benefit from the product standardization that is critical for secondary or securitized financing.

The nature of the risks involved cannot be generalized easily. Different aspects of the process, such as entitlement or sales, involve very different kinds and levels of risk. And among projects, local circumstances make risk comparisons difficult. Some of the potential risks that can prove catastrophic to an AARC include environmental issues, political uncertainty, and changes in economic or market conditions.

Develop Common Ways to Describe Risk

If risk cannot be quantified easily, at least it can be described. The common elements of the entitlement process can be communicated and understood. For example, developers can adopt common terminology to describe the entitlement process, they can document both the direct and indirect likely costs associated with obtaining entitlements, and they can create a system for analyzing the project's financial performance that is specific to land development and for-sale housing, as contrasted with income-producing property.

Anticipate Policy, Social, and Technological Changes

AARCs of the early 21st century will address smaller market segments. Real growth of personal income, changing demographics, the increasing number of age-qualified retirees and empty-nesters, greater regulatory risks, and changing technology will require the AARC developer to change the product to meet the market and to alter the process through which that product is brought to market. The crux of the issue is "who will pay the costs of residential growth?" Unless another solution is found, the politically expedient alternative will be to force more of the cost burden back to the AARC, thus further reducing the residual land value and making the financing of AARC developments an even greater challenge.

Source: Ehud G. Mouchly, chief executive officer, READI, LLC, and REProjectCapital.com, development and financing companies based in Santa Monica, California. This feature box was adapted from "The Business of Master-Planned Communities," in *Trends and Innovations in Master-Planned Communities* (Washington, D.C.: ULI–The Urban Land Institute, 1998).

Most important, because they do not add children to the school system, active adults do not impose the single greatest tax burden typically created by new residential development. Even for developments that are age-targeted rather than age-restricted, the difference in the number of school-age children (and thus the costs of educating them) and the number of school-age children in "all households" is dramatic.

In addition, older people drive less, especially during peak traffic times, creating less of a burden on local roads and less traffic congestion. In 1997, for example, the Institute of Transportation Engineers estimated that during the evening rush hour, 100 single-family homes generated 101 trips, whereas when the households were restricted to those aged 55 to 74, the same number of single-family homes generated 23 trips.[5] NAHB reports that older adults also use somewhat less water, sewer, and trash removal service than the members of an average household (as reflected in their monthly costs for those services).[6]

As part of their efforts to seek public approvals for AARCs, many developers provide analyses that outline the expected effect of the proposed project on the local economy. A Del Webb study, reported in a press release, estimated that its Sun City Grand development in Surprise,

Arizona (in the Phoenix area), would have a total regional economic impact of almost $5 billion over its 13 years of development, while imposing less demand on municipal services than a typical master-planned community (except for emergency medical services):

Del Webb Corporation's Learning Center at Sun City Hilton Head, in South Carolina, includes several classrooms that can be adapted to community residents' interests.

Demand category	Level of demand (as a percentage of the demand generated by a typical master-planned community of similar size)
Traffic volume	33
Street maintenance	35
Water consumption	60
Wastewater generation	74
Solid waste generation	67
Police protection	25
Fire protection services (nonmedical)	33
Emergency medical services	110

The feature box on page 28 summarizes information prepared by Robson Communities for its PebbleCreek community.

Government Regulations and Relationships

Because of the economic benefits that senior residents bring to a community, the American Association of Retirement Communities was formed in 1994 to promote the attraction of retirees as an economic development strategy. In addition, at least eight states have initiated programs to encourage older people to relocate within their borders. Mississippi, for example, through its Hometown Mississippi Retirement program (which the state refers to as "the most aggressive retiree attraction program in the nation"), certifies "retirement cities" within the state and then markets them to "active, amenity-seeking, out-of-state persons aged 50–65."[7] As part of its strategy, the state has also instituted an income-tax exemption on qualified retirement income. Finally, it offers to assist AARC developers with everything from permitting to financing.

At the local level, some jurisdictions that are familiar with the economic benefits of retirement communities have incorporated designations for AARCs into their zoning ordinances and have zoned land to encourage this type of development. However, Bill Slenker, president of Slenker Land Corporation, of Burke, Virginia, cautioned that very few jurisdictions have a zoning classification for age-restricted AARCs. His firm has written new zoning text amendments tailored to enable the production of specific AARC developments, but found this approach laborious and time-consuming. "Each jurisdiction is very cognizant of the litigious environment and is slow to grant approvals for zoning changes, because they are concerned about the reaction of neighboring citizens."

Developers proposing an AARC development should expect opposition from the surrounding community. Some people will object to *any* development on a previously vacant site. Others will be concerned about massing, scale, or density. A wise developer will approach elected officials and neighborhood organizations early, so that their objections can be addressed during the planning process. Often it is possible to "sell" the neighbors on the idea of the community and to enlist their support, particularly if the developer is prepared to respond to community concerns and to provide something—such as a nature preserve or a small park—that the community wants. If properly informed and encouraged, organizations such as the American Association of Retired Persons or the area agency on aging may endorse the development and may even be willing to testify in favor of it at public hearings.

Over time, large-scale AARCs affect the balance of political power in the host community. Older people tend to vote in greater numbers than younger citizens and to take a keen interest in local politics. Although some communities fear that older citizens will not support bonds and taxes that benefit schoolchildren, the record on this issue is mixed. In some places, residents of AARCs have indeed voted down school bonds or seceded from school districts rather than pay school property taxes. In other places, seniors are strong supporters of local schools, serve on school boards, and volunteer in the local school system. A key factor appears to be whether or not a relationship between the schools and the senior citizens is developed early in the life of the AARC.

Market and Marketing Considerations

Perhaps the most striking difference between AARC developments and intergenerational communities, and the one that drives the other differentiating characteristics, is the age—and there-

PebbleCreek's Economic Impacts and Contributions to the Local Economy

PebbleCreek is a 6,500-unit AARC being developed by Robson Communities outside of Phoenix, Arizona.

Economic Impact (1997)

	Direct impact +	Induced impact =	Total economic impact
	550 jobs	2,100 jobs	2,650 jobs
Earnings (in millions, 1994 $)	$16	$50	$66
Expenditures (in millions, 1994 $)	$91	$83	$174

Construction activities and the operation of the PebbleCreek community provide direct contributions to the metro Phoenix economy of 550 jobs with a payroll of more than $16 million. Annual expenditures from construction activities, PebbleCreek operations, and PebbleCreek households results in $94 million in purchases of goods and services from local business firms.

The primary impacts induce additional activity that spreads throughout the local economy. This re-spending of the original injection of dollars creates secondary effects that will produce an additional 2,100 jobs, $50 million in earnings, and $83 million in spending in the other sectors of the Phoenix economy.

The combined effects of primary and secondary impacts associated with the PebbleCreek community create 2,650 jobs, earnings of $66 million, and $174 million in expenditures in the Phoenix area.

Tax Revenue Contributions

Tax revenues from primary activities (in millions, 1997 $)

	1997	2010	2020
State income tax	$8.2	$31.8	$48.2
Sales tax	$2.8	$8.7	$60.2
Total	$11.0	$40.5	$60.2

Projected Annual Expenditures (in millions, 1997 $)

Year	Jobs	Earnings	Expenditures
1997	2,650	$66	$174
2020	11,000	$273	$813

At buildout (by approximately 2020), ongoing service and maintenance activities and consumer spending by more than 11,000 residents of the PebbleCreek community will provide 11,000 jobs for local workers, with annual earnings of $273 million (1997$), and will generate annual expenditures totaling $813 million.

Source: Prepared for Robson Communities by the Center for Business Research, L. William Seidman Research Institute, College of Business, Arizona State University, Tempe, Arizona, July 1998.

Note: Except where noted, amounts are in 1994 dollars.

fore the nature—of the market. By definition, the people who buy in AARCs are older—55 and over. (Developers interviewed for this book reported that the average age of buyers in their communities was somewhere between 59 and 65, and getting younger all the time.) Most are financially secure married couples who buy a home in an AARC because they want a different lifestyle, not because they want to own a home or because they need a place to live. It is a purely discretionary decision: there is no real requirement or urgency to purchase, and mature consumers can—and do—take their time deciding whether and where to buy. The discretionary aspect of the motivation to purchase means that developers are not filling a need: instead, they must create a desire for the lifestyle that they offer.

It is a truism in this business that mature buyers do not purchase promises: the lifestyle being offered must be in place at the time of sale. Thus, AARC developers must create and present the community's amenities up front. And to target those amenities effectively, developers must do the necessary research to understand the current preferences of the specific market segments they hope to reach.

The village center at Solivita, the first amenity-rich active adult retirement community built by Avatar Retirement Communities, is located within Avatar's Poinciana development in central Florida. The center contains more than 100,000 square feet of recreational facilities, including a spa and fitness center, a golf clubhouse, arts and crafts areas, meeting spaces, and a full-service restaurant. Future expansion plans call for a 1,000-seat professional theater.

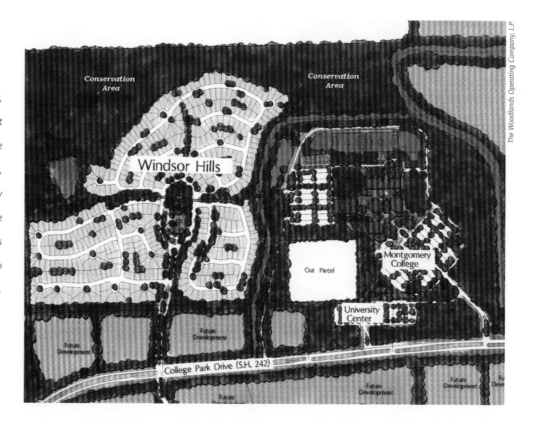

The site plan at right is of Windsor Hills, a 458-home active adult community that is located in The Woodlands, a 26,000-acre master-planned community north of Houston, Texas. The site is adjacent to Montgomery College and The University Center, where the Academy for Lifelong Learning provides continuing education programs geared to active adults.

At the same time, the members of the mature market are more sophisticated and demanding than their younger counterparts. In Hanneman's words, "These are black-belt consumers." They have bought homes in the past, often several; they know what they want; and they have the time, expertise, and inclination to thoroughly investigate their options before making the purchase decision. They take their time and ask a lot of questions. Moreover, the market includes not only prospective buyers but often also their adult children, who tend to accompany them on visits to AARCs and advise them on purchase decisions.

Because the purchase is discretionary and the prospect is informed and deliberate, the home sale process is an exercise in relationship-building, and, as Larry Comegys, president of the Florida region of Pulte Homes Corporation, advises, "developers must ensure that their companies are staffed with people who can interact well with these buyers." A hard-sell approach is not merely ineffective with this market: it is counterproductive. From initial visit to purchase can take from six months to two years; involve many visits; and require lots of time, information, and patience from the sales team. Experienced developers report that, typically, the conversion ratio (the number of actual sales that result) for every 100 qualified first-time visitors will be in the single digits.

On the positive side, people over 55 often own their own homes free and clear, and thus have the means to finance a move and to purchase a new home, often for cash. For many, this is the time of their lives to enjoy what they have earned. Increasingly, they want luxury, choice, and new experiences, and they are quality-sensitive. For the developer, the expectations of the mature buyer offer an opportunity to gain additional profits through the sale of upgrades and options.

Del Webb Corporation

A massive stone fireplace warms conversation areas inside Prairie Lodge, the clubhouse at Sun City at Huntley, just outside of Chicago.

After the homes have been sold, the customer-service orientation required to serve this market continues. As Dave Schreiner, Del Webb's senior vice president and general manager of Sun City at Huntley, explains, "People underestimate how hard it is. We get ten times as many calls from customers as do other builders; it's exponentially more difficult."

1. Susan Bady, "Coming of Age," *Professional Builder,* May 1999, p. 50.

2. National Association of Home Builders, "Executive Summary," in *Profile of the Active Adult Housing Market: Analysis of the US Census Bureau's 1997 American Housing Survey* (Washington, D.C.: National Association of Home Builders, n.d.).

3. D. J. Burrough, "The New Golden Years," *Urban Land,* March 2000, p. 51.

4. National Association of Home Builders/National Council on Seniors' Housing, *Winning Strategies for Approval: Impact on Schools* (brochure).

5. Institute of Transportation Engineers, *Trip Generation,* 6th ed. (Washington, D.C.: 1997).

6. National Association of Home Builders/National Council on Seniors Housing, *Winning Strategies for Approval: Impact on Water and Sewage Usage* (brochure). The figures were based on tabulations from the 1995 American Housing Survey.

7. Quotations in this paragraph are from marketing materials put out by Hometown Mississippi Retirement.

Gauging the Market for Active Adult Communities

Gregg T. Logan, Senior Vice President, Robert Charles Lesser & Company, Atlanta, Georgia

Developers of retirement communities are eagerly anticipating the expected dramatic increase in the number of older people in the United States during the next 30 years. The baby boom generation has dominated consumer demand for all products at every stage of its life cycle so far, and will soon affect market demand for active adult retirement communities (AARCs). This chapter will describe the size and nature of the active adult market, discuss the various segments within that market, and suggest how developers can determine and analyze likely demand for a specific project.

Anglers can while away the afternoons on the fishing pier at Sun City Hilton Head.

THE EISENHOWER GENERATION AND THE BABY BOOMERS

From 1990 to 2000, the U.S. population aged 60 years and over increased by about 3.5 million. However, during the next ten years, the total increase in persons aged 60 and over will be over ten million—almost three times that of the past decade.[1] Looking further ahead,

With its primarily single-story living area, front porch, garage, and small lot, the Hidcote model offered at Village Greenes, an active adult community in Ocean County, New Jersey, developed by Kevin Scarborough Homes, exemplifies a type of home that is popular with many active adults.

the increases in the mature population will be even more dramatic. By the year 2030, persons aged 65 and over will number about 70 million, almost double the number in 1987.

Among active adults, two large age cohorts, which can be grouped according to life experience, make up the market for current and future leisure-oriented retirement communities: the Eisenhower generation and the baby boom generation. People in the Eisenhower generation—those born between the Depression and World War II—are now aged 55 to 70 and make up most of the current market for active adult retirement communities. The baby boomers are the 76 million Americans born between 1946 and 1964. Though some of the older baby boomers are beginning to buy homes in age-targeted active adult communities (especially in preretirement resort developments), they are not yet a significant force in this market.

The Eisenhower Generation

The members of the Eisenhower generation (or "Ikes") represent about 14 percent of the U.S. population, or about 38 million persons (the group is about half the size of the baby boom generation).[2] Ikes are the most affluent retirement-age generation in history, with average annual spending levels that are higher than those of any other age group. In fact, their financial outlook for retirement is much stronger than that of baby boomers, in part because more Ikes than boomers have actively saved for retirement.

According to the Census Bureau, the majority of the members of the Eisenhower generation (79 percent) are homeowners. Some may "move down" to a smaller home more suited to

The luxurious homes at Sun City Grand, in Phoenix, Arizona, appeal to affluent active adults from all over the world.

FIGURE 2-1

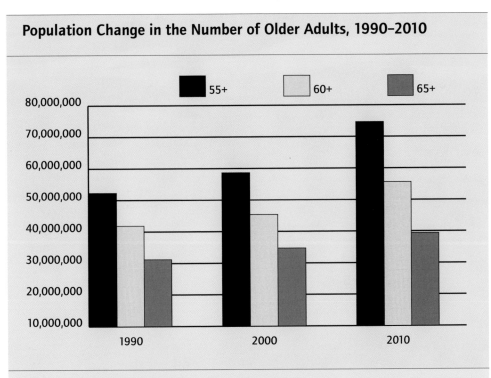

Population Change in the Number of Older Adults, 1990–2010

| | 55+ | 60+ | 65+ |

Source: U.S. Bureau of the Census, *Current Population Reports*, P25-1130, "Population Projections by Age, Sex, Race, and Hispanic Origin," February 1996; and PPL-21, "U.S. Population Estimates, by Age, Sex, Race, and Hispanic Origin: 1990 to 1994," March 1995.

this stage of their lives, while others may buy a second (or seasonal) home, add on to, or remodel their current home. Two factors place Ikes in a strong position to buy homes: first, they owned their homes during periods of high appreciation in housing values; second, they earned pensions during one of the most stable periods for corporate America.

The members of the Eisenhower generation have gone through (or soon will) a number of major life changes—becoming grandparents, leaving a corporate work environment and perhaps starting a home business, moving into a smaller or lower-maintenance home, and so on. In most

cases the kids have left home, and the parents have an opportunity to spend more on themselves, for housing as well as for other items. The more affluent members of this group spend freely on travel and on new cars and homes, while also planning for retirement. If they move at all, they need a good reason, since this may be their last housing purchase. Their housing criteria have changed over the years, and the last home that they purchase must meet specific requirements.

The Baby Boomers

The oldest of the baby boomers have now reached age 54. Beginning in 2006, when the first of the boomers turn 60—the age at which many will be candidates for purchasing in an active adult

The Bonita Bay community, in Bonita Springs, Florida, which won a ULI Award for Excellence, includes a handsome golf clubhouse with a "Florida lodge" theme. The clubhouse is adjacent to the Tom Fazio Golf Course.

community—there will be rapid growth in the number of households headed by persons 60 and over. (The median age of retirement in the United States today is about 63 years.) By 2020, the majority of the baby boomers will be aged 55 to 74. By 2020, the population aged 65 to 74 will have grown 74 percent, while the population under age 65 will have increased only 24 percent.[3]

Since the boomers represent about one-third of the U.S. population, the impact of their aging is going to be felt by a wide range of consumer products, including housing and community development. A key market for new housing for decades, boomers are responsible for the explosion in demand for primary housing in the 1980s. The coming "age wave" of baby boomers entering their senior years is expected to create unprecedented opportunities for community developments that target their needs. As the leading edge of the baby boom generation nears retirement, developers of retirement communities are beginning to assess the impending impact on the demand for their products.

Though the full effect will not be apparent for several more years, aging baby boomers will begin to have a tremendous effect on the demand for AARCs after 2006. At present, the boomers are more concerned with raising their children, succeeding in their careers, earning money, and staying physically fit (the baby boomers entered their most economically productive years in the 1990s). When they reach their early 60s, in 2006, traditionally the prime age for AARC homebuyers, will they behave similarly to the generation that preceded them, or will generational differences moderate their impact on the demand for AARCs?

The members of each generation have unique motivations, desires, and preferences that will affect the kind of retirement lifestyle they seek. Thus, the simple fact that the baby boomers are aging does not guarantee that they will behave in the same way as previous generations. Even boomers' current views on how and where they would like to spend their retirement are not necessarily a reliable indication, as their attitudes are likely to change as they reach retirement age. That demand for retirement housing will increase is a given; but because the types of housing and communities that will appeal to boomers may not be the same as those that appealed to previous generations, the trick will be to identify desirable characteristics for those communities that have yet to be developed.

There are indications that the boomers will remain in the workforce longer than their parents did—because of better health and a sense of "staying younger" longer, as well as out of sheer financial need. Many have simply not saved enough—or, because they had children late in life, will be paying for college tuition when they would ideally be saving for retirement. Thus, basic economics may postpone retirement for some baby boomers. Nevertheless, despite delayed retirement for some, boomers' sheer numbers will dramatically affect the demand for AARCs.

Meanwhile, many boomers will continue to be attracted to developments—such as suburban country-club communities—that offer them the opportunity to enjoy an active adult lifestyle while remaining in their traditional family home. In addition, many second-home communities that are now weekend getaways will evolve into retirement residences as the population ages, providing an attractive alternative for both younger and older segments of the market. Such communities will compete with AARCs for boomer buyers.

MARKET RESEARCH

To evaluate specific development opportunities in light of both the current market and the expected dramatic increases in the older population, builders and developers of AARCs undertake market and consumer research. While developers have historically used market studies as support for financing, the most successful among them also rely on market and consumer research to

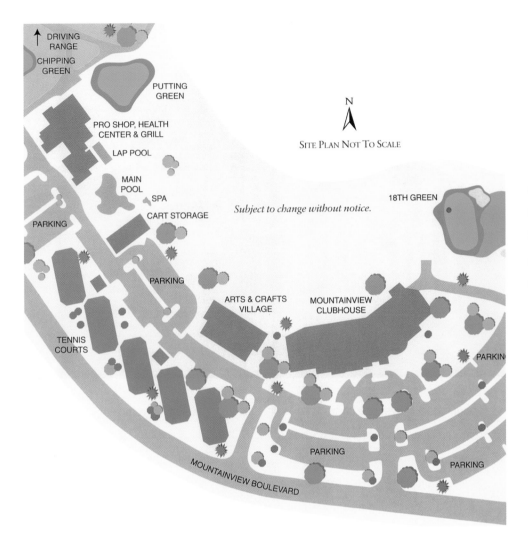

Labels in image:
DRIVING RANGE
CHIPPING GREEN
PUTTING GREEN
PRO SHOP, HEALTH CENTER & GRILL
LAP POOL
MAIN POOL
SPA
CART STORAGE
PARKING
PARKING
ARTS & CRAFTS VILLAGE
MOUNTAINVIEW CLUBHOUSE
18TH GREEN
PARKING
TENNIS COURTS
PARKING
PARKING
MOUNTAINVIEW BOULEVARD

N
SITE PLAN NOT TO SCALE
Subject to change without notice.

At Robson Communities' SaddleBrooke development, outside Tucson, the MountainView Country Club includes an arts and crafts village and a golf and fitness center in addition to the main clubhouse.

inform the creation of the master plan, the selection and design of amenities, product program-ming, and the development of a marketing strategy. In addition, ongoing market and consumer research throughout the life of a project enables developers to keep abreast of changes and main-tain the community's competitive position in the marketplace. Even developers and builders who have a somewhat standardized approach to community and product design find that there are enough differences among geographic markets to warrant market studies at each location.

Market Evaluation: Objectives and Components

The specific objectives of any given market study will vary depending on the needs of the devel-opment team. Typically, the objectives will include

- Achieving a better understanding of the consumer so that the project can be tailored to the target market
- Forecasting the potential depth of the market, both for active adult housing in general and at the subject property specifically

Sales of this popular model at Mirage at Holiday City Barnegat active adult community, in Barnegat Township, Ocean County, New Jersey, developed by Menk Corporation of H. Hovnanian Industries, demonstrates that homes with second-story guest areas do appeal to a segment of the active adult market. At right and on the facing page, the exterior and interior of the model.

- Gauging the interest of a particular market audience in a variety of community and product characteristics, including age-restriction

- Determining what development standards should be required and which products and amenities should be offered to position the community competitively in the marketplace

- Establishing or refining the information that will guide the community's master planning and marketing and sales strategies.

With those objectives in mind, key ingredients of a thorough market evaluation will likely include the following components. (The evaluation assumes that the developer has a site and wants to test a project concept for that site.)

- A definition of the community's specific target market and its needs

- An evaluation of the suitability of the subject site for the proposed use

- The identification of demand-related market characteristics, such as demographic factors (population by age, income, number of households, etc.)

- An assessment of the size and nature of the existing and planned supply of AARCs (obtained via competitive market analysis)

- An overall evaluation of supply and demand, including an assessment of specific types of housing products in price ranges that are appropriate to the identified market audience

- A determination of the appropriate competitive positioning strategy

- An analysis of all the information to create development program recommendations.

The Market Audience

Developers of communities that target retirees and empty-nesters need to understand who their buyers are, what makes them unique, what they want, and what motivates them to purchase housing in an active adult community. The most successful AARC developments are market-driven, and developers use market and consumer research to ensure that is the case.

In general, such research confirms that retiree buyers are purchasing a lifestyle rather than simply buying shelter. They want to satisfy lifestyle needs that cannot be met in their current living situation, and they are seeking quality and value, as they—not the builder or developer—define it. In terms of product, research indicates that most prefer detached housing, although duplexes, condominiums, and other configurations also sell well under certain circumstances. In particular, small-lot, villa, and detached patio homes have been popular in many communities, especially with buyers who want a maintenance-free, move-down lifestyle at a slightly lower density than is characteristic of attached housing developments. Finally, research indicates that active adults want to live in a community that suits their unique interests, which may include golf, exercise walking, gardening, entertaining guests at home, arts and crafts, attending the theater, photography, or other pursuits.

If there is a common theme to discussions about the retiree homebuyer market, it is this: the market is composed of not one, but multiple market segments. Developers cannot assume that the market is monolithic and that they can succeed by offering one development program.

The various market segments each have specific characteristics, and, through market and consumer research, the segments can be targeted for each new community development project.

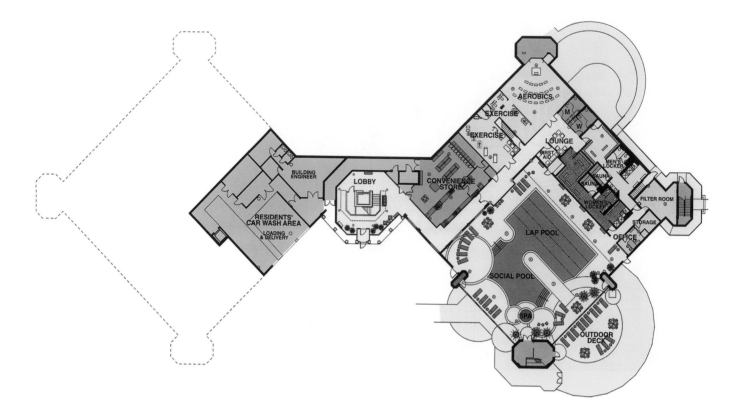

Market success does not require that all facilities be in place when a project opens. The IDI Group Companies is phasing development of its luxurious Clubhouse West at Leisure World of Virginia. Phase I of the clubhouse, which includes an indoor pool, fitness areas, meeting and hobby rooms, and a library, bank, and convenience store, has been completed and is buzzing with activity. As community development progresses, the second phase of the clubhouse will be built. A second, future clubhouse is also planned. Above and on the facing page, the first and second floors of the clubhouse.

So, for example, the market audience for retiree developments built in the 1990s was composed largely of financially secure, mobile households who wanted to enjoy this unique period of their lives in a highly social, recreation- and leisure-oriented community setting.

To understand the market for a particular project, it is essential to realize that different age cohorts within the active adult market are likely to have different needs and preferences. So, for example, though the active adult market is generally considered to encompass those aged 55 to 74, outlooks and needs vary among those aged 55 to 59, 60 to 64, 65 to 69, and 70 to 74. In addition, developers of active adult communities, particularly those that are age-targeted rather than age-restricted and those that will require many years to build out, will need to consider the needs and preferences of prospective buyers—those in the 50 to 54 and perhaps 45 to 49 age cohorts—as well.

Along with membership in an age cohort, geographic location is another consideration: generally speaking, buyers' preferences vary by region. This is especially important in light of the fact that among retiree homebuyers in the 1990s, those that relocated across state lines represented an affluent minority.

CONSUMER RESEARCH

Too many developers have become enamored of a project solely on the basis of demographic studies that indicated a large number of age-qualified households in the vicinity. While that may be a good start, it may not be enough to demonstrate that the market is sufficiently large to

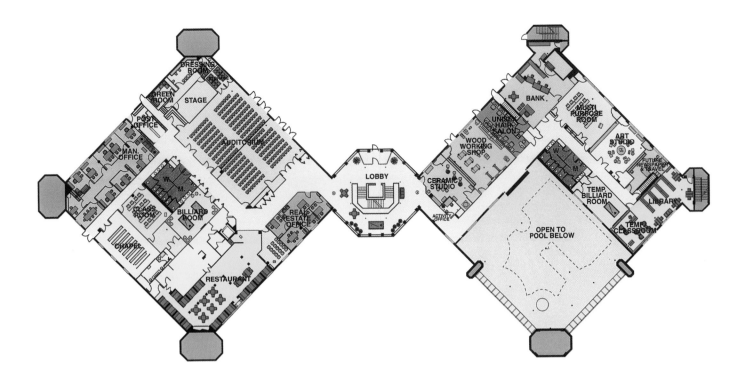

ensure the viability of a project. Just because people are of a certain age and income level is no guarantee of future behavior.

Consumer research is a useful tool for gaining a more accurate forecast of the depth of the market for a particular AARC project, as well as for understanding the preferences of the local or regional market audience with respect to type of community, housing products, and amenities. Consumer research involves developing a survey instrument for the specific market area, implementing the survey, analyzing the results, and using them to prepare product, pricing, and amenity recommendations. Techniques used to conduct consumer research include, in addition to the collection of statistical information, attitudinal surveys, focus groups, and one-on-one interviews. Analyzing the results of statistical surveys may include cross-tabulations of the data to provide a more in-depth understanding of the potential consumers. Information from local and regional demographic studies, consumer research findings, and competitive market data can be used to prepare forecasts of demand for residential products, by type and by price range, at a particular subject property.

Although consumer research often relies on statistical information, surveys that segment the market merely on the basis of such measures as age and income are missing opportunities to better understand what really motivates people. The most sophisticated surveys also delve into consumers' psychographics, or attitudinal profiles. There are distinct attitudinal segments within the over-50 market, some of which are more open to the idea of active adult community living than others. For example, the 60 percent of households age 55 and over who are still married represent a stronger market for AARCs than the overall market—a piece of information that must be factored

Homes at Rancho Resort, a manufactured-home community for active adults being developed within the master-planned community of Rancho Sahuarita, just south of Tucson, resemble conventional homes. The stucco exteriors and concrete tile roofs are compatible with southwestern architectural styles and are virtually maintenance free.

into the demand equation. Developers who simply qualify the market by age and income while attempting to forecast market depth are likely to overstate the opportunity. Indeed, attitudinal surveys indicate that large segments of the potential market audience have, at present, no interest in living in a retirement community—yet another factor that must be considered when forecasting future sales for a particular development. Focus groups, which are among the techniques described in the first feature box in this chapter, are particularly useful for exploring qualitative factors. Unlike quantitative surveys, focus groups do not produce statistically valid results; they do, however, provide important information that can be further tested in a quantitative study.

The major players in the AARC industry, such as Del Webb Corporation and US Home, conduct ongoing research to better understand emerging trends as well as extensive consumer research for each new development project. In 1997, Del Webb Corporation surveyed boomers who had recently turned 50 on a wide range of attitudes and interests.[4] The results included two significant findings that could substantially affect the assessment of future demand for AARC housing. First, 18 percent of respondents said that they would consider moving to another state to purchase a retirement home (less than 10 percent of current retiree households move to another state); whether they will follow through on those intentions remains to be seen, but their doing so could increase the demand for retirement community development, particularly in warm-weather destinations. Second, only 8 percent of respondents said that they would prefer to live in an age-restricted active adult community, compared with about 14 percent of current retirees.

Will boomer households be twice as likely to move out of state but only half as likely to buy in an age-restricted community? If the planned project will be age-restricted, then understanding the proportion of the local market that will prefer an age-restricted environment is critical to forecasting demand. With respect to age-restriction, studies by Robert Charles Lesser & Company have found some variability from one market to the next. In addition, responses seem to be influenced by how the question is asked and by the life-stage of the respondent. Boomers' stated lower propensity to choose an age-restricted AARC could be merely a function of their

Tools for Qualitative Research

Real estate professionals use market research to tap the pulse of consumers and professionals and learn their opinions about products, services, issues, and concepts. When people think of market research, they typically remember the telephone call they received at dinnertime that asked their opinion about a proposed new development in the neighborhood. Such surveys or polls are quantitative consumer research. Quantitative research measures the volume of response to specific questions, for example, what proportion of people prefer fourplexes or townhouses. This type of research is valuable because it can produce numerical data on preferences and product appeal based on a large number of responses. But while the quantitative research can tell us how many senior citizens prefer to buy rather than rent a retirement home, it cannot explain why or under what circumstances golf memberships should be "bundled" into the sales price of a home in an AARC.

Qualitative research can provide that explanation. Considered by some to be "soft" because results cannot be tabulated, measured, or projected, the qualitative method explores the nature and nuances of underlying attitudes, opinions, beliefs, and values. This knowledge can provide direction or generate ideas in:

- Creating new products, services, designs, or plans;
- Changing existing products, services, designs, or plans;
- Identifying and exploring attitudes about national, regional, or local issues;
- Testing specific marketing and advertising strategies, concepts, materials, and packaging; and
- Understanding reasons for consumers' unexplained behavior.

A qualitative study can be undertaken *before* a quantitative study to identify key issues to be measured and ensure that the survey's terminology will be properly understood. It can be used *after* a quantitative study to explore and better understand the findings of a survey. Qualitative research takes the form of in-depth one-on-one interviews and focus groups.

A focus group is a directed discussion among a small group of participants, usually eight to 12, who were selected to participate because they have common characteristics of interest to the focus group's sponsor. For example, the developer of a retirement community might wish to hear the opinions of a group of married females who are between the ages of 50 and 60 with household incomes over $40,000 who reside within a specific geographic area. A professional moderator focuses the discussion on the desired topics and encourages respondents' participation and interaction. For a given project the sponsor typically commissions a number of focus groups involving different categories of respondents. At the conclusion of the series of focus groups, the sponsor is given a written report analyzing the findings of the study.

Typical objectives for a focus group might include:

- Identifying and ordering what is appealing or unappealing about a particular community;

- Understanding what would motivate homeowners to move from their present residences to a nearby community;

- Exploring respondents' attitudes toward specific aspects of the product or different designs;

- Understanding the image a development community projects;

- Understanding competitors' images;

- Ascertaining the components of "curb appeal";

- Asking for comments on floor plans, community designs, elevations, or amenities;

- Testing respondents' reaction to certain key marketing terms or materials;

- Understanding the lifestyle, attitudes, and preferences of the target market.

Focus groups are an expedient and cost-effective tool of qualitative research. In addition to helping the sponsor understand the target market's values and attitudes, focus groups often uncover unexpected issues. For example, the developer of a retirement community might not have considered including transportation services until a focus group of senior citizens identifies it as an important need. Another benefit of focus groups is that the turnaround time is convenient for the client; usually a study can be completed within six to eight weeks from recruiting respondents to the final report.

Respondents' erroneous observations or faulty judgments revealed in the findings are still valid—and especially valuable. Such responses provide insights about inappropriate perceptions and may identify a need for clarification or consumers' education. Because of the nature of the qualitative research and its small sample size, findings from the qualitative study are not meant to be generalized or projected. By exploring attitudes, insights, and opinions, however, focus groups can provide real estate professionals a greater understanding of potential consumers' needs and behaviors.

Source: Excerpted from Barbara G. Rosenthal, president, Rosenthal Qualitative Research, Potomac, Maryland, "Focus Groups: A Tool for Qualitative Research," in *Residential Development Handbook,* 2nd ed. (Washington, D.C.: ULI–The Urban Land Institute, 1990), 29–31.

current stage of life, and their attitudes may change as they grow older; or it may reflect a genuine desire for more diverse living circumstances. It is difficult to tell how people will actually behave when their circumstances change, and even boomers themselves may be unable to predict accurately what they will want five to ten years from now. It is just as likely that when boomers retire, they will behave like the members of previous generations. Clearly, boomers' preferences will need to be monitored carefully as they age.

MARKET ANALYSES FOR SPECIFIC DEVELOPMENTS

The four sections that follow cover the principal areas of concern for the market analyses under-taken for a specific development: market area determination, site evaluation, competitive positioning, and forecasting future sales absorption.

Market Area Determination

The primary market area, or PMA, is the geographic area or areas from which the majority of buyers will be drawn. Sometimes it is important to consider additional, secondary market areas (SMAs), from which additional buyers may emanate—for example, in a situation where most of the market is local or regional, but additional sales may result from in-migration. The PMA and SMA may also be distinguished from the competitive market area (CMA), which is defined as the area within which similar real estate developments may compete for available consumer demand on a more or less equal basis. With AARCs, competition is broader than for most other kinds of developments, and may in fact include properties in other parts of the country. For example, AARCs in the CMA of southwest Florida may compete for buyers from the PMA of the midwest-ern United States and the SMA of the northeastern United States.

Unfortunately, there are no hard-and-fast rules that can be used to define these distinctive areas: the definition of market areas remains, to a large extent, a matter of educated judgment, based, in part, on good research. For example, to define the PMA for a development, the analyst must look at the target market in the site's immediate sphere of influence (meaning the geographic range suggested by his or her professional experience), in-migration, tourism, and other data that indicate where people in that market area are coming from. Interviews to determine where buyers in existing communities came from are also helpful. Asking all potential competitors which projects they consider their competition, and plotting the responses on a map, also helps define the most rel-evant CMA. As a rule, larger projects with greater marketing budgets have larger PMAs and CMAs.

Site Evaluation

Understanding the suitability of a specific property for an AARC development in relation to two factors—other potential sites and regional competition—is an important starting point for any market assessment. In fact, if the site does not pass muster in this phase of the evaluation, there is no point in going further. A sample site evaluation schedule is shown in figure 2-2.

The characteristics in a site evaluation schedule typically relate to the proposed develop-ment and to its location. For example, a retiree household living in Atlanta, Georgia, may decide to stay in the immediate area; move to a second-home community just outside the metro area, in a lake or mountain setting; or move to a Del Webb retirement community near Hilton Head, South Carolina. So a developer with a proposed new community targeting Atlanta-area retiree households must evaluate the relative desirability of each of these options and contrast them with the proposed project. Understanding the relative appeal of each of the options from the consumer's perspective will help the developer to plan and execute the project competitively.

Obviously, location is one of the first considerations. Affluent retirees who relocate tend to purchase properties in "warm and wet" climates, other areas with temperate climates, and college towns. For those who relocate, the fastest-growing areas are in the South and West, where 76 percent of the total increase in older residents took place over the past ten years. College towns are popular, including those outside the South and West, particularly those that have cultural activities and facilities that appeal to older people.[5] Nonetheless, the majority of retirees do not move out of their home state.

Another consideration is the depth of the potential demand within the proposed project's PMA in comparison with that of other reasonably accessible areas that offer the consumer simi-

FIGURE 2-2

Sample Site Evaluation

Locational factor	Target	Subject site rating	Subject site assessment
Access to significant employment cores	Drive time of less than 1 hour from metropolitan area	4	Good: travel time less than 1 hour
Access to major highways or other transportation routes	Direct access (less than 5 minutes' drive time)	3	Fair: estimated 15 minutes to interstate
Drive time to major airport	Less than 60 minutes' drive time	4	Good, and airport proximity is a plus
Quality of surrounding land and natural resources	Above-average scenery (mountains, water)	5	Exceptionally attractive site with several lakes
Climate	Region lends itself to four-season activity	4	Good: golf and boating opportunity year-round
Presence of historic charm or local character	Regional flavor manifest in built environment	2	Limited
Tourist destination	Local features that draw in significant population	2	Some regional draw to nearby recreational lake
Presence of social and cultural outlets	Above-average regional arts, music, etc.	1	Poor: limited in this quadrant
Proximity to shopping facilities	Regional malls, outlets, high-end local retail facilities	2	Fair: convenience retail is a significant need
Proximity to medical facilities	Important—facilities should be better than local-serving facilities	1	Poor: limited in this quadrant
Proximity to colleges and universities	Local institution with outreach	1	Poor: limited in this quadrant
Tax conditions	Property and sales taxes favorable	4	Good: property taxes relatively low
		2.75	Average

Source: Robert Charles Lesser & Co.

lar alternatives. In other words, how deep is the pool of prospective buyers, and how much access would the project have to that pool? Proximity and access to the major concentrations of prospective buyers are critical. For example, a project targeting Atlanta-area consumers that is located close to existing concentrations of retiree-age households may have an advantage over a community at Hilton Head hoping to attract the same potential buyers. A number of factors can affect depth of demand: for example, does the area around competing developments have a history of in-migration of retiree-age households? Similarly, being in a market area with substantial tourist activity would be positive, since repeat visitors may be a source of buyers.

An inviting clubhouse, such as this one in The Fairways at Lake Ridge, a Kokes Family Community in Tom's River, New Jersey, can serve as the focal point for enjoying an active adult community's lifestyle.

It is also critical to examine the marketing effort at each competitive community. For example, a developer who knows that the regional competition is spending $3,500 to $4,500 on marketing per sale can use that information to prepare budgets for a new development as well as to forecast the portion of available market demand that the proposed community is likely to capture. Such information is especially valuable if the developer had not anticipated a similar level of marketing expenditures.

A project with regional competitors will also need to examine such issues as the relative cost of living in one jurisdiction versus another, including the potential effect of state and local taxes. Other, more site-specific variables include local crime rates and the proximity of medical facilities, major highways, a major airport, and retail and cultural facilities.

The site evaluation methodology summarized in figure 2-2 considers factors that, on the basis of experience, are most indicative of a site's future success as an AARC. The criteria will vary depending on a variety of factors, including whether the community is located in a retirement destination, such as Florida, or in a "home market" within a metro area that targets consumers who live there now. The analysis may include a specific score for each criterion and may assign weights to certain criteria according to their relative importance; the combined value of all scores is the development's "opportunity quotient." Factors or criteria to be scored would likely include accessibility, visibility, surrounding land uses, proximity to source markets, availability of shopping and other services, college or university presence, climate, taxes, planned road improvements, and area crime rates.

To establish baselines against which to measure the subject property, the analyst needs to score a panel of local or regional AARC developments as well. In preparing such case study evaluations, the analyst, to the degree possible, assesses the conditions of the competitive properties at the time that the developments were initiated, not when they are in a more mature phase. Next, alternative sites under consideration by the developer, as well as the competitors' planned future developments, must be similarly evaluated and compared to the subject property. The score that is assigned to a property being considered for development as an AARC only makes sense in relation to the scores for alternative or competitive developments. A low score in relation to either existing developments or the sites of competitors' future projects may indicate that a particular property is not suitable. Conversely, a high score may indicate an opportunity for premium pricing relative to selected competitors.

Competitive Positioning

Because a new AARC will likely compete for the available market audience with other local or regional developments, it is important to evaluate a specific site and location in terms of location-related variables. In addition, to determine the share of the market that can be captured by a particular project, the analyst must evaluate various characteristics of both the proposed development and competing projects. This information can also be used to create the master plan for the development and to determine the price position of the community in relation to that of other communities in the local area or region.

The analyst must compare the development to the competition in terms of housing product, pricing, and natural and man-made amenities. Each of these factors must be evaluated in relation to the project budget and the desires of the consumer market. Understanding the quality and features of the competitors' products is important for two reasons: first, to be aware of the minimum standards in the marketplace, and second, to devise possible ways to make the competition obsolete. Knowing what is important to the consumer is critical because it enables the developer to make adjustments to community programming, design, amenities, and other items

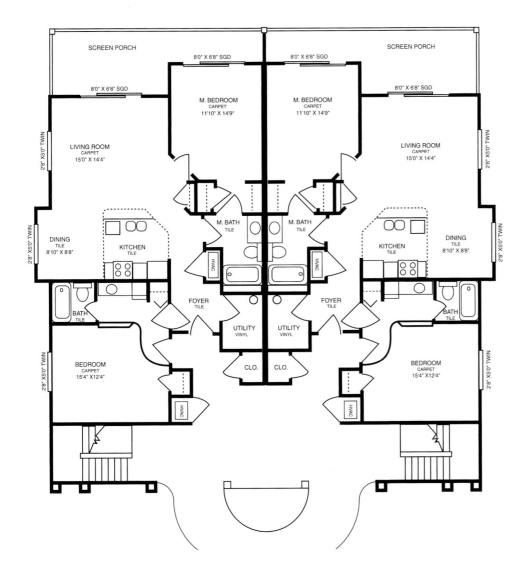

Two-family homes, such as the Club Villas at St. James Plantation, in Southport, North Carolina, are also a popular choice in active adult retirement communities.

that are not being adequately addressed by existing options. The importance of understanding the consumer underscores the crucial role of both market and consumer research.

Evaluating the proposed amenities in relation to local and regional competition is important both for project planning and competitive positioning. Since golf courses tend to be a basic feature of many AARCs, the golf facilities of competitors should be carefully evaluated. For example, does the competition feature first-rate clubhouse facilities of over 20,000 square feet, with impressive interior design, multiple dining options, and extensive space for clubs and activities? Or do competitors offer separate facilities for golf and social activities, with both a clubhouse and a community center? Other considerations include the quality of the tennis program; whether or not there is a full-time activities director to conduct a "soft amenities" program; the presence of a health and fitness center (an amenity of increasing importance); the availability of neighborhood pools, bocce courts, on-site water amenities, and, in some locations, perhaps even a beach club or beach access.

Depending on the project's size, whether competing communities feature a town center and how the town center is designed are also important evaluation criteria. As discussed in

Though lifestyle is generally considered to be the primary reason that people choose to live in an active adult retirement community, good home design is essential. In Bellasera, in Scottsdale, Arizona, the living and dining area of the Coralina model shows the open floor plan, high ceilings, window walls, and luxury finishes preferred by this market.

chapter 3, a town center is an increasingly important community focal point, which typically includes some combination of recreational amenities, retail stores, services, facilities for civic activities, and community gathering spaces.

The quality of the community's site plan is also a measure of its competitiveness. If competitors' site plans do not foster both a sense of individual neighborhoods *and* community, or do not offer amenities that are sited for residents' convenience, there may be an opportunity for a new, better AARC that would attract a greater market share. Conversely, communities with well-conceived master plans—that include features such as walking and bike trails and pedestrian and cart-path access to the major amenities—will be more competitive.

Last but not least is an evaluation of the quality and market responsiveness of the housing products. While buyers' initial interest in the community will be based on their perception of its ability to provide a lifestyle that appeals to them, ultimately they must find a housing product that offers the quality and value they seek.

Forecasting Future Sales Absorption

Specific market-area characteristics, which must be defined for the particular PMA, provide important context for the demand side of the supply/demand equation. A central aspect of any market study involves determining whether the market depth in the property's defined market areas can support an AARC, as well as forecasting what can be captured at the specific site. In order to forecast demand, the developer must know not only the number of age- and income-qualified households but their propensity to choose an AARC. Achieving this level of under-standing requires an analysis of key demand variables—for example, existing and potential new households in the core market audience of those aged 55 to 64 (and the five-year age cohorts within this range), and their migration patterns, income distribution, homeownership, housing values, turnover rates, propensity to remain in the metro area, and potential interest in living within an age-restricted community. (While households younger and older than the core market range are also important to understand, most people who first purchase in an AARC are between 55 and 64 years old.)

Before conducting direct consumer research, the analyst may have to make preliminary esti-mates by applying national trends to local data. For example, if 13 percent of households in the nation with persons aged 60 to 75 will seriously consider living in an age-restricted AARC, that percentage can be applied to household statistics for the subject site's PMA to suggest, at least at a macro level, what the demand might be. While such an exercise is not sufficient for a final eval-uation of supply and demand, applying national trends to local household data is often useful to obtain initial estimates of market demand in the preliminary "go/no-go" stage. Ultimately, factors such as the propensity of age- and income-qualified households to move to an AARC should be derived from consumer research conducted specifically for the subject site's market area.

Figure 2-3 shows an example of a demand-forecasting model. As the forecast indicates, a hypothetical project in Harbor County can capture 131 sales per year. Because they will vary, the factors used in the analysis need to be determined for each geographic area for which demand is to be forecast. A key variable is, of course, the total number of age-qualified households in the market area—in this case, 22.5 percent of the total 355,568 households. The estimate of the "probable home purchase" price range was based on the number of households in each "current home value" category. As shown on the chart, it is assumed that buyers will purchase a home of lower value than that of their current residence. (Surveys of competitive developments and inter-views with potential purchasers indicate that active adult buyers generally do not want to roll over all of their equity.) Households that meet the age and home-value criteria are then further

FIGURE 2-3

An Example of Annual Demand Potential in an Active Adult Community in the Harbor County Market Area

This table shows how potential demand for a given AARC can be estimated. First, the analyst estimates the number of age-qualified households in the area that, if they sold their existing homes, could afford to purchase homes of various prices in an AARC. On the basis of past behavior patters, the analyst estimates the number that would actually purchase a home in an AARC, and, finally, estimates the number that would purchase in the subject property.

	$75–99,000	$100–124,000	$125–149,000	$150–174,000	$175–199,000	$200–249,000	$250,000+	
Value of current homes	$75–99,000	$100–124,000	$125–149,000	$150–174,000	$175–199,000	$200–249,000	$250,000+	
Probable home purchase price	$75–90,000	$90–115,000	$115–130,000	$130–150,000	$150–175,000	$175–200,000	$200,000+	
								Totals
Number of owner households in county	355,568							355,568
Percentage of age-qualified buyers[a]	22.5%							22.5%
Number of age-qualified households in the primary market area	80,003							80,003
Percentage of households with a qualified existing home value[b]	21.7%	16.5%	7.8%	5.4%	3.9%	4.1%	7.9%	67%
Number of age- and home-value-qualified households	17,361	13,200	6,240	4,320	3,120	3,280	6,320	53,842
Annual turnover rate (%)[c]	9.6%							9.6%
Annual turnover (number)	1,667	1,267	599	415	300	315	607	5,169
Percentage likely to remain within metropolitan statistical area[d]	90.0%							90.0%
Number likely to remain within metropolitan statistical area	1,500	1,141	539	373	270	283	546	4,652
Percentage that would consider South Harbor County	18.7%							18.7%
Number that would consider South Harbor County[e]	280	213	101	70	50	53	102	870
Percentage interested in an age-restricted community	39%	45%	45%	43%	37%	35%	33%	42.5%
Potential demand for AARC units	110	96	45	30	19	19	34	352
Percentage captured by this project[e]	25.0%	35.0%	45.0%	50.0%	55.0%	50.0%	45.0%	37.3%
Annual project capture by price	27	34	20	15	10	9	15	131

a. Local planning department estimate.
b. Local planning department estimate.
c. Estimated from census statistics.
d. Based upon consumer research responses.
e. Estimate based upon competitive market trends.

Source: Robert Charles Lesser & Co.

qualified by the turnover rate—the percentage that will move in a given year—and by whether they are likely to remain in the region or relocate. They are still further qualified according to whether they are likely to be interested in an age-restricted community. Finally, the model assigns an estimated capture of the available demand, by price range, based on the number of new housing options that will be present in the market at the time the subject property is being marketed.

Even when there are few or no competing developments, it is unlikely that any project will capture 100 percent of the potential demand. But well-conceived developments that are based on a thorough understanding of both competitive standards and consumer desires can realize substantial market shares that will lead to healthy financial returns.

---

1. "Population Projections of the United States, by Age, Sex, Race, and Hispanic Origin: 1995 to 2050," *Current Population Reports,* P25-1130, February 1996.

2. During the 1990s, the rate of growth in the population aged 60 and over actually slowed because fewer babies had been born during the Depression years of the 1930s.

3. U.S. Department of Commerce, Bureau of the Census, *Aging in the United States: Past, Present and Future* (Washington, D.C.: GPO, n.d.).

4. "Baby Boomers Eye Retirement," *Third Age News and Opinion,* February 1997.

5. William H. Frey, "New Sun Belt Metros and Suburbs Are Magnets for Retirees," *Population Today* 27, no. 9 (October 1999).

3
Creating Lifestyle

Diane R. Suchman

Talk to developers of active adult retirement communities (AARCs),

and they will tell you that what they are selling is not housing but

lifestyle. Thus, what constitutes lifestyle is important to understand

in targeting, planning, and marketing of an active adult retirement

community. What creates lifestyle is more than simply a clubhouse,

a swimming pool, and a calendar of social events. For example,

lifestyle also embraces the residents' image of the community and

of themselves within it—including the people they are with and how

they spend their time. This chapter will array the various compo-

nents of an active adult lifestyle and suggest the circumstances in

which each is likely to be important to a development's competitive

position.

People who move as they enter their retirement years often want

something different from what their current home offers. Typically,

they seek a lifestyle in which they can pursue their own interests,

The range of activities older people enjoy is no longer limited to such standbys as shuffleboard and canasta.

Surroundings such as these, in Sun City Palm Desert, create the environment that sets the stage for an active adult community's lifestyle.

try new experiences, and socialize with their peers. Often they want a resort environment where their life will resemble a perpetual vacation, providing comfort, quality, independence, companionship, choices, security, and freedom from responsibility. They feel that they have worked hard and saved all their lives to earn this new lifestyle: they deserve it, and they can afford it.

While this description applies to many active adults, it is also true that the market is not monolithic. The active adult market—here assumed to be people aged about 55 to 75 who are interested in and can afford to live in an AARC—is made up of a number of distinct groups, or market segments. Each market segment can be defined in terms of age, income, interests, and expectations, and each has its own values, desires, and recreational, social, and emotional needs. Furthermore, market preferences are continuously evolving. The diversity and evolution of the market explain the range of AARCs being developed and the variety of lifestyle offerings.

Market diversity also underscores the importance, for the developer, of basing development decisions on extensive and ongoing market research, including statistical analysis, surveys, focus groups, one-on-one interviews, solicited feedback from buyers, and analyses of competitors' successes and failures. In addition, a developer's decisions about lifestyle components will depend on the community's site and size, the region in which it is located, whether "lifestyle" will be enjoyed mostly within the development or will be location-dependent, what competitive developments offer, and unique development opportunities or constraints. However, with due consideration of each of these factors, amenity decisions will ultimately be determined by the buyers' ability and willingness to pay for them and the developer's resources, capabilities, and tolerance for risk.

A prospective buyer's impression of a community's lifestyle often springs from the preconceived image, or "brand identity," that the developer or the community has created over time. The brand identity enables retirees to envision a future way of life. Developers who seek to create or maintain a brand identity also base decisions about amenities on the requirements dictated by that identity. (Creating a brand identity is discussed in chapter 5.)

The features and amenities that create lifestyle within a community can be "hard" or "soft." Hard amenities are the physical structures—golf courses, clubhouses, swimming pools, and so forth. They are expensive and largely fixed, and their presence is obvious. Because of the costs and risks involved, developers must assess carefully the value and cost-benefit of hard amenities to their target market. Soft amenities, such as excellent community management and extensive social programming, are less expensive and less readily apparent from the outside, but they are no less important. Soft amenities can greatly enhance the community's value and, at the same time, be easily adjusted to meet the market's changing needs and preferences.

To create the elusive and much-touted lifestyle that buyers seek in AARCs, developers must give careful thought to providing a market-responsive array of both hard and soft amenities. The overall amenity package will be composed of a number of elements, including location, design features, physical amenities, security, a sense of freedom, camaraderie and social interaction, and opportunities for personal growth; the sections that follow discuss each of these elements in detail.

LOCATION

The oft-repeated three most important real estate purchase considerations—location, location, location—apply as well to prospective purchasers in AARCs. A community's location—both in terms of the geographic region where it is located and in terms of its specific site and immediate surroundings—is a key amenity and the first element that defines the lifestyle that is offered.

As a rule, older adults nearing retirement who decide to move out of the family home after the children are grown will move either within their existing community—close to family, friends, and other established ties—or will choose a retirement destination. In some cases, people who leave their communities will choose to retire in an area where they have vacationed in the past. The reasons for their choices help to explain the lifestyle that they seek.

Retirement Destinations

When they move to a retirement destination in a different location from their previous home, often in a different state, active adults tend to choose resort locations with warm climates and natural recreational and visual amenities such as water (lakes, rivers, beaches) or mountains. Sales brochures typically describe AARC locations in terms of two factors: a key natural feature, such as a mountain range, and distance to a major city (and its airport). Other factors in the location decision are the tax structure, the cost of living, and family issues. And, according to George Fulton, president of Fulton Research, Inc., of Oakton, Virginia, one of the major draws of "destination" markets is price: buyers can get more for their money in Phoenix or Florida than in many major metropolitan markets in other parts of the country.

Communities built in retirement destinations that are not within a metropolitan area tend to

John Ormond/Courtesy of JBZ Architecture + Planning

be larger and more comprehensive in their offerings than communities near cities. They may, for example, provide not only a full range of recreational programs and amenities but a small shopping center (or at least a convenience store), dining facilities, some health care services, and perhaps a gas station and post office. The largest of these communities become small cities in their own right, with a full complement of commercial, institutional, and public facilities. The Villages, in central Florida, for example, offers—in addition to recreational facilities and amenities—a Town Square retail and entertainment district, a regional medical center and wellness center, two grocery stores, a pharmacy, a hardware store, more than a dozen restaurants, a travel company, an insurance company, a bank, a furniture store, medical and legal offices, three houses of worship, a theater, a hotel, two bowling centers, a gas station, and more. Thus, in a very large-scale project, location can sometimes be created by the development's own critical mass.

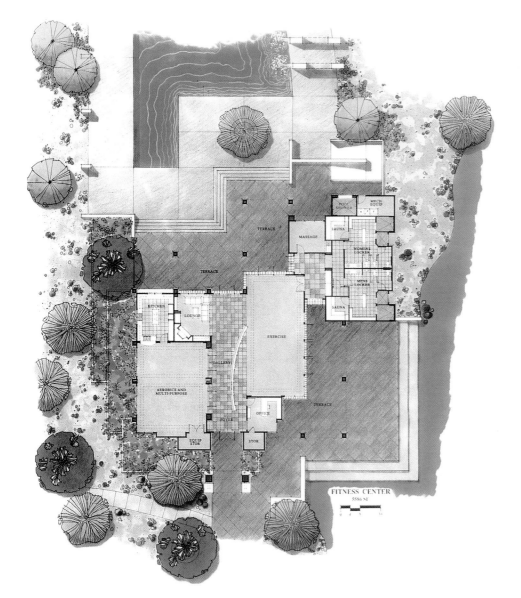

The luxurious 5,586-square-foot fitness center at the active adult community of Bellasera, in Scottsdale, Arizona, features an outdoor pool and terraces for socializing (photo on facing page); inside, there are exercise facilities, an aerobics studio, a kitchen, a lounge, and a massage room.

Relocation within Metropolitan Areas

In recent years, developers have observed that many retirees who are willing to relocate are not willing to give up proximity to children and grandchildren. For these active adults, being close to "the kids" is a major component of lifestyle. In addition, for some, the ability to continue to work on a part-time basis is important. (According to a recent survey, 80 percent of people who are approaching retirement plan to work at least part-time during retirement.)[1] Many retirees also prefer to maintain their longtime associations with religious institutions, medical professionals, and other familiar ties.

As noted in chapter 1, AARCs in nontraditional locations—that is, in metropolitan markets—tend to be smaller than those in retirement destinations and to offer fewer physical amenities: the metropolitan area itself—through cultural facilities, educational institutions, and sports events—augments what is available within the boundaries of the community.

Del Webb Corporation (4)

Golf, bocce, tennis, and swimming are among the extensive outdoor recreational facilities offered at Sun City Hilton Head.

If the community is located outside a major metropolitan area but near a village or town, the "natural amenity" might be the town itself, with its shops, churches, community activities, services, and educational, cultural, and volunteer opportunities.

Immediate Surroundings

Though AARCs typically offer substantial leisure activities, much of an active adult's recreational activity actually takes place beyond the community's gates. Thus, there must be outside opportunities for recreation and education, as well as access to culture, sports, shopping, and the public realm. The "Site Evaluation" section of chapter 2 outlines specific location factors that contribute to a desirable active adult lifestyle in the area immediately surrounding the AARC site: these include access to employment centers, access to major highways, drive-time to the nearest major airport, attractiveness of the surrounding land uses, climate, historic charm or character, "destination" features that draw local tourists, social and cultural outlets, a variety of shopping opportunities, medical facilities, educational institutions, and the comparative tax environment.

According to William Parks, of PDC, Parks Development Consulting, in Scottsdale, Arizona, most retirees shop frequently for groceries in order to have fresh foods and smaller amounts to carry per trip, so the preferred time-distance to a grocery store is 15 minutes or less. Parks also recommends a location that is no more than 30 minutes from a shopping district or regional mall, both for shopping and possible employment. Because active adults tend to travel, he recommends that the community be located within an hour's drive of an international airport.

Parks also cautions that adjacent land uses such as schools, large commercial districts, and employment centers, while desirable for the intergenerational home market, may deter sales in an AARC because older people will be concerned about traffic congestion, noise, excessive light at night, and privacy and security. In addition, adults in the AARC market do not want to see uses that are associated with aging, debility, or death, so locations adjacent to a nursing home, cemetery, or medical institution are generally not desirable.

Visually pleasing views and green spaces near or within AARCs are especially important. As noted earlier, developers often select sites for AARCs that are within viewing distance of natural amenities such as mountains, rivers, wooded areas, and lakes, or where "natural" open space amenities such as ponds, golf courses, gardens, and nature preserves can be established.

The community should be easy to reach and easy to find. Because driving is the primary mode of access, an ideal location for an AARC would be on a secondary road that interchanges with a freeway—or, if necessary, one turn off that secondary road, with good signage pointing the way. More complicated locations may deter older drivers who are unfamiliar with the area. Considerations in locating AARCs within master-planned communities are outlined in chapter 4.

DESIGN AMENITIES

Lifestyle is determined to a great extent by the design of the community and its components. Though chapter 4 discusses design issues in detail, this section will briefly describe the elements of community and home design that contribute to the distinct lifestyle appeal of AARCs.

Nature is a key amenity for active adults, appealing to their aesthetic sense and contributing to a feeling of relaxation. The resort or country-club atmosphere that distinguishes AARCs is created to a large extent by the quality of the natural or enhanced environmental features—such as open space, trees, water features, and landscaping—and the way that these features are incorporated into the project design. As Art Danielian, president of Danielian Associates, in Irvine, California, explains, "Because the residents spend a lot of time in active adult communities, the setting should be beautiful and there should be beauty to discover— for example, along walking trails." The outdoor environment is important not only for aesthetic reasons but also because it can provide the setting for activities residents enjoy, such as fishing, boating, or hiking. (According to Robert Snyder, senior vice president of JWT Specialized Communications, in Dallas, Texas, freshwater fishing is the fastest-growing sport among the mature population.)

Smith Aerial Photography, © 1994 (2), courtesy of DiVosta and Company

By creating a system of artificial lakes, DiVosta and Company converted the flat, featureless tomato field in Naples, Florida, shown at left into the attractive, water-oriented active adult community of Village Walk, shown at right.

Some AARCs have made the natural environment the focal point of community design. St. James Plantation, in Southport, North Carolina, for example, is located on an intracoastal waterway near the Atlantic Ocean; the site is heavily wooded and includes marshes and wetlands. These features made possible an environmentally sensitive, water-oriented development that features lakes, a marina, a beach, and a nature preserve.

In other developments, uninteresting land has been brought to life with imaginative site development that produces the valued "natural" amenities. In the Village Walk development, in Naples, Florida, the developer, DiVosta and Company, began with a square, flat, featureless tomato field and created a community around a system of finger lakes connected by lighted walking trails and bridges that converge at the town center. At Indian Ridge Country Club, in Palm Desert, California, a flat parcel of desert land became a community of undulating green golf courses, gardens, and heavily landscaped boulevards.

Older buyers look for quality, both in real terms and in terms of the image that is conveyed. The development concept should produce an appealing, consistent, and identifiable character, theme, style, and atmosphere. Overall project design should be aesthetically pleasing; have a resort-style look; be appropriate to the local historical and architectural context; and be well-landscaped and well-maintained.

Mature buyers are drawn to AARCs in part because they are controlled environments. To help create the desired sense of order, the community should be designed with readily identifiable entrances; a sense of arrival; well-defined boundaries; a hierarchy of spaces, public to private; and clear, readable signage that makes it easy for residents to find their way.

Because socializing is so important, the overall community design should encourage interaction among residents. There are many approaches that work, including clustering homes in
neighborhoods and creating places where people will naturally congregate. Such places can be
as obvious as miniparks with seating areas or as imaginative as the satellite postal facility at
Village Walk where every resident must come to collect mail.

Though many observers contend that the homes in AARCs are not as important as the choice
of amenities, others caution that a market-responsive home product is a key component of the active
adult lifestyle. Active adults generally like two- to three-bedroom ranch-style single-family homes,
though preferences vary by market. Depending on the location, AARCs might also include high-rise
or mid-rise condominiums, garden apartments, manufactured homes, or a mix of product types.

Typically, active adults who are relocating nearby prefer home designs that are familiar;
those who are moving away prefer designs that reflect the history, culture, and architectural
style of the new location. Quality, privacy, and opportunities to customize are particularly important. Active adults like a sense of luxury and choice. To provide the choices that make up the
amenity and lifestyle package of today's AARCs, many developers offer homes in three tiers of
price and quality and often include hundreds of optional features from which to choose. Some
will also move walls or otherwise customize interior space. Specific home features that are particularly compatible with an active adult lifestyle include usable front porches and rear decks or
patios for socializing, eat-in kitchens, great-rooms for entertaining, office space within the home,
and subtly incorporated universal-design features to accommodate the needs of aging residents.

Amenities for Small Active Adult Communities

As the residential construction industry scurries around, worrying about how to provide homes for the colossal number of aging baby boomers, the question begs: "What amenities should I provide?" And that question leads to the next, "How many dwellings do you plan to build?"

Of course, if thousands of homes are proposed, the revenue generated can support many amenities—golf courses, indoor and outdoor swimming pools, tennis courts, a clubhouse, spas, and the list goes on and on. But what about smaller communities that consist of 500, 200, 100, or even 50 units?

Let's say the parcel of land will accommodate a nice "tight" community of 250 to 300 units. A 5,000 to 7,000 square foot recreational building will accommodate a community of that size. But, how do you know which amenities to include in it? Typically, the building would provide areas for social activities, a small library, an exercise room, a portable dance floor, a small meeting area that could also be used for an auditorium. It would contain furniture for parties, a catering kitchen, an area for card games, and a separate area for billiards. The building may also include an area for arts and crafts. However, you must conduct the necessary research to find out the amenities that your target market wants.

As for external amenities, this size community could support a small social swimming pool, a bocce court, or perhaps even a putting green. Again, research, research. Find out what your potential customers want and what they are willing to pay.

Many communities are springing up on small parcels of land that accommodate fewer than 100 dwellings. What amenities are appropriate for a small community? To begin with, for most markets, luxury facilities are out of the question. A concept that is gaining acceptance is the meeting hall or social hall of 1,200 to 1,500 square feet. This structure contains an efficiency-type kitchen and restrooms. The building is constructed with large sliding glass doors on the

The clubhouse at the Village Greenes community, in Ocean County, New Jersey, includes a combination library and computer room.

perimeter walls. The roof usually has substantial overhangs (four to six feet) around the four sides of the building to provide an indoor-outdoor atmosphere. The balance of the indoor space is no more than open space for parties, dances, and meetings with minimal indoor and outdoor furniture provided by the builder. This building usually has central heat and air conditioning.

Another amenity that is gaining popularity is the old-fashioned, covered picnic pavilion with open sides, hard surface ground covering, and substantial overhangs around the roof. Essentially, the structure is a roof supported by surrounding posts. Barbecue pits and picnic tables are provided, as well as overhead lighting and paddle fans.

Amenities cost money, hence, conduct research to determine what your target market is willing to pay. Amenities like golf courses and swimming pools, and the staff to maintain them, are expensive. A picnic pavilion for a small community is very inexpensive. A social hall is a bit more in monthly cost, but still well below a total of $100 a month fee structure. In addition, the cost of services such as grass cutting, snow clearing, garbage collection, and maintenance of the common areas adds to the amenity charges. And, since a guarded entry gate is so labor-intensive, it is the most expensive amenity of all.

The active adult market segment, particularly those on fixed incomes, are very sensitive to that monthly fee. A certain common sense enters the project pro forma, when ultimately, the question is asked, "What will residents pay and what amenities will be provided for that sum?"

Source: David S. Wolff, president, Real Estate Diagnostics, Inc., Toms River, New Jersey. This feature box was reprinted from *Seniors Housing News* (fall 1998), pp. 28–29.

In addition to a community clubhouse, each condominium building in Leisure World of Virginia, in Landsdowne, Virginia, has its own space for social gatherings. A multipurpose room within the community's Riverbend building can serve as a card room, library, or classroom. Because the room has a dance floor and an adjacent kitchen, it is also an ideal place for parties.

"HARD" AMENITIES

Because people are living longer and staying healthy longer, "old age isn't what it used to be." Older people tend to be more active and more physically fit. The advertisements of some developers, like Del Webb, feature images of senior adults engaged in activities such as rock climbing and scuba diving. This approach underscores the fact that, even if they do not use such amenities themselves, people in the active adult market view themselves as vigorous and want to see the kinds of amenities in their community that represent a highly active lifestyle.

Though the practices of successful AARC developers differ, the common wisdom is that most—if not all—of the community's planned amenities must be delivered upfront. Because AARC buyers are older and more experienced, feel that their "good years" are limited, and are making a discretionary purchase, they generally do not settle for less than they want—and it is lifestyle that they want. Developers such as Del Webb have succeeded in part because they invest tremendous amounts of money to create the communities' amenities and present the lifestyle to prospective buyers upfront. Others have found that a certain amount of phasing is possible: for example, the clubhouse can be built in two phases, or a golf course nine holes at a time. According to William B. Renner Jr., Associate Principal of EDSA, in Fort Lauderdale, Florida, larger communities with longer life spans must build in a greater degree of adaptability in the master planning and permitting to adjust to changes in market demand. In every case, decisions on the phasing of amenities must be based on a careful assessment of the community's market and the lifestyle expectations of potential residents.

Because the cost can be spread among more homebuyers, larger communities tend to include more of the physical elements that contribute to the creation of a particular lifestyle. A community that constitutes a subdivision within a larger, master-planned community often shares some of the amenities of the larger community—a town center, for example—so the developer may need to build less extensive offerings within the active adult development itself. Freestanding communities, in contrast—especially those located in exurban areas—must provide all the elements of lifestyle internally. Developers of active adult developments located near the downtowns of villages and small towns may view the proximate area as part of the community's lifestyle and amenity package. Depending on the specific location, active adult communities located within metropolitan areas may, similarly, have lifestyle-enriching facilities and activities that are sufficiently nearby to augment what is offered on site.

Golf and Other Outdoor Recreational Facilities

High on the list of physical amenities and facilities typically chosen to create lifestyle in an active adult community are sports and recreational facilities. Among the options, golf is often the first one considered.

Golf. Large AARCs, especially those in retirement destination locations, are often built around one or more golf courses. In these communities, the golf course serves as the focal point of community design, the major feature in the community's image, and the primary visual amenity. Depending on the target market and the project economics, AARC golf courses range from a single, nine-hole "executive" course for the exclusive use of community residents to a multi-course golf club that is located within the community but draws its membership from the population of the entire area. Or, as in the case of Sun City at Huntley, outside of Chicago, the golf course may be open to the public but offer residents preferential rates and tee times.

Though golf is a popular amenity for inclusion in AARCs, even in "golf destinations" a large percentage of buyers do not play golf. According to Ed Robson, president of Robson Communities,

Viewing stands adjacent to tennis courts at Indian Ridge Country Club, in Palm Desert, California, provide an opportunity for viewers to socialize as they watch the games.

only 25 percent of the residents in Robson communities—all of which include golf courses—actually play golf. The proportion of golf players will, of course, vary by market and even by development. Survey responses on the subject also vary (no doubt in part because different surveys ask different questions). According to Jim Migliore, president of US Home's Special Projects Division, responses to company surveys indicate that golf is "critically important" to only 5 percent of the market, while 60 percent indicate that it is "not important." In Del Webb's 1997 survey of baby boomers—people born between 1946 and 1964—only 11 percent indicated that they play golf frequently.[2] A 1994 national survey of homebuyers that was not age-specific indicated that a golf course within a community was "very" or "extremely" important to 39.5 percent of respondents.[3] By comparison, the same survey showed that 78 percent of respondents valued open space and natural areas.

Nonetheless, golf remains a popular organizing amenity in AARCs because of the country-club image it conveys and because it creates a large swath of landscaped open-space views that all residents can enjoy. According to Phillip K. Smith Jr., president of Sunrise Colony Company's Coachella Valley division, once the decision has been made to include golf, providing "really great" brand-name championship golf courses, designed by a celebrity architect, makes a difference because it broadens the market to include more serious golfers and golfers from a wider geographic region. Where there are golf courses, related amenities such as putting greens and driving ranges (with or without lights) and pro shops may also be included—depending, again, on the target market and project economics.

AARCs that do not include golf courses among their on-site amenities may compensate with a location that is near to golf clubs or public courses. For example, Leisure World of Virginia is located adjacent to the Lansdowne Resort, which features a Robert Trent Jones golf course as well as an array of other amenities that Leisure World residents can use on a fee basis.

Other Outdoor Recreational Facilities. Swimming pools are a focal point for exercise, especially because aquatic activity is easy on aging joints. Even more important, swimming pools foster socializing. Many residents who do not swim like to gather around the pool to visit with one another and enjoy looking at the water. For that reason, most AARCs include an outdoor recreational or "social" swimming pool—heated, well-landscaped, and with ample deck space to accommodate lounge chairs for sunbathing during the day and parties during the evening. Depending on the community's size, location, and market preferences, there may also be an indoor pool, a lap pool, a wading pool for grandchildren, and whirlpool spas. Sometimes indoor and outdoor swimming-pool areas and their associated "aprons" will be connected by a sliding glass wall to create a larger recreational area that can be used more flexibly, especially for large gatherings.

Tennis courts (preferably lighted) are popular in AARCs, though many observers feel that demand for this amenity has been declining in recent years. Like swimming pools, tennis courts are important not only for people who participate in the sport but for those who gather to

SaddleBrooke, located 14 miles outside of Tucson, includes its own commercial center.

watch and socialize. For that reason, communities such as Village Walk and Indian Ridge Country Club include viewing stands in their tennis facilities. Communities with tennis courts may also include a pro shop.

Other amenities enjoyed by players and kibitzers alike are bocce, lawn bowling, and horseshoes. Shuffleboard, once a staple, has become less popular outside of Florida. In addition, AARCs may include outdoor amphitheaters; shaded picnic areas (perhaps with barbecue grills); gathering places, such as gazebos; and "tot-lots" for visiting grandchildren.

Without doubt, the most popular outdoor recreational amenities, which are nearly universal in AARCS, are walking trails.[4] Walking trails respond to active adults' desire to exercise and to experience nature. Typically, a trail system winds through and connects various destinations within the community, taking advantage of open spaces and views. Ideally, trails should be 12 feet wide—wide enough to accommodate walkers, joggers, bicyclists, in-line skaters, and strollers full of grandchildren. How a trail system is designed and used can be adjusted over the life of the community to adapt to residents' changing interests and preferences. For example, a simple walking path might later be developed as a fitness course or a nature trail.

Clubhouses and Town Centers

As the physical, social, and symbolic focus of the community, the clubhouse or town center is an extremely important element of the community's lifestyle. For that reason, decisions such as where it should be located, what it should look like, what spaces and activities it should include, and how it should be furnished should be made with careful consideration of the target market's values and preferences. Regardless of its design and components, the function of the clubhouse or town center is to create a "club atmosphere," providing spaces and activities that encourage social interaction and enable residents to pursue their various interests.

Even in small communities, the clubhouse will need to include an entry foyer, a social hall, a kitchen, rest rooms, a fitness center, multipurpose activity spaces, and administrative offices.

Most communities will also want to include a library and a computer center (which often share space). Libraries are especially popular with this age group, as demonstrated in Village Walk, where, to fill this need, the residents themselves gradually converted a small meeting room within the town center into a community library.

Fitness centers are also particularly popular. As LeRoy Hanneman Jr., president and chief executive officer of Del Webb Corporation, noted, "We can't build health and fitness facilities large enough." A number of developers have had to add space to existing fitness facilities to meet demand. In addition to being outfitted with a variety of types of exercise equipment, fitness centers should provide staff to help residents use the equipment and should offer ongoing programs to motivate residents and to make their exercise more sociable, fun, and safe.

Depending on the size of the community and the interests of the resident population, clubhouses might also include an indoor swimming pool, lounge areas, arts and crafts facilities, a

In the Village Walk community, in Naples, Florida, landscaped 12-foot-wide trails connect residential areas with each other and with the town center. Because the trails are so wide, they can easily be shared by walkers, bicyclists, in-line skaters, and grandparents with strollers.

ACTIVE ADULT RETIREMENT COMMUNITIES

restaurant or café (possibly with both indoor and outdoor seating), a theater (usually as part of the social hall), a health spa, aerobic exercise rooms, saunas or steam baths, pro shops, card rooms, a billiards room, a woodworking shop, a snack bar, and so forth. According to William E. Becker, managing director/president of The William E. Becker Organization, in Teaneck, New Jersey, clubhouses in AARCs should include "amenities that they remember from their thirties, forties, and fifties—billiards, card rooms, and sports bars."[5] Some AARCs, such as Indian Ridge Country Club, also include facilities and activities designed for visiting children.

Many clubhouses include retail uses for the convenience of residents. For example, the clubhouse at Leisure World of Virginia includes space for a beauty salon and barber shop, a bank, and a mini-market. SaddleBrooke, located just north of Tuscon, includes a small shopping center that is owned by the developer, a gas station, a dry cleaner, a restaurant, a barber shop and beauty salon, a resale shop, and a bank. At Dee Why Gardens, in New South Wales,

DiVosta and Company

Australia, community residents operate a kiosk that sells convenience items. Typically, clubhouses in AARCs do not include space for medical services, though wellness centers, such as the one at Sun City at Huntley, are gaining popularity.

To accommodate groups of different sizes and residents' changing preferences, spaces should be designed for flexible use. In particular, the social hall should be "expandable" to accommodate large gatherings—and such expansion should be possible on one floor. (In several of the case studies featured in this book, social gathering space within the clubhouse was originally planned on two levels. In subsequent AARC clubhouses, both developers created single-level expandable social halls instead.)

Some AARC developers "deconstruct" the clubhouse and related facilities and create a town center instead. The distinguishing features of a town center are its multistructure design, visual prominence and identity (town centers often incorporate a symbolic element such as a bell tower), and the inclusion of retail as well as recreational space; town centers also often include a "village green." At Village Walk, for example, the developer built a town-hall-type complex of connected low-rise buildings, inspired by traditional neighborhood development design, that includes a convenience store and café, meeting spaces, office space, apartments, a bank, a beauty shop, a gift store, a U.S. postal facility, an automated teller machine, two gasoline pumps, and a nearby car wash.

Retail space within an AARC is typically owned by the developer, although it is sometimes eventually taken over by the community homeowners' association. Either way, it may be necessary to charge operators below-market rents to make it feasible for them to provide the services and conveniences that community residents desire. Similarly, restaurants, cafés, and snack bars may not prove profitable, but because they are part of the lifestyle desired within the community, profit should not be the determining factor in the decision to retain those uses. If retail facilities will eventually be controlled by community residents, the developer must educate the homeowners' association about reasonable financial expectations for these uses.

"SOFT" AMENITIES

The term *soft amenities* refers to qualities, services, and activities that may not be reflected in the physical form of the community but that nonetheless contribute to the residents' enjoyment of the community's lifestyle. Soft amenities include, for example, security, recreational programming, education and volunteering opportunities, and health and fitness programs.

Security

One of the reasons older people choose to live in an AARC, suggests Roger Galatas, president and chief executive officer of Roger Galatas Interests, LLC, is to seek "refuge from a changing world." They want to live among their peers: people of similar socioeconomic backgrounds who

have shared some of the same life experiences, think the way they do, and are at a stage when they have the time and inclination to enjoy their lives. An AARC also offers a clublike atmosphere that not only "includes us" but "excludes them." Part of the appeal of an AARC is that it is a controlled environment, where the way of life is safe, consistent, predictable, comfortable, and less rushed and stressful than life in the larger, workaday world.

Developers can foster a sense of safety and security in a number of ways. Most obviously, they can enclose the community with fencing or walls and allow access only through gates that are secured by guards, electronic devices, or both. Though they provide the appearance of safety rather than actually deter unwanted visitors, such features are much valued by the AARC market. In addition to giving a feeling of security, the gated-community approach reinforces the sense of exclusivity that is part of the AARC lifestyle. Within the community, security is typically maintained by roving professional or volunteer ("neighborhood watch") security patrols.

Nonetheless, not all AARCs are gated. Sun City at Huntley is an open community, in part to make possible public access to the golf course, the use of which is not restricted to community residents. Use patterns sometimes dictate complicated access and security arrangements. At Indian Ridge Country Club, for example, a guarded entrance controls access to the community. Within the community, only residents have access to the residential areas. Access to the golf club—which serves a different, though overlapping, population—is through a separate internal gate.

Within the community, passcards or passkeys may be used to limit use of the clubhouse to residents and their guests. For example, at Heritage in the Hills, in suburban Detroit, residents can gain access to the clubhouse 24 hours a day, entering with a magnetic passkey that records

Club Windsor is the centerpiece of Windsor Hills, a community for active adults in The Woodlands, a master-planned community in Houston, Texas. The clubhouse features a heated swimming pool, a billiard room, meeting space, and a full schedule of social activities. Each month, a "homeowner happy hour" provides new neighbors with an opportunity to get acquainted.

the person's identity and time of entry on a computer. At other communities, the use of the clubhouse is less restricted. At Sun City at Huntley, for example, because parts of the clubhouse (such as the restaurant and pro shop) are open to the public, security is maintained by the watchful eyes of the professional staff rather than by restricted admission.

In addition, providing home security systems, preferably as a standard feature in all homes, reinforces the feeling of community-wide security. The value to the mature buyer will far exceed the cost to the builder (especially if such systems are bought at bulk prices). In multifamily buildings, all entryways to the building should be electronically secured, and in some markets, residents will feel more comfortable if building security is augmented with peepholes and dead-bolts on individual entry doors.

Though active adults do not feel "old," part of the sense of security that they seek in an AARC is knowing that medical care will be available if and when they need it—though, as noted earlier, they do not want to see any on-site or adjacent health care facilities. Thus, an AARC should be located within a reasonable distance of a hospital and in close proximity to medical offices. This requirement is not universal, however. As Hanneman points out, having a hospital nearby is "not a major concern at the point of sale. Medical facilities will follow us, because our customers pay their bills."

Recognizing a potential market, hospitals near AARCs will often provide outreach services on an as-needed basis and may also offer wellness programs either in the hospital itself or, by special arrangement, within the community. Such services help residents to monitor and maintain their health and to age in place. In addition, the communities' fitness centers, especially if staffed by professionals who understand the capabilities and limitations of older people, provide residents both with valuable health benefits and with a much-valued sense of vigor.

Back to School and Loving It

Today's retirees have discovered that retirement provides them with an opportunity to share their knowledge and expertise and to explore new areas of learning.[1] They are knocking on the doors of educational institutions and saying, "We want to learn."

In 1999 alone, through dedicated "learning in retirement" programs, some 70,000 retirees attended more than 4,000 courses each term at over 263 colleges or universities throughout the country. Learning in retirement programs are separate programs established specifically for seniors, and many are taught by retirees with expertise in the subject matter. In response to demand, new programs for retirees are appearing at an additional 25 universities each year.

The concept of a program for learning in retirement began over 30 years ago, when the New School for Social Research, in New York City, agreed to sponsor the first Institute for Retired Professionals. Though the university provided space, credibility, and guidance, the courses and workshops were planned and taught by the retirees themselves. Over time, other colleges formed similar institutes, many of which adopted essentially the same format. In 1988, these colleges created a nonprofit, voluntary network to communicate and share their experiences and know-how.[2] The network now includes 263 institutes; 57 more are being planned with guidance from the network. (Not all retirement learning programs participate in the network.)

The colleges structure retiree learning programs in various ways. Some sponsor independent programs, others create distinct programs within their continuing-education departments, and still others involve seniors in the college's regular class offerings. The examples that follow illustrate different approaches to learning in retirement programs.

Eckerd College: The Academy of Senior Professionals at Eckerd College

At Eckerd College, a small liberal arts college in St. Petersburg, Florida, the Academy of Senior Professionals at Eckerd College (ASPEC) is a private membership organization with especially strong links to the college. The academy offers its members more than 40 different courses and workshops on topics ranging from modern physics to creative arts, social issues, international relations, computers and applied technology, religion, archeology, and even boat and light-airplane construction. In addition, to capitalize on the vast resources of knowledge represented by ASPEC, faculty may ask an academy member to participate in one of the college's regular classes as a "discussant/colleague." Members provide students with real-life guidance in selecting careers, help develop the course material, and work with students on research; often, ASPEC members become friends, colleagues, and inspiring role models for the young people. To foster intergenerational learning further, the school provides a "student-colleague interchange" program, which links incoming freshmen with ASPEC members before the students reach the campus.

The Fund for the Improvement of Post-Secondary Education has awarded Eckerd College a grant to help six other colleges create intergenerational collegiate learning programs.

A number of ASPEC members live in College Landings, an active adult retirement community located adjacent to the Eckerd College campus.

Duke University: The Duke Institute for Learning in Retirement

The Duke Institute for Learning in Retirement (DILR) was established in 1977, when retirees from the picturesque active adult retirement community of Fearrington Village, in nearby Pittsboro, North Carolina, approached the university in search of courses and study groups keyed to their interests. The current director of the DILR program, Sara Craven, explains that the students "come into retirement today with 25 or 30 years of active living ahead of them," she said, "and they are still exploring . . . still thinking what they might want to do with the rest of their lives."

DILR classes are open to adults age 50 and over and encompass a wide range of subjects. About half of the classes are taught by the members themselves (topics are selected by the DILR board of directors); other courses are taught by Duke faculty members or graduate staff, or by experts from the community.

Response has been enthusiastic. One student reported that she had moved to Fearrington specifically because of the rich cultural and educational opportunities available in the area. During the previous semester, she said, she had taken courses in Italian civilization; the great composers (taught by a former Julliard faculty member); a course on Faulkner and Tolstoy; and an exploration of the Psalms, led by a rabbi—"all things I would never have had the opportunity to learn." Another Fearrington resident, retired from his staff job at the United Nations, talked about the privilege of being in an "intellectual environment," and the additional benefit of access to the cultural and educational opportunities a university like Duke has to offer, including the wide selection of concerts and theater and other entertainment events that are part of the university scene.

DILR's classes, which are offered three semesters each year, are noncredit, require prerequisites, and give neither tests nor grades. Requirements include class preparation and participation and sharing the results of one's own research. Though supported by membership fees, DILR is jointly administered through the Continuing Education Department of Duke University (which houses its offices) and Duke's Center for the Study of Aging and Human Development.

About 20 percent of the participants in the DILR programs are residents of Fearrington.

Montgomery College: The Academy of Lifelong Learning

One of the nation's newest learning in retirement programs is the Academy for Lifelong Learning at Montgomery College, in Conroe, Texas. Located at the school's campus within The Woodlands, a large, master-planned community, the academy resulted from the joint efforts of The Woodlands Development Company, Montgomery College, and representatives of the larger community.

The "marriage" between The Woodlands Development Company and the fairly new Montgomery College was almost inevitable when The Woodlands added two new age-restricted communities to its roster, one of them almost immediately adjacent to the college campus. As Kenne Turner, dean of the continuing education department, describes it, it was a "perfect meeting of the minds" when The Woodlands management approached the college with the possibility of establishing a learning in retirement program. Dean Turner points out that, as a community college, the role of the school is to "serve the community," and he talks with great enthusiasm about the rewarding experience of establishing a new educational program that will offer all area retirees education and training, study groups, social interaction, and "the opportunity for people with similar interests to get together." He sees the new learning in retirement program as "a chance for the retirees to pick up where they left off in their growth and learning and development."

Response from potential members and students has far exceeded expectations. When the concept was first announced at a small reception, it was expected that perhaps 40 or 50 people would attend. Instead, 220 came to give their overwhelming support.

Membership fees for the Academy of Lifelong Learning at Montgomery College are low—only $25—to make it widely accessible. Courses are free, except for those taught by college faculty or outside experts (which charge a small fee). Courses with the largest enrollment include computers, the classics, Spanish for tourists, philosophy, German, wellness-related courses, and "Bonehead Bridge."

George Mason University: Program under Construction

The Prince William County campus of Virginia's George Mason University is currently in the process of creating a special learning program for retirees. As with Montgomery College, the concept was brought to the college by a development company, Coscan-Brookfield Homes, which is building Dumbarton, a new, age-restricted active adult community nearby. The college has responded enthusiastically, and has even agreed to share the cost of expanding the bus service between the new community and the campus.

Dorothy Harper, vice president for active adult development at Coscan-Brookfield Homes, has made learning opportunities for residents one of her top priorities. Even though a separate institute for learning in retirement is not yet established, she had already negotiated price breaks for retirees on college-sponsored cultural events and on seminars and workshops on topics of particular relevance to the older student (such as financial planning, estate planning, living wills, living trusts, and personal improvement).

Because the larger area that surrounds the college and the new community is becoming home to increasing numbers of retirees, many of them from the close-in Washington, D.C., suburbs, Harper expects considerable interest in peer learning opportunities not only from within Dumbarton but from larger communities nearby.

Princeton University: A Retiree Auditing Program

For a number of years, Princeton University, in Princeton, New Jersey, has been quietly and informally permitting retirees to audit regular college classes. Many local residents, including a very large contingent of retirees living in nearby active adult communities, eagerly took advantage of this opportunity. The program offered them the chance to learn from the country's top educators at one of its most prestigious universities. Participants paid no fee, had to obtain the professor's permission to audit the class, could not participate in class discussion, and earned no college credit.

In response to growth in the number of retiree auditors, the university has developed a more formal structure for the auditing program, and it now charges participants $50 per course. The university has also set forth parameters for participation and established a volunteer community auditing council, composed of 13 participants in the retiree auditor program, to serve as policy advisors.

Though the more formal structure of this program may be disappointing to those who have had the advantage of auditing the Princeton classes without interference or fees for many years, the extraordinary increase in the number of retirees seeking to audit also testifies to the importance retirees place on lifelong learning and ongoing personal growth—not only in the Princeton area but throughout the country.

Source: Myril Axelrod, president, Marketing Directions Associates, New Fairfield, Connecticut.

1. Many of "today's retirees" are not fully retired, but still work part-time or on a consulting basis.

2. For more information about the network, contact Deborah Rodgers at Institutes for Learning in Retirement Networks, Boston, Massachusetts; (617) 422-0784 or (617) 426-0549.

Incorporating universal-design features into homes and community facilities also helps provide a sense of personal security and enables residents to age in place.

To AARC residents, access to emergency medical care is even more important than access to a hospital. In locations where hospital facilities are not within quick response distance, developers might want to consider other alternatives. For example, SaddleBrooke is serviced by Northwest Hospital but maintains on-site emergency response paramedic services as well.

Because health care is a delicate topic for mature buyers, who know that they will need to have it available in the not-too-distant future but do not want to be reminded of their approaching old age or frailty, some developers reserve land on site for the future development of facilities to accommodate their residents' changing health needs. For example, the Village by the Arboretum, in Guelph, Ontario, has set aside a parcel of land for an extended-care facility.

Clubhouses in adult retirement communities often provide space for ceramics, one of the many activities that are popular with active adults.

Freedom

As observed earlier, people who choose to live in an AARC rather than to stay in their family home are seeking something: a fresh start, new activities, new friends, and new opportunities. But they are also fleeing something: unwanted responsibilities. They want time to enjoy their new lives. One of the lifestyle benefits of living in an AARC is that residents retain the benefits of homeownership without the burdens.

Homes within AARCs are typically designed inside and out for ease of maintenance—through, for example, choice of materials or use of the latest technological innovations. Lots are typically small and may be fitted with sprinkler systems. Often, developers include maintenance of the homes' exteriors and landscaping as part of the services provided, both to relieve home-owners of this burden and to ensure that the community retains its desired appearance and value. In northern climates, snowplowing of streets and driveways is often either included among services provided or is offered on a fee basis.

Depending on the market served, other fee-based services that may be available include housekeeping, dog walking, package pickup, valet services, plant watering, personal training, trans-portation services (including on-call shuttle service to and from the airport), and home checks. Many developments provide concierge services that will perform almost any chore or attend to almost any service need on a fee basis. As a rule, such services should be provided on an as-needed basis because active adults, though they want freedom from responsibility, are also resistant to the idea of being dependent and to paying for services that they do not want or need.

Fun, Social Interaction, and Personal Growth

For most people, retirement is a time to shed responsibilities and seek new experiences. Retirees want to have fun and learn new skills. This may mean learning to play a new sport, such as golf or fishing; learning to use the computer; taking on a part-time job; or pursuing a new hobby. Many older people find that for the first time in their lives, they have the opportunity to explore their creative side: they may take up painting, pottery, jewelry-making, or wood-crafting. Others want to sing or play music. Still others want to play bridge or canasta, or shoot pool. Some want to test their skills in competitions, such as Senior Olympics, bridge tournaments, or juried art shows.

In addition, AARCs give residents opportunities to enjoy new friendships—for example, through organizations of people with like interests and experiences. Many AARCs have clubs for people from the same state, ethnic background, or religious group; clubs for singles, specific kinds of sports enthusiasts, or members of service organizations such as Lions or Rotary; or hobby groups for thespians, gardeners, toastmasters, and on and on. Support groups may be established to help fellow residents through illness or bereavement. Other clubs may organize trips—from around town to around the country or the world. A social calendar filled with community parties and celebrations of special occasions creates a festive atmosphere and an opportunity to mingle and create community traditions.

Cultural activities are especially important at this stage of life. In addition to what is available in the surrounding community, active adults often enjoy concerts and lectures that can be brought to the AARC from, for example, a nearby university. They will want opportunities to visit museums, art exhibitions, theaters, and special events. Many older people welcome the chance to explore new educational opportunities, and universities have responded to this yearning with a range of programs targeted to retirees.

Active adults also like to spend time doing volunteer work, and a wise AARC developer will establish relationships with institutions and organizations that make those opportunities available. Many Sun City communities operate volunteer bureaus to link community volunteers with groups that would welcome them. As a result, Hanneman explained, "the hospital in the original Sun City actually had more volunteers than employees." Overall, about 40 percent of the 90,000 residents of Sun City communities nationwide volunteer regularly.

The list of potential activities that active adults may want to pursue is long and almost infinitely expandable. The implication for AARC developers is that they need to provide the setting in which these kinds of choices and activities can be nurtured and enjoyed.

The physical design of the community, the choice of recreational facilities, and the design of the clubhouse or town center—augmented by facilities outside the community's environs—can provide residents with opportunities to pursue an array of activities. And, as outlined in chapter 6, sound community management is essential to creating the "soft goods."

In every case, this means that someone must take responsibility for making a program of choices available and ensuring that activities are scheduled and physically accommodated. Though residents must make their wants known, most developers hire professional staff to facilitate the organization and scheduling of recreational activities, programs, and events. "Left to their own devices, people will hibernate in the home," commented Hanneman. "Getting them involved is key. We invest time and money in nurturing their interests through our professional social staff."

Professional staff also make it possible for the developer to respond to specific interests that may not have been identified during the market research process. As part of its commitment to customer service, Robson Communities' senior vice president, Michael Osborn, explains, "Anybody can build golf courses and swimming pools. We listen to our homeowners and provide what they ask for. Our guiding principle is, 'If you want to do something and we don't have it, get six people together and we will help you organize it.'"

In communities where the developer continues to own or manage the clubhouse after the development is completed and sold, paid staff typically continue to oversee social programming. In other cases, it is up to the residents, individually or through their homeowners' association, to volunteer to organize and manage the social programs themselves.

HONING THE COMPETITIVE EDGE

In creating the lifestyle that defines an AARC, offering the usual array of amenities is not enough to stay competitive in today's expanding and creative marketplace. Developers who want to stand out from their peers must go the extra mile. As Michael Rubin, president of Avatar Retirement Communities, explains, "Ultimately we will all build the same product: there's no intellectual capital with respect to floor plans. There's only so much the land yields in density, only so much you can do with planning and architecture. How you will distinguish yourself is by surprising the customer." Kathleen B. Cecilian, of KC & Associates, in Flemington, New Jersey, agrees, advising developers to "go overboard, give the customers more than they expect. Forget what people need or want: Give them what they would love."

1. Roper Starch Worldwide, Inc., for American Association of Retired Persons (AARP), "Baby Boomers Envision Their Retirement: An AARP Segmentation Analysis," February 1999, <research.aarp.org/econ/boomer_seg_1.html>.

2. Del Webb Corporation, *Similarities and Differences among the Boomers: A Survey of Attitudes and Opinions of People Born between 1946 and 1964* (Phoenix: Del Webb Corporation, October 1997), 27.

3. The survey, conducted by American LIVES and InterCommunications, Inc., was described by Brooke Warrick and Toni Alexander in "Changing Community Preferences," *Trends and Innovations in Master-Planned Communities* (Washington, D.C.: ULI–The Urban Land Institute, 1998), 15–16.

4. According to the survey referred to in endnote 3, walking and biking paths were the most valued amenity, rated "very or extremely important" by 75 percent of respondents.

5. William E. Becker, "Build Your Adult Community Success on These Marketing Basics," *Seniors Housing News*, summer 1998, p. 9.

Design Issues

William R. Parks, PDC, President, Parks Development Consulting, Inc., Scottsdale, Arizona;

with contributions from Kenneth Rohde, AIA, KTGY Group, Inc., Irvine, California;

and Donald Jacobs, President, JBZ Architecture + Planning, Newport Beach, California

When planning an active adult retirement community (AARC), it is essential to keep in mind that an AARC is not a traditional family-home community; thus, many of the principles used in planning such communities do not apply. The overall organization of an AARC is different, from street patterns to lot configurations and product mix; in particular, the way that the nonresidential areas are integrated into the plan differs from the approach that would be used in a family-home community. These differences arise because the residents are older and pursue a different lifestyle.

As discussed in chapters 2 and 3, the attitudes, financial position, and preferences of people who are likely to live in a retirement community determine the kind of lifestyle that the developer will seek to create. To a large extent, the desired lifestyle is created through design—the design of the community, the homes, and the recreational facilities.

Regional architecture and a landmark clock tower characterize the Town Center of Village Walk in Naples, Florida.

The other key design determinant is the residents' age. The members of the "young senior" population targeted by developers of AARCs generally feel vigorous and resist seeing themselves as subject to the infirmities of age. Yet planners and designers of AARCs need to understand and plan for residents' eventual physical limitations. Although often very active, the members of this group are no longer young at the time of purchase and will continue to grow older in their new home. Most are beginning—or will soon will begin—to experience some of the changes commonly associated with aging. Their joints may be less mobile and their physical movements less quick. Reflexes are beginning to diminish. Muscle mass declines, as does strength. Many older adults have mild arthritis, which is likely to worsen as they age. Their eyesight is weaker, and many need more light to perform routine tasks. Hearing may also be less acute. And for some, cognitive ability may begin to decline.

Once they are settled in the community, most residents prefer to "age in place" until and unless they can no longer function well in their homes and in the community. As the discussions that follow illustrate, designs for AARCs accommodate and assist residents as they continue to age.

COMMUNITY PLANNING AND DESIGN

Design Context and Relationships

Regional vernacular and market perceptions. A well-designed AARC reflects the architectural style and materials of the region; good architecture and design are important not only for their own sakes but as part of a successful marketing program. Retirees generally want the style of their homes and communities to be strongly associated with the area in which they choose to live. For those who relocate to an AARC from other areas of the country, living in a style that is associated with their new location reinforces their sense of the lifestyle that they have chosen. They often select home elevations that reflect their image of the area's history or architectural flavor, and many will even pay premiums for an upgraded elevation that very closely reflects the area's architectural character.

Indigenous landscaping. For the same reasons, trees, shrubs, and grasses that are indigenous to the local area (or those that have been adapted to the local climate) should be the primary landscape materials for AARCs. Native vegetation also tends to be less costly to maintain. For the most part, nonnative materials will require more maintenance, watering, or preparation—and their survival can still be tenuous at best.

The use of indigenous vegetation can also help minimize the cost of maintaining the community's common areas. When a homeowners' association (HOA) takes control of a community or neighborhood, it often makes changes to reduce maintenance costs and HOA dues, and community landscaping has often been a prime target of cost-conscious associations. Several years

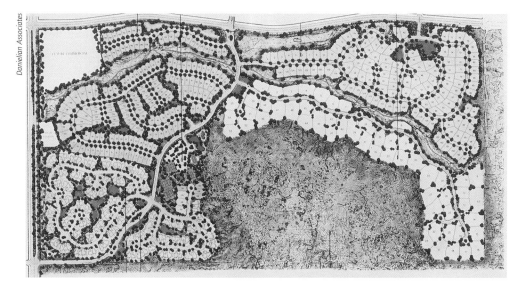

The site plan for Winfield, a 300-acre Pulte Homes Corporation community in Scottsdale, Arizona, emphasizes the preservation of open space and the enhancement of the natural environment.

ago, a neighborhood association in Sun City West, Arizona, decided that the grassy frontyards of their townhomes where too expensive to maintain in a desert environment. When the neighborhood residents took control of their sub-association, the grass was removed and replaced with a material that did not need cutting or watering: rocks!

Character, Theme, Style, and Atmosphere

AARCs should be designed to create a character, theme, style, and atmosphere that will appeal to the target market. These terms may be defined as follows:

- Character—a distinguishing feature or asset
- Theme—an implicit or recurring idea; a motif
- Style—the way in which something is said, done, expressed or performed
- Atmosphere—overall ambience and feeling.

What is essential in an AARC is for all four elements to work together. Although, for example, the common areas will have more of a resort ambience and will include structures that differ in scale from those in the residential areas, both the residential and common areas must be tied together through a shared theme and style. The overarching element—community character—thus embodies continuity, consistency, and completeness, all of which are expressed in the quality of design and its execution. It is through the creation of a visually and aesthetically cohesive whole that an AARC achieves the comfort level and sense of place that the senior buyer seeks.

Character. Quality—and the value perceived in that quality—is important to retirees. Active adults have years of experience buying homes and assessing neighborhoods, and they have a good understanding of quality in a physical environment. From the inside of the living room to

The lushly landscaped swimming pools adjacent to the Indian Ridge Country Club clubhouse, in Palm Desert, California, include patio areas and seating that can be used for large gatherings or more intimate socializing with friends.

the curb and gutter in front of the house, they have seen many examples of construction and have come to appreciate the best for its longevity, beauty, and substance.

Theme. The architectural theme of the community must create a sense of comfort and desire in the eyes of the prospective purchaser. Deciding on the appropriate theme for a community depends heavily on market research results, but the rule of thumb is that the theme derives from a combination of climatic conditions and the local vernacular architecture. A well-thought-out and well-executed design theme that reflects the best qualities of the local area is one that will be most appreciated by potential buyers. Heavy "theming" that fails, in the eyes and minds of buyers, to create a sense of place, will have difficulty succeeding. Regardless of the type of theme employed, the active adult market will not be attracted to or value efforts that appear contrived, over- or underdone, or out of place; as noted earlier, active adults have considerable experience in buying homes and choosing neighborhoods, and they expect high-quality design and construction.

Style. The style in which the theme is carried out—down to the signage, landscaping, sales brochures, and collateral details—can be considered the defining element that ties the theme together.

Atmosphere. The overall atmosphere of the community has the difficult task of embracing both the residential area, where the active seniors will live, and the community area, where they will play. Successfully combining the two depends on the ability of the theming elements to create the desired atmosphere. To residents, their new home must *feel* like "home"; it should also be conducive to socializing, exercising, and showing their friends around this great community where they now live.

Neighborhood Planning

Neighborhoods and Product Mix. For the retired market in general and those interested in lifestyle communities in particular, retirement can be a great equalizer. Gone are the pretensions and status symbols of the corporate world. By retirement, goals have been met and achievements recognized. Many retirees are much more open to self-expression and less rigid in their need to define their place in society. Therefore, the "status" neighborhoods typically found in conventional master-planned communities, in which neighborhoods are segregated by product price, are not important to the retiree in an AARC. That residents have attained the status of "successful retirees" is clear from the very fact that they are living in the community; no further distinction is necessary.

As a result, the lot mix for an AARC should reflect a fairly balanced distribution of lot and product sizes. However, in larger communities where several product lines are offered for sale, the developer should take care to avoid placing the largest lot or product type adjacent to the smallest lot or product type if the price difference is more than double. For example, lots with product prices starting at $125,000 should not be adjacent to lots with products starting at $250,000. Buyers of larger products will resist living next to lower-priced products because they believe that their property values will be negatively affected. The differences in size and price are generally not as large in smaller communities, so different lot and product sizes can be inter-mixed to gain advantages in design and density.

Neighborhood Identification. For communities with more than 300 homes, creating smaller neighborhoods within the community helps residents find their way and identify with their immediate neighbors as the community grows. Again, the design of these neighborhoods should be "status neutral," and the placement of lots and houses should be balanced in relation to the entire range of products so that no one neighborhood is perceived as being "better" than another. While creating distinctive neighborhoods within a community of any size is not an essential ingredient to success, some builders have found such neighborhoods useful in sales and marketing and in phasing construction.

Lot Configurations and Design. Efficiency and privacy are two critical elements to consider when planning residential lots. Efficiency means not being oversized in relation to the home. Privacy means limiting visibility into the house or into the private yard area from neighboring houses. As long as good window placement and effective screening maintain privacy between houses, lots can be kept small.

Older adults will accept small lots because they have little use for them, and large lots are costly to maintain. For single-family detached homes (which is what the market overwhelmingly prefers), side yards can be as narrow as five feet where local codes and markets will allow. Frontyards can also be kept to minimum local standards and expectations. Rear yards, however, are a different story. Regardless of region, many retirees view their rear yard as part of their living area. Homeowners in AARCs will often have a deck, patio, or porch projecting into the rear yard of the home, which becomes an extension of their indoor living space. Because privacy and quiet are important in this part of the lot, unfenced rear yards should be at least 20 feet and preferably 25 feet from the back of any roofed structure; for fenced or walled rear yards, the distance can be reduced to 15 feet.

Cul-de-sac lots are very popular in conventional family communities because they offer large yards and relatively safe and quiet streets. However, in active adult communities, large yards are expensive to maintain, children do not play in the streets, and neighborhoods tend to be quiet. Thus, the appeal of the cul-de-sac to the active adult market is limited. As a rule, only about 2 to 3 percent of all lots should be on culs-de-sac in active adult communities.

Circulation and Access

Accepted principles of circulation, street design, and signage apply to AARCs, with some important additional considerations.

Street Circulation. Finding one's way easily is important in AARCs, both for marketing purposes and to make life easier for residents as they age. Certain conventional community planning designs—winding streets, "T" intersections, offset intersections, loops, and long culs-de-sac—should be used sparingly, as they can make it more difficult for residents to find their way around the community. Though many of these techniques were developed to enhance street scenes, slow the speed of traffic, and create quiet, safe neighborhoods for children, they can also be confusing and difficult to navigate. Confusion is especially likely when street names change in the middle of a block.

Way-Finding. In AARCs, the most practical internal circulation system is a modified grid with four-way intersections, slightly curving streets, and minimal culs-de-sac and "T" intersections. This system not only makes it easier to find one's way, but its more conventional approach is also familiar and reassuring to the market. A modified grid system can also allow more north/south, solar-oriented lots, which are highly preferred by the market, especially in warm climates.

Street Design. Residential street widths are typically narrower in conventional communities than in active adult communities. Streets should be sufficiently wide—32 to 36 feet—to allow

two comfortable travel lanes and at least one parking lane; streets narrower than 30 feet are generally not good practice in AARCs. Although the residents are active adults, their age-related limitations will affect their ability to maneuver an automobile and negotiate tight streets. With the exception of those in golf-course communities, arterial and collector streets may be designed to local municipal standards.

Because many states allow golf carts on public streets as long as the carts are equipped to local standards, golf-course communities can expect a fairly high number of private golf carts in the community. Some communities separate cart paths or cart trails by putting stripes on collector and arterial streets, but this approach has had mixed success. Generally, when a golf cart is licensed to operate as an ordinary vehicle, the cart owners will drive anywhere an ordinary vehicle can go. Most communities have found that the best way to create a safe environment for golf carts is to widen the outside lanes by four to six feet on collector and arterial streets and to

Homes such as this one, in the Winfield community, complement their southwestern location in color, form, and texture.

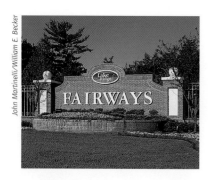

Clear signage and attractive landscaping mark the entrance to the Lake Ridge community, in Tom's River, New Jersey.

lower the speed limits. This approach brings regular traffic down to the speed of the golf carts and allows automobiles to pass the golf carts safely.

Trail Systems. Walking is the most popular form of exercise in the senior market today. Communities that can provide off-street trail systems with a comfortable walking surface in a natural area will be highly valued by the retirement market. Any network of trails should connect to residential and arterial streets to provide a complete and well-integrated system that all residents can easily access. Although trail construction will vary from region to region depending on climate, conditions, and materials, the overall goal is to create a comfortable, low-maintenance, all-weather walking surface. Generally, concrete is not recommended.

When providing trails along arterial or collector streets, it is good practice to separate the trail from the roadway with a landscaped parkway. Planners and designers may also consider adding seating areas along the trail system. In the King's Ridge AARC, in central Florida, the trails that are located on the main arterial throughout the community include nicely designed and well-executed seating areas. In addition to serving as an amenity, the seating areas are visually interesting elements of the landscaping along the arterial.

Bicycling is another popular form of exercise in AARCs, and developers should consider a bike trail system that is separate from the walking trails. If the walking and bike trails are combined into a single system, the trails should be at least eight feet wide, preferably with a center stripe. For example, in the Village Walk community in Naples, Florida, DiVosta and Company connected the residential areas and the town center with a lighted trail that accommodates walkers, bicyclists, and in-line skaters.

The Project Entrance

The image that is created at the main entrance to an active adult retirement community is very important: for retirees, the entrance is the front door of their new lives, and it should reinforce their sense of what the community is like and why they chose to live there.

The entry monuments should be designed to support large graphics. Especially if the community is located along a busy thoroughfare, the identifying signage should be large enough for older residents and prospective buyers to read easily. The public approach to the main entry—its "presentation"—is also very important and should complement and enhance the entrance itself. The landscaping along the approach to the community should set the tone for the quality of the landscaping within. "Windows" into the community from the main access road should be strategically designed to allow views of community amenities such as a golf course, lake, clubhouse, or natural open area. Windows can also provide distant views of the housing within the community.

Security

Retirees tend to prefer to live in communities that have security features. Among communities surveyed for the *National Directory of Lifestyle Communities,* 43 percent had automatic gates, a security guard, or both. Of those that were not secured in these ways, 34 percent had roving patrols within the community.

A gated and guarded entry should include a structure large enough to house at least two people; it should also include a toilet facility and storage. Often, the guardhouse is the security headquarters for the community. Screened parking for several cars and security vehicles should also be provided. There should be easy turnarounds both before and after the gates. A separate visitors' entry lane should be provided in addition to the lanes in which residents enter the community.

AMENITIES

The choice and design of community amenities in an AARC is central to establishing an environment where residents can enjoy the active and sociable lifestyle they seek.

The Clubhouse

More than any other amenity, the clubhouse or community center embodies the lifestyle that is created in the community. The hub of all activity, the clubhouse is the predominant marketing element in presenting to sales prospects the potential of the active adult community.

Size and Phasing. The size of the clubhouse relative to the number of homes in the community and the level of quality in the design, fittings, and finishings will have a direct impact on the potential buyer's perception of value. Through economies of scale, larger communities can provide a multitude of facilities and amenities for their residents. Builders of smaller communities, in contrast, must be particularly judicious in the planning and design of facilities to provide, within a more limited budget, a desirable lifestyle and, at the same time, present facilities that will appeal to potential buyers.

There are no magic formulas to determine the size of a clubhouse on the basis of the number of people it will serve. Not all of the residents of an AARC use the facilities every day, and some do not use them at all. However, data from the *National Directory of Lifestyle Communities* does suggest a rule of thumb for sizing facilities: for communities with fewer than 300 units, the ratio is approximately 21 to 23 square feet of clubhouse for every home. For communities with between 300 and 1,500 units, the ratio is 16 to 18 square feet per unit. And for communities with more than 1,500 units, the ratio goes down to 13 to 15 square feet per unit.

Timing. Building the facilities early is very important for the initial marketing of the community. Over the past three decades, broken promises—in both the general real estate industry and

The Valencia Falls Clubhouse

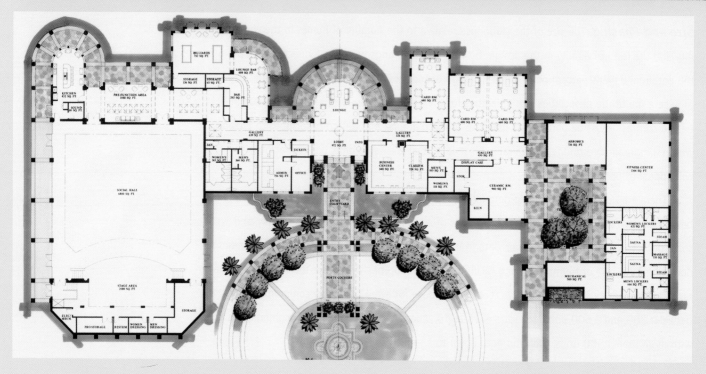

Source: Kenneth Rohde, Principal, KTGY Group, Inc., Fort Lauderdale, Florida.

ACTIVE ADULT RETIREMENT COMMUNITIES

The Valencia Falls active adult retirement community, in Coral Springs, Florida, has a 25,000-square-foot clubhouse for a community of 800 homes. The clubhouse's Spanish Colonial Revival style was chosen to establish the character and lifestyle of the community.

SWIMMING POOL

FORMAL GARDEN

MAIN LOBBY

AUDITORIUM

SERVICE ACCESS

PORTE COCHERE

PARKING

ENTRY DRIVE

SAND BEACH

SHADE GAZEBO

SPA

BATH HOUSE

SHADE GAZEBO

LAP POOL

FITNESS CENTER

PUTTING GREEN

CENTER COURT

TENNIS PAVILION

TENNIS COURTS

The clubhouse includes a sandwich bar and lounge, a billiards room, activity areas, a fitness facility, card rooms, a community kitchen with a display kitchen for cooking classes, and a large auditorium for professional productions. The floor plan is shown on the facing page.

Exterior amenities, shown in the site plan at left, include a swimming pool, a lap pool, a sand beach, gazebos, a spa, tennis courts, a putting green, and a formal garden.

the AARC industry—have made the buying public wary of plans and renderings promising grand communities. Completing the clubhouse—or at least a substantial portion of it—at the onset of development will alleviate buyers' concerns and demonstrate that the developer has the financial wherewithal to complete the community as planned. Developers of larger communities, where facilities will eventually total more than 25,000 square feet, have the luxury of building only a portion of the facilities during the initial phase of development. However, that portion still needs to be substantial enough to provide the first residents with the promised lifestyle. A recommended rule of thumb is to build enough of the facility to accommodate the first one-third of the homes, but not less than 20,000 square feet.

Location. The location of the clubhouse and other major amenities is important from the standpoint of both marketing and use. To maximize the value of the clubhouse from both of these perspectives, a developer must consider and balance a number of factors. Best planning practice places the clubhouse in a central location within the community where all residents can reach it easily. For marketing purposes, the clubhouse should be located near the sales center and where it has the highest visibility for sales traffic. Location decisions may also be influenced by the natural features of the site.

Clubhouses are easy to locate in smaller communities, where the center of the community is not far from the main entry. In larger communities, however, the cost of developing the roadways and infrastructure to reach into the center of the community in the initial phase can be a financial burden. Nevertheless, a central location has benefits. Because prospective buyers must drive further into the community, they can better appreciate the size and nature of the property that the community will eventually encompass. Also, centrally locating the clubhouse allows the developer to place more of the community's amenities—such as a golf course, preserved areas, greenbelts, and walking trails—along the "marketing trail." And in some cases, on their way to visit the clubhouse, prospective buyers can drive past future commercial, professional, or emergency services, which can be noted with appropriate signage. Finally, a lengthy marketing trail leading into the center of the community can send a subtle signal to prospective buyers that the developer has the financial wherewithal to be successful.

Relationship to the Sales Center. Because the clubhouse is one of the developer's best marketing tools, it should be located as close to the sales center as possible, even in the same building. However, developers should take care not to allow residents' activities and sales activities to mix. If the two functions are in the same building, they should have separate entrances, separate signage, and separate parking. If they are in separate buildings on the same campus, the sales center should not be between buildings that serve the residents. Potential buyers will want to visit the clubhouse, but residents generally dislike having the builder's sales activities directly in their midst.

The developer of a large community who is planning an extended sales operation should consider constructing a building to house the sales and operating functions. If it is located close to the clubhouse, this building can become part of the community's recreational and office facilities when the sales operation is complete. This approach can reduce the overall size of the recreational facility that the developer has to build.

General Design Considerations. The clubhouse is the primary vehicle for presenting the community lifestyle: it creates prospective residents' first impressions and helps them determine whether the community is right for them. The clubhouse can convey an image that is casual, elegant, or somewhere in between. A casual style creates a strong sense of invitation and ownership; elegance creates a feeling of exclusivity. The appropriate balance of "casual elegance" will create a successful clubhouse for a specific market.

Like any community center, the clubhouse is the primary social gathering place for residents. The clubhouse must be carefully planned to maximize visual impact, functional flexibility,

Soaring ceilings, expansive windows, and fine interior finishings and furnishings create an elegant ambience in the clubhouse at Sun City Grand, in Phoenix, Arizona.

97

and operating efficiency while minimizing maintenance and energy costs. The clubhouse must be designed to allow a number of simultaneous activities to take place without any one activity disrupting others. A clubhouse that is always "humming with activity" creates a feeling of vitality and contributes to the synergy that is needed to achieve the active adult lifestyle.

Generally speaking, the clubhouse is divided into three areas, each of which serves a specific function: an area for fitness facilities, an area for social activities, and an area for hobbies or other activities. (The clubhouse should also include offices for community administration and operations. Though the amount of office space will vary with the size of the community and the activities offered, at least one office and a conference room will be needed.)

In larger communities, fitness, social, and hobby areas can be housed in separate buildings in a campus setting or in one large building with a separate entrance for each activity area. (One advantage of separate entrances is that they allow residents wearing fitness clothes or golf attire to avoid mixing with those who are attending dressy functions in the restaurant or ballroom.) Although some spaces may be used for more than one purpose, distinct spaces are associated with each of the key activity areas.

Even where separate entrances are provided, however, all users should be able to enter through a main lobby. The exterior approach to the lobby should be designed and furnished to welcome residents and guests and at the same time convey the image of the lifestyle that the community seeks to provide. There are numerous ways to achieve both effects—among them, water features; striking landscape design; and strong architectural elements, such as a *porte cochère* or detailed fenestration. The main lobby should create a strong visual cue indicating all

Because room dividers make possible the flexible use of space in the main social hall, the clubhouse at Heritage in the Hills, outside of Detroit, can accommodate functions of various kinds and sizes.

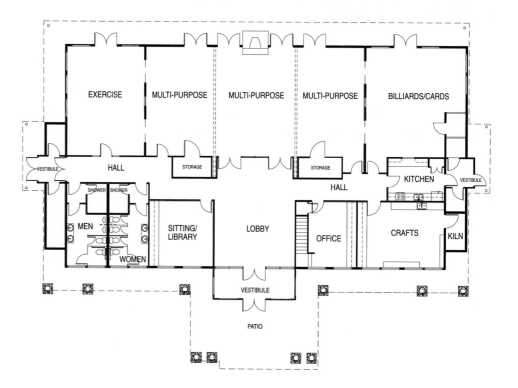

ACTIVE ADULT RETIREMENT COMMUNITIES

the opportunities offered within. A reception desk and an informational kiosk describing the available activities and facilities are excellent ways to orient visitors.

Because it plays such a strong role in creating the visitor's first impression, the main entry area should be designed with the highest possible level of fittings and finishings. Inside the main entry, a high-ceilinged area with clerestory windows creates a lively ambience during the day; in the evening, a combination of indirect lighting and illumination from chandeliers creates a beacon that enhances the approach to the community center.

Golfers who arrive by car should be directed to the golf entry, and a bag drop should be located within easy view of the starter's desk and pro shop. A terrace can be designed to create a view of the first tee, putting practice area, and—if the community is large enough—a driving range. Circulation spines and clear signage should be used to direct golfers to use hard-surface walkways to reach the greens, the starting area, and the restaurant patio.

Parking. To minimize walking and make access easier, parking spaces can be grouped around the building near each of the separate entries. Covered walkways can be provided in climates where these are desirable. Parking areas should include large diagonal spaces and two-way driveways rather than small, perpendicular parking spaces. Parking stalls and bays should also be wider than standard: nine-foot stalls and 60-foot perpendicular parking bays will allow residents greater comfort and safety when negotiating the parking lots. To satisfy the higher level of need in an AARC, it is good practice to increase—by 10 to 15 percent over code requirement—the number of parking spaces designated for the use of handicapped residents. Such spaces can

Clubhouse design should provide for a separate entrance for golfers and a parking area for golf carts.

then be distributed around the building and not grouped together in one location, which can create the sense that the facility is for "older people."

In golf-course communities, parking lots should also include parking stalls for golf carts, as many residents prefer to use their carts for general transportation within the community.

Fitness Facilities. Health and fitness amenities are essential, and most of the developers whose projects are featured as case studies in this book reported that fitness facilities are the most popular clubhouse amenity. Depending on the size of the community, fitness amenities range from modest exercise rooms to large exercise, dance, and health club facilities.

Exercise equipment should be placed so that outside activities are visible from within the facility; however, occupants who are exercising should be able to observe outside activity rather than be observed. In fitness rooms that are adjacent to outdoor activity areas (such as the pool, the golf starting area, or the lounges within the fitness area), large glass walls can increase the sense of connection to outside activities; treadmills, weight machines, and other equipment should be oriented to windows rather than to blank walls.

Weight equipment should include both free weights and top-of-the-line hydraulic weight machines. A service desk staffed by professional trainers can monitor access to the exercise facilities and observe the area for emergencies.

Low-impact and dance aerobics are very popular forms of exercise in AARCs. A well-designed dance and exercise studio should have at least one mirrored wall with a ballet barre; storage for mats, steps, and swing weights; good air conditioning distribution; and controllable indirect lighting (because many aerobic exercises are performed lying on one's back). A well-cushioned wood floor should be provided to reduce stress on older joints. Lastly, because older exercisers may be self-conscious about being seen in tights, users should be able to limit visibility into the aerobics studio if they wish.

Shower and locker areas can be shared by golfers and fitness exercisers. Although minimal locker facilities are needed in smaller communities, where most residents come dressed for the workout and then return home for their shower, at least a small facility must still be provided. Medium-sized and larger communities should provide sauna areas and massage rooms as well as showers, lockers, and changing facilities.

In larger facilities, there is a growing trend toward partnering with a health care provider to staff and operate a wellness center within the fitness facility. The wellness center typically provides residents with literature, counseling about exercise for their age group, information on aging, and limited health screening.

Activity and Hobby Spaces. The clubhouse must also provide space and facilities to enjoy a wide range of hobbies and activities. The activities program will vary according to the interests

Designing Health and Fitness Facilities

The following is a descriptive list of desirable elements that could be included in a health and fitness facility designed for active adults. The types and number of components offered in any given development will vary, depending on the size and location of the community and the preferences of the specific target market.

Pools: Indoor and Outdoor

1. Pool depth for water aerobics: 3½ to 4½ feet, sloping across the pool.

2. Competitive length for "Senior Olympic" competition: 25 yards.

3. Access for handicapped residents:

   Ramp with handrails on both sides.

   Removable hoist or sling.

   "Zero-level" entry for outdoor pools.

4. Indoor pool environment:

   Sliding roof or skylights.

   Sliding walls and windows.

   Noninstitutional décor.

   Low-velocity air movement; air should never blow directly on the water.

   Good acoustics for water aerobics instruction.

5. Indoor spas: These demand intense programming and extensive design considerations. They need considerable space because safety requires access on three sides. They generate considerable heat and moisture, so they need to be in a separate space if they are anywhere other than in an indoor pool environment.

Aerobics and Multiuse Rooms

1. High-impact aerobics are relatively unpopular; mat activities, yoga, stretching aerobics and exercises, and low-impact aerobics and activities based on dancing or gliding are the norm.

2. Requirements:

   Cushioned wood or other hard-surface floor system.

   Mirrors on three walls, a ballet barre on one.

   Storage for mats, steps, swing weights, and audio equipment.

   Adjustable lighting.

   Cubicles for personal effects.

   Controllable window treatment for privacy; active adults prefer not to be viewed from the outside or from adjoining circulation areas.

Fitness Center

1. General requirements:

   Control desk for check-in and monitoring.

   Lounge area for "cool-down."

   In larger facilities, an office for the fitness director.

   Cubicles for personal effects.

   Room should be oriented toward view, and equipment should be oriented toward windows.

2. Cardiovascular equipment:

   Primarily treadmills and exercycles (both recumbent and upright), with less emphasis on stair-step machines and rowing machines than would be found in intergenerational facilities.

   Recessed treadmills.

   Cardio "theater": TVs with individual earphones.

3. Strength training:

   For larger facilities, "full-circuit" equipment stations; for smaller facilities, multistation equipment.

   Free weights and benches (free weights should be primarily dumbbells, with few barbells).

   A floor area and a wall area for stretching, with mats and progress charts.

Indoor Walking Tracks

1. General requirements:

   Cushioned, "running track" surface.

   Level floor; no banking.

   Views.

   Specific length is not important; provide distance measurements (i.e., "X number of laps to a mile").

   Alcove seating at appropriate intervals.

Source: Richard Diedrich, AIA, executive vice president, Diedrich/NBA, a subsidiary of Niles Bolton Associates, Atlanta, Georgia.

of the residents and the skills of the activity director, so the physical spaces should be flexible enough to accommodate changes in use. As a rule, the level of fittings and finishings in the arts and hobby rooms can be somewhat lower than that in the social areas.

Common activities include ceramics, painting, quilting, woodworking, and photography. The ceramics room should be outfitted with equipment for mixing, molding, glazing, and firing ceramics. The art studio should be oriented to obtain north light and should be near outdoor shaded patios, which can provide an ideal setting for sketching, painting, and other forms of art. A gallery for the display of their art and craft work offers residents an opportunity to show their work within the community. The main entry lobby and the corridors that connect the primary amenity zones offer good spaces for exhibits and display cases.

Computer facilities are becoming more and more common in clubhouses as seniors become increasingly interested in surfing the Internet, corresponding with their grandchildren by e-mail, using computer graphics, and designing Web sites. Computer facilities in clubhouses can take various forms. Computer rooms often include multiple networked stations, printers, scanners, and copiers. Classes can be offered for the novice or experienced user and can focus on particular topics, such as financial planning, or on specific computer application programs.

Social Areas. Social areas within the clubhouse should convey a sense of casual elegance. A multipurpose room is generally used for functions such as banquets, dances, theatrical performances, and resident-directed gatherings such as travel talks and community meetings. So that it can be used for functions of varying sizes and types, the multipurpose room should be divisible into separate spaces. High-grade sound partitions can be used to control sound transmission between the divided spaces.

Clubhouses in larger communities should include a formal stage with a curtain; medium-sized communities should have at least a platform and a staging area. Multipurpose rooms in medium-sized to large communities should have backstage dressing rooms and prop areas to support a range of different programs. The clubhouse design should include a large area outside the multipurpose room where people can gather and socialize before and after events.

Because the multipurpose room is used for banquet functions, an adjoining catering kitchen is desirable. In larger communities, the restaurant operator should be able to prepare banquets. For example, in the Village at the Arboretum, in Ontario, the kitchen is sufficiently large and well-appointed to allow the preparation of meals for some 400 guests. In medium-sized and smaller communities, where the kitchen is more modest, it may be used primarily for catered events and potlucks.

Billiards rooms and adjacent media areas with large-screen television sets offer additional opportunities for socializing. Card games are popular, and rooms for this activity are essential. Ideally, the clubhouse would include flexible spaces that can be expanded into double-sized card

This restaurant, in the clubhouse at Sun City Hilton Head, illustrates the importance of light, color, and contrast in the design of interior spaces for AARCs.

rooms when tournaments and special functions are held. Depending on the size of the community and the interests of the residents, clubhouses might also include game areas and media rooms.

Lounge areas, whether they are bar areas or fireside reading lounges, are important spaces where residents gather to socialize or while they wait to participate in other activities. Lounges should be easily accessible from the main lobby of the clubhouse; because they should offer the opportunity to observe rather than to be observed, lounges should not be placed in the center of the lobby area but off to the side.

Contiguous to the lounge area, many larger communities include a restaurant, which often overlooks the golf course or a water amenity. Such views contribute the kind of elegant touch that is characteristic of a country club, adding to the ambience of the restaurant and reinforcing the "resort" aspect of the community lifestyle.

Another feature that provides an excellent opportunity for social interaction is a library, which can include used books provided by residents as well as books from traveling public libraries. Seniors love to learn. Where libraries are not specifically included, residents may create one: in the Village Walk community in Naples, Florida, for example, residents converted a small card room into a community library. Libraries typically include lounge seating areas that create a warm, welcoming ambience.

Interior Design for Clubhouses

The clubhouse in an active adult retirement community should have a country-club look, offering a "members only" appeal but within a casual environment. As a general rule, the interior should be furnished with warm colors, timeless design, and a style that is appropriate to the location. For example, in southern California, an effective clubhouse would be designed with a Mediterranean look and furnished in desert earth colors, with stone accents and beamed ceilings.

The following are some rules of thumb to guide the interior design of clubhouses:

- Involve the interior designer early in the planning process, along with the architect, as part of the clubhouse design team.
- The clubhouse amenities and design should be upbeat, bright, and fun, and the tone should be casual rather than formal.
- Establish good curb appeal with high-quality exterior lighting and landscaping.
- Materials should reflect the history and architectural character of the project's location. For example, in Florida, to "feel like Florida," the interior design should be contemporary, light, and airy.
- If the design is based on a theme, carry it through and be authentic.
- Good lighting is essential, indoors and out. Use decorative fixtures that give off lots of light. Lighting should be stronger in task and reading areas such as arts and crafts rooms, multi-purpose rooms, and card rooms. Dimmer switches make it possible to adjust the level of light to the needs of specific activities.

Accessibility. By law, all common facilities, including fitness areas, must provide access for people with disabilities. Many older residents have physical limitations or develop temporary physical disabilities. Stages or platforms should have ramp access. And in swimming pools, a ramp not only provides wheelchair access but also allows bathers to enter the water slowly and to the depth of their choice. As an alternative to a swimming pool ramp, the developer can install a "handicapped hoist" or a transfer bench and pool curb. One side of the curb is raised approximately 14 inches from the pool deck, and the other side is at water level. This arrangement allows a person to sit on a raised bench outside the pool and then swing over to the water level at the high side of the bench to make an easy transfer. This detail can often be incorporated into creative landscaping to create a "horizon water line" pool.

- For good acoustics, stay away from finishes that can echo; always soften noisy areas with carpet, wall upholstery, or drapery.

- In selecting seating, lounge chairs are preferable to sofas. (Sectional sofas are especially difficult for older people and should not be used.) Chairs should have arms; and, because older people benefit from visual distinctions, chair patterns should contrast with carpet patterns.

- Place seating groups close together to facilitate conversation.

- Provide benches or other seating along long corridors and walkways.

- Bright colors are best. Avoid tones of gold because colors tend to take on a more yellow cast when viewed through older eyes.

- Add character with signage and graphics that are customized for the facility. All signage should be located and designed to be easy for older eyes to read.

- Millwork items are important to create a clubhouse atmosphere; reception desks, bookcases, and bars also help convey a sense that the design quality is high.

- Make generous use of indoor plants, especially to "warm up" large indoor spaces. The taller the ceiling, the taller the plants should be.

- Keep the look fresh and in good repair: replace carpeting, fabrics, upholstery, and other "soft goods" every five or six years. "Case goods" (tables, desks, cabinets, etc.) should be replaced within ten years.

- Nothing in clubhouses for active adults should hint at any design or furnishing accommodation for aging.

Source: Sue Firestone, president/chief executive officer, Sue Firestone & Associates, Santa Barbara, California.

Interior Design. The quality of the interior design sets the tone for the community clubhouse—and therefore for the entire community. An appealing ambience can powerfully motivate residents to use and enjoy the clubhouse, and a clubhouse that is bustling with activity is a much stronger marketing tool than one that stands empty.

The successful clubhouse interior design of today strikes an appropriate balance: it is neither too "institutional" nor excessively ostentatious. As noted earlier, casual elegance is the dominant note.

Outdoor Recreational Amenities

The selection of outdoor recreational facilities for an AARC depends on the preferences of the target market, the characteristics of the site, and the available budget. Typical outdoor recreational amenities include golf, swimming pools, and court games.

Golf. Many retirees play golf, and a golf course is the central amenity in many retirement communities; nevertheless, not all communities can or want to revolve around golf. In AARCs with golf courses, approximately 30 percent of the residents play the game. Because golf-course lots provide green vistas, they are popular and enjoyed by golfers and nongolfers alike. If the development site is large enough to contain more than one golf course, the first course should be a full-length, regulation course with a driving range. Second and third courses may take different forms, depending on market conditions and land availability.

The character and topography of the land typically dictate the location of the golf course, with stormwater drainage being a key consideration. In fitting the golf course within the site plan, it is important that the golf course be visible from the marketing trail and, if possible, from the front entrance to the community as well.

Swimming Pools. Outdoor swimming pools should be designed as integral components of the campus or clubhouse site, much in the way that a hotel pool is positioned in relation to the lobby. Thus, the pool itself should be rendered visible without putting the people around the pool on display, especially to nonresident visitors or passersby. Economical use of space dictates that the pool be easily accessible to the shower and locker facilities in the health and fitness center. Often a contiguous waterscape feature such as a lake, waterfall, or fountain helps to show off this amenity.

Swimming pools in AARCs are used for two primary activities: (1) exercise (water aerobics, water walking, and lap swimming) and (2) socializing. For smaller communities that can support only one pool, a good choice would be a multifunctional, free-form outdoor pool with separate areas for exercise and bathing. Outdoor pools should also include ample decks and generous shaded areas, furnished with tables and lounge chairs, for socializing and "around-the-pool" events. (Many seniors enjoy the outdoors but are concerned about the effects of sun on their skin.) In cold-weather climates, an indoor pool is a highly desirable feature.

Builders of larger communities should consider providing at least two swimming pools, one for fitness and exercise and one primarily for socializing. To garner the best use from a fitness pool, an indoor, fully climate controlled environment is recommended. Whirlpool spas within the swimming pool complex are highly desirable.

Every facility should have at least one large outdoor patio area: such areas are not only functional but contribute to a pleasant ambience, especially when they are designed as an integral part of the campus or site. The outdoor gathering area should be easily accessible from the main circulation area of the clubhouse and supported by the clubhouse's food service operations or catering kitchen.

Other Outdoor Recreational Facilities. Court games, especially tennis, bocce, and shuffleboard, continue to be very popular recreational pastimes in active adult retirement communities.

Designing Golf Courses for Active Adult Retirement Communities

Because there has been no in-depth research on active adult or baby boomer golfers, Ron Garl, a Lakeland, Florida, golf course architect, worked with *Senior Golfer* magazine to conduct a survey of older golfers, asking them to "Help Build A Course That You Can Play!" Over 4,000 people responded. Using the data from these survey responses, Garl designs courses that are tailored to the capabilities of senior golfers—and at the same time, offer the same shot-making quality and golf experiences that players at other levels of ability enjoy.

The first way Garl designs golf courses to accommodate the needs of older golfers is to include multiple tees. For example, a golf course might have five sets of tees, numbered one through five, placed at different distances from the holes. The various tees enable a golfer to choose the course he or she would like to play without engendering a feeling of playing from a "senior" or "women's" tee.

Another approach is to create holes that incorporate multiple tees into a curved linear design. This design system places the tee boxes in such a way that each set of tees offers the same shot quality in terms of visualization, yet a golfer need never hit over another set of tees. And, perhaps more important, curved linear design makes the play of the course equally challenging for players of different skill levels. The tee placement changes the degree of challenge by changing the angle and length to the landing area. For example, if the hole angles to the left, the tees, in progressive positions going forward, are all set to the right. In this way, as a player moves forward from the furthest to the closest tee, the hole not only becomes shorter, but, because the angle to the landing area is less sharp, the hole becomes less difficult. At the same time, this design technique results in reduced "carries" for the forward tees: that is, the back tee may require a 200-yard carry over a hazard, whereas the "senior" tee may only be 140 yards. Thus, the design "levels the playing field" for golfers of different abilities.

The survey also provided insights into how senior golfers play and how far they hit with different clubs. The overall favorite golf club was the 7-iron, while the favorite for chipping was an 8-iron. One of the big surprises was that 39 percent of seniors hook the ball. This information can be incorporated into designs to make them enjoyable and challenging, yet rewarding to play.

Specifically, the survey enables designers to create holes for play with a given club. For example, knowing that the majority of senior golfers hit a 5-iron 155 yards, a hole can be designed with that in mind. The goal is to design the various holes so that every club in a golfer's bag will be used at some point on the course.

The chart at right shows how far, on average, senior golfers hit using various types of clubs. Based on the preferred course length indicated in the survey, Garl normally designs golf courses with five sets of tees, one set of which results in a total course length of 6,280 yards.

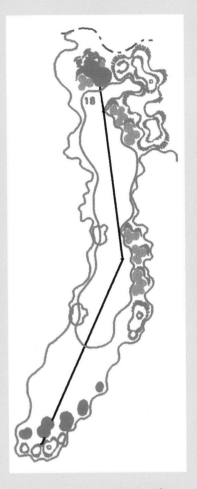

Curved linear design for designing golf tees.

Club	Distance (yards)
Driver	216
3-wood	197
4-wood	185
5-wood	178
3-iron	176
4-iron	165
5-iron	155
6-iron	145
7-iron	135
8-iron	123
9-iron	111
P-wedge	96

Source: Ron Garl, golf course architect, Lakeland, Florida.

Certain games have regional appeal, and the choice of which to include should be based on an assessment of market preferences. Bocce, for example, is particularly popular in the New Jersey area; shuffleboard is favored in Florida.

For the convenience of residents and to take advantage of nearby parking, game courts are typically located adjacent to the clubhouse. This location also makes for a stronger marketing presentation by creating a visual massing of amenities. Tennis courts should be located in a quiet area, away from activities that produce noise and distraction. However, the bocce and shuffleboard courts should be located in more active spots, as they are more social games.

Because activities such as bocce, tennis, and shuffleboard provide both participants and observers with opportunities for social interaction, facilities for these activities should include shaded observation areas, preferably with seating. In addition, game courts should be easily accessible and within view of the major areas of the clubhouse.

RESIDENTIAL PRODUCTS

Designing a home for the active, mature homebuyer is not a difficult task, but it does require an understanding of the market's needs, desires, and lifestyle, which differ significantly from those that most builders are accustomed to addressing in the conventional family-home market. Usually, there are only two people living in the home, typically husband and wife. Since they are now retired or semiretired, they spend much more time in the home during the day. And, many of the leisure activities in which they engage take place in the home. Their lives are more relaxed and casual, and many want the home's design to reflect that.

Though retirees are generally receptive to changes in their lifestyle, the basic values, beliefs, and principles that have guided their lives remain steadfast—and, in fact, usually strengthen as they age. Thus, although they want a home with a fresh style and a new ambience, their long-standing values require the home to be of high quality and to function efficiently and cost-effectively.

General Design Considerations

The vast majority of mature buyers prefer single-family detached homes, though, as the case study on Leisure World of Virginia demonstrates, this preference is not universal (see chapter 7). They also prefer to live on one level, although two-story homes can be offered if all primary living spaces—especially the master bedroom and den or office—are on the first floor. Typically, a second floor will contain a second bedroom and bath. A basement is generally not a popular option. However, if the topography of the site allows, a walkout basement that can be used for additional living space may be desirable. In cold climates, foundation depths may make basements almost a requirement.

Good indoor-outdoor relationships are important for the homes of active adults. Even in regions where there are four distinct seasons, people want to enjoy the outdoors through a

Well-designed homes for active adults offer views of open space from the breakfast nook off the kitchen.

patio, deck, porch, or balcony. Patios and decks should be strongly connected to interior living spaces and easily accessible through the kitchen; to ensure privacy, they should be screened from side and rear neighbors. From a functional standpoint, front porches can suffice where site constraints make other options difficult. Front porches are especially popular where they face attractive natural or built features.

Ample light provides a contemporary feel and better accommodates the needs of aging eyes. A light, bright, and airy home offers a strong contrast to the dark, low-ceilinged, more compartmentalized homes that many retirees have left behind. Ceilings should be nine or ten feet high—high enough to add volume without being inefficient. High windows should be used above upper kitchen cabinets, over mirrors and showers in bathrooms, and on other outside walls where privacy needs to be protected. Skylights are important in inner rooms to let natural light into the house during the day. Although borrowed light—via transoms and high internal "windows"—can also be effective, such features should be used judiciously, where they are the most effective and where privacy will not be disturbed.

Floor Plans

Less formal room arrangements are a hallmark of the retirement lifestyle. A casual, relaxed, and open plan, supported by strong visual connections, allows the main living spaces of the home to flow together. Low walls, wide passages, and internal windows should be used to connect rooms that in more traditional homes would be separated by solid walls. These windows should create a sense of spaciousness, providing glimpses into other rooms and accenting views through the house.

The popular "great-room" plan is probably the best example of the casual style. A well-designed great-room, which generally opens to both the kitchen and the outdoor area, offers distinct spaces for conversation, dining (both casual and formal), and viewing television. The entry foyer should open directly onto the great-room, but the kitchen should not be visible from the entrance. Depending upon the needs of the buyer, the great-room can also incorporate a home office or hobby area. Great-room plans make sense for the retirement lifestyle because they fulfill the same function as a conventional, compartmentalized plan without the additional space and upkeep.

Although the great-room plan is popular, family-room plans and formal living- and dining-room plans are still in demand and should be a part of a builder's line. However, those plans should also be opened visually, with internal windows and wide passages connecting the various living and dining spaces.

A single plan that accommodates everything that a retiree wants and needs may be impossible to achieve. The market is very diverse, and the lifestyles and home activities of retirees are marked by considerable variety. There are, however, several key home activities that should be addressed by a range of floor plans.

Because many retirees still work part-time, the home office is an increasingly important offering. A good location for a home office is adjacent to or close to the front door: not only does that provide easy access for visitors and deliveries, but it is also easier to isolate from other living areas of the house.

The guest bedroom should be large enough to accommodate an extra portable bed or cot because it may be used not only by children but by grandchildren. Hobbies and crafts, an important part of the retirement lifestyle, can be accommodated in an extra bedroom, a larger utility room, or extra space in the garage.

Scott Mitchell/Courtesy of Danielian Associates

The Morganite model in Winfield, an AARC in Scottsdale, Arizona, is a two-bedroom plan with options to accommodate two additional bedrooms, including a detached "casita." It features a pre-entry courtyard, 12-foot ceilings, and living spaces that are designed for flexible use.

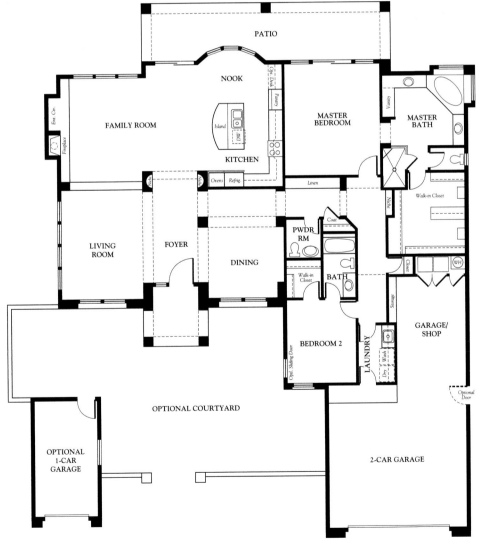

To take advantage of rear-oriented views and of patios, decks, and other outdoor living spaces, the primary living areas should be open to the rear of the house. The master bedroom should be located at the rear of the house as well, both to provide protection from traffic noise and to offer access to views. The areas in the home that should be oriented to open space are the great-room (or living room and family room) and the breakfast nook. In the retirement lifestyle, the breakfast nook is considered the most important room in the house. It is where the couple generally enjoys the morning paper over a leisurely cup of coffee while planning the day's activities.

Good circulation patterns through the house and good transportation between the garage, the kitchen, and the rest of the house are key elements of a successful floor plan. The garage entry should have convenient access to the main hall, the kitchen, and the family room (if included) and should lead directly through or past the utility room. Having the garage close to the kitchen is very important to reduce "grocery lugging" distance. Situating the utility room close by allows for convenient cleanup after a day of gardening or working in the "shop." Convenient passage from the kitchen to the outdoor living area or patio is also important. The route should be as direct as possible so that residents need not walk around furniture or negotiate a flooring change while carrying food.

Because members of the active adult market do not like to go through one room to get to another, circulation from the kitchen to the rest of the house should, where possible, be through hallways. Even in the open and casual home, hallways or defined circulation patterns are still important to provide a route between (as opposed to through) rooms. However, through the use of low walls, internal windows, and wide archways, hallways can be visually joined to adjacent rooms and still function in the way that the mature market wants them to.

Another element of circulation is the entry foyer. A well-designed foyer will enhance an open and casual plan by setting the stage for the rest of the house. It should open to the main living areas but be sufficiently contained to accommodate appropriate furniture.

Privacy

Even in open, casual floor plans, home design should protect the residents' privacy, indoors and out. Since the active adult market favors small lots because they require less maintenance, side windows may be so close that residents get to know their neighbors all too intimately. In such cases, homeowners may be forced to cover up windows that would otherwise make the home light, bright, and airy. To avoid side-to-side facing windows, plans should be designed as for zero-lot-line products. However, lots should be conventionally platted because many seniors are confused by the complexities of use easement transfers and irregularly shaped lots. Another technique to increase privacy is to place high windows on one side of the house that face low windows on the neighboring house.

Internal privacy can be just as important as external privacy. When the second bedroom is used for visiting family and guests, many people like the privacy of "split bedrooms." A good split-bedroom plan puts the master and guest bedrooms as far from each other as possible. However, as Donald Jacobs, president of JBZ Architecture + Planning, in Newport Beach, California, points out, one of the realities of senior couples is that many of them sleep in separate bedrooms, though this is something they may not want to discuss with a salesperson. Sometimes this is a permanent arrangement, but it can also happen when one of the pair is recovering from an illness or surgery. In some cases, particularly when one member of the household is the caregiver, senior couples don't necessarily want the second bedroom located away from the master bedroom. Thus, a developer should offer floor-plan options that include split bedrooms for those who want privacy and adjacent bedrooms for those who prefer bedrooms in closer proximity.

Another aspect of privacy that is important for aging residents is the separation between the bathroom and the sleeping area in the master suite. The suite should be designed so that the connection between the two areas does not allow light and noise to awaken the sleeping partner during the night. If there is limited flexibility for positioning the entry, a door or a pair of doors can provide a more gracious entry.

Storage

Because homes in active adult communities are generally smaller than "the family home" from which residents moved, every home plan, large or small, should address storage needs. When retirees move into their new home, they rarely abandon all the memories, collections, and possessions that they have accumulated over their lifetime. In addition to walk-in clothes closets, linen closets (at least one large one per bath), a kitchen pantry, and a coat closet, the design should include broom closets, built-in cabinets and shelves, display ledges, and art niches. Higher ceilings make it possible to add high storage shelves in walk-in closets and garages for seasonal items and luggage. Storage options such as floored attics with fixed or pull-down stairs, full or partial basements (where feasible and cost-effective), extra cabinets in the utility room, and expanded garages should also be designed into the home. Although many of these are optional features offered by the builder, they must be considered in the planning and design of the home.

Garages provide important storage space for belongings as well as automobiles. Although a retired couple can generally manage with one car, they prefer two-car garages so that they will have ample room for storage, a golf cart (in golfing communities), or a workshop.

Along with the smaller items that retirees have collected over the years, their furniture—particularly the antique pieces—requires ample space. Dining and living rooms should have enough wall space to accommodate a large hutch, an extra server, a large sectional sofa, and overstuffed lounge chairs. The master bedroom should be large enough to hold two dressers, and the headboard wall should provide sufficient space for twin beds with a nightstand in between.

Universal Design for the Active Adult Home

Builders of active adult communities are often challenged by the difficulty of providing universal design features in their units that will help residents age in place and enhance rather than detract from the residential feel of the homes. The following is a list of universal design features, any of which can be incorporated into a new home easily and without great expense:

General

Level access

Garage-door openers

Lever door handles

9' high garage door; van height option

3' wide exterior and interior doors

Minimum 36" wide hallways (42" preferable)

Front-loading laundry appliances

Wider, deeper stairs

Closet shelving in adjustable heights

Non-slip flooring with level thresholds

Dual cueing (both visual and audio indicators) for doorbell and security and smoke alarms

Electrical

Outlets a minimum of 18" above floor

Light switches 42" above floor

Touch or toggle luminous light switches

Thermostats at easy-to-read locations and elevations

Security

Home wired for security

Direct wired to police, fire, and emergency medical services (as option)

Security at guardhouse

Flashing porch light and/or 911 switch

Bathrooms

Extra-wide entry

Shower designed for transfer (36" wide by 36" deep) or roll-in (minimum 36" wide by 48" deep)

Consider options for flush-threshold, no-door shower seat

Hand-held spray with 60" long hose

15" extension at side of bathtub for easier entry

Raised toilet heights as option

Do not enclose toilet; or provide option to open up

Kitchen

Single-lever faucets

Pulls (no knobs) on cabinets and drawers

Counter-height oven

Raised dishwasher

Countertops at a variety of common heights— 30", 36", and 42"

Roll-out shelves or drawers in lower cabinets

Glass doors or open shelves in upper cabinets

Vertical (pantry-style) cabinets for most-used items

Waste and recycling containers on pull-out drawers in lower cabinets

Built-in desk

Side-by-side refrigerator (24" deep preferred)

Safety shut-offs and dual cueing on appliances

Pull-out step stool

Roll-out carts

Contrast edge on counters and flooring

Varied light sources and adjustable controls

Source: Mary Jo Peterson, president, Mary Jo Peterson, Inc., Design Consultants, Brookfield Connecticut. This information was originally published in *Seniors' Housing News* (fall 1999):27.

Aging in Place

Home design to accommodate the limitations associated with aging can be a marketing as well as a design issue. Active retirees don't want to think of themselves as old or growing old, so designs to help them age in place should be incorporated subtly and tastefully. Since not everyone will age in the same way or remain in the home for the same length of time, a plan for aging in place should include only those elements that would be the most difficult and costly to add when the need arises.

A cardinal rule is to keep the home on one level. Single-story plans outsell two-story or split-level plans in the active adult market by a margin of ten to one. Other key elements are wider doors into the house and into the bedrooms and baths, wider halls and passageways, and wider bathrooms. A short ramp in the garage can make it possible for possible for people who use wheelchairs to enter and leave the house with assistance and can also be used to wheel large objects in and out of the house.

DESIGNING AN ACTIVE ADULT RETIREMENT COMMUNITY WITHIN A MASTER-PLANNED COMMUNITY

Developing an AARC within a larger, conventionally master planned community has advantages, especially if the AARC is too small to support a golf course by itself. To ensure that the active adult portion of the community fits into the master plan in a way that is beneficial to both the AARC and the larger community, it is best to begin working with the master developer during the initial master-planning process. Unless the unique planning requirements of active adults are successfully incorporated from the outset, conventionally master planned communities may not be suitable environments for an active adult subdivision.

Amenities

In master-planned communities that incorporate AARCs, there are typically two levels of amenities: those that are shared by all residents of the master-planned community and those that are developed for the exclusive use of the residents of the active adult subdivision. The way in which amenities are used is typically reflected in fees and in the structure of the homeowners' associations. Thus it is important, within the AARC, to ensure that the amenities are reserved for the

Diedrich/NBA, a subsidiary of Niles Bolton Associates

Natural light in the exercise rooms is an important feature of Del Webb's fitness areas. Note that the treadmills are placed so that exercisers have views of the golf course.

exclusive use of the active adult residents: these amenities are paid for by the active adult buyers and supported through their dues, and residents do not like outsiders using "their" clubhouse.

Typically, the amenities for the larger master-planned community—such as a golf course, tennis courts, parks, trails, and other facilities—are designed to serve an intergenerational market. Through cooperative arrangements with the master developer, the active adult residents may be able to use the golf and tennis facilities during off-peak hours at reduced rates. If such arrangements can be made before planning for the AARC amenities is undertaken, the need for some of the AARC amenities may be reduced or eliminated.

Identity and Design Context

In general, retirees who are interested in living in an AARC are looking for a community with its own special identity, and they are unlikely to find an undifferentiated neighborhood within a master-planned community appealing. Because community identity is an important aspect of marketing and design, the active adult developer must work with the master developer early in the development process to establish the specific design characteristics of both the larger community and the AARC.

Creating a unique identity within the master developer's overall design scheme is not difficult. The main emphasis should be reflected in a well-defined entry with monuments and graphics, community landscaping and special hardscaping (distinctive paving), and the architecture of the community facilities. At the same time, the active adult neighborhood should fit into the master plan. Radically different design will draw negative attention.

Location

When negotiating the location of the active adult neighborhood within a master-planned community, it is recommended that the active adult community be located

- Close to but not directly adjacent to any commercial sites.
- As far as possible from any planned school sites and industrial areas.
- Close to but not directly adjacent to any public parks.
- Accessible to but away from busy streets.
- Not directly adjacent to high-density residential areas such as apartments or mid-rise or high-rise condominiums.
- Adjacent to high-end or empty-nester residential neighborhoods.
- Adjacent to any master-planned golf course but not too close to the clubhouse. (Also, it is preferable that an adjacent golf course be buffered by a wetlands or open space preserve to separate the public course from the residences of the active adults.)
- Adjacent to any wetlands or other natural open space.

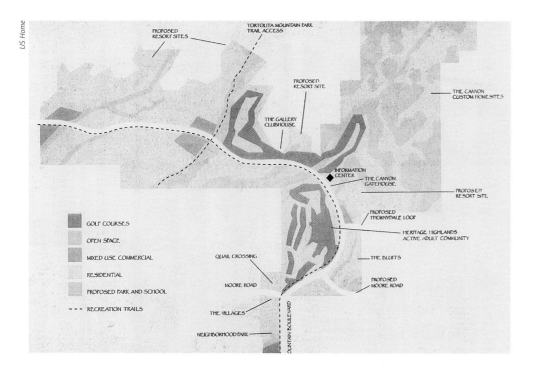

PROPOSED
RESORT SITES

TORTOLITA MOUNTAIN PARK
TRAIL ACCESS

PROPOSED
RESORT SITE

THE CANYON
CUSTOM HOMESITES

THE GALLERY
CLUBHOUSE

INFORMATION
CENTER

THE CANYON
GATEHOUSE

PROPOSED
RESORT SITE

PROPOSED
THORNYDALE LOOP

HERITAGE HIGHLANDS
ACTIVE ADULT COMMUNITY

QUAIL CROSSING

THE BLUFFS

MOORE ROAD

PROPOSED
MOORE ROAD

GOLF COURSES

OPEN SPACE

MIXED USE COMMERCIAL

RESIDENTIAL

PROPOSED PARK AND SCHOOL

RECREATION TRAILS

THE VILLAGES

MOUNTAIN BOULEVARD

NEIGHBORHOOD PARK

US Home's Heritage Highlands active adult community is one subdivision within the larger master-planned community of Dove Mountain, in Arizona.

Circulation

The entry to the active adult neighborhood should be directly off the main arterial road within the community. It is wise to have the main entry controlled by a traffic signal, both for convenience and as a safety measure for residents. If the master developer has a program for community-wide directional signage, graphics should be enlarged within the active adults' neighborhood to accommodate the needs of the senior market.

Circulation should loop internally within the active adult neighborhood. The entrances into and out of the neighborhood should be limited, regardless of whether the community is gated, to provide a greater sense of security and to discourage accidental traffic and unwanted incursions.

5
Marketing

Kathleen B. Cecilian, President, KC & Associates, Flemington, New Jersey

For any given development, the developer's goal is to sell the product. This chapter discusses briefly the concept of marketing strategy; describes an array of tools that developers can use to create an integrated marketing strategy for active adult retirement communities (AARCs); and highlights aspects of the sales experience and process that are especially important for this type of development.

A well-conceived marketing strategy is the foundation of all successful AARCs. Creating a marketing strategy means much more than merely selecting an advertising agency: it means deliberately creating an image for the community in the eyes of the outside world. Marketing strategy determines how a development enters the market and goes forward, which battles are fought and which are avoided. Integrating the marketing strategy into all areas of the development—including planning, development, and operations—creates a seamless impression that consumers respond to well.

At Winfield, in Scottsdale, Arizona, floor-to-ceiling windows in the sales office provide views of the community's outdoor amenities.

In the SaddleBrooke community, outside Tucson, homebuyers can choose among various elevations that are based on the architectural heritage of the Southwest.

There should be no disparity between the community as it is represented in the advertising materials and the community as it really is. If the marketing strategy is savvy and well-planned, a consumer will not only understand the community but aspire to live in it.

At the core of the marketing strategy is "positioning": positioning determines a community's place within the competitive environment. Will the community be high-end? Provide European service? Be value-based? Environmentally friendly? The developer must be courageous and take a market position, but must also understand that the position must remain fluid and will be modified to adjust to market changes as the years go by.

THE TOOL BOX

A developer can use a combination of tools to market an AARC successfully. These include the development of a brand identity, the use of market and consumer research, the creation of unique selling propositions, and various forms of advertising and public relations.

Tool 1: The Branding Iron

The single most important objective in marketing an AARC is to build a brand identity in the minds of prospective buyers. A brand is a name, readily recognized by consumers, that is associated with a style and a set of practices that identify and differentiate the company and its developments. The brand's purpose is to create a kind of prepackaged understanding of the company in the minds of the people it sells to and works with, as well as in the minds of the public at large.

Branding an active adult community is not unlike branding cattle on a ranch. A rancher wants to differentiate his cow from the other cows on the range, even if all the cows look pretty much alike. Creating a unique image in the buyers' minds of the company and what it represents is the foundation of a successful branding program. The brand image will guide the planning, development, and sale of individual communities to ensure that they represent and reinforce the development company's unique image, culture, and set of disciplines in the mind of the potential buyer.

Simply stated, most industry observers agree that if a developer can build a powerful brand, the homes in that developer's communities will sell faster. In addition, purchasers are more confident about buying a product that bears a recognized brand name: because it is well recognized, the brand name carries the implication that the product is superior. Superior does not mean premium-priced: it simply means superior, whatever the category or price range, as long as the product is positioned correctly in the competitive marketplace. Because of a brand's power to convey information, developers must take care to ensure that it is associated with positive impressions and experiences.

Branding is not achieved through advertising alone. Everything the company does contributes to the perception of its brand. A developer may attract customers to a sales office through spiffy "brand-building" advertising, only to have the perception of its brand forever marred by the on-site experience. To ensure that the image created is reinforced by both the sales process and by the products offered, developers need to conduct a "brand reality check" and ask themselves these questions every week:

- Do competitors covet the brand?
- Does the company under-promise and over-deliver?
- Does the company keep its word? Does the company do what it says it will do, on time?
- Do people aspire to own the products that carry the brand?
- Is the brand associated with good value?
- How are the telephones answered?
- Is the company customer-focused?
- Would the last customer refer the company to a friend?
- Does the company's culture create a memorable brand impression on all its visitors?

These questions will help to build a powerful, consistent brand that will translate into more sales. Mature buyers take questions like these seriously: they want to do business with professional people of integrity who can provide a community that is in keeping with the retirees' traditional value system. Everyone can name brands that influence their purchasing decisions and lifestyle. From Ritz Carlton to Wal-Mart, from Nike to Rolex, people know what brand is right for them. The challenge for a developer of AARCs is to create a brand identity that will inform and draw buyers.

Building a Brand

To build a brand, developers need to do the following, in the order given:

1. Conduct research (market, product, and consumer).
2. Create unique selling propositions.
3. Apply the research findings to product design and advertising.
4. Create a "marketing trail" (signage, a sales center, a sales presentation, collateral materials).
5. Conduct database marketing (including relationship marketing, follow-up marketing).
6. Manage spheres of influence (government, builders, realtors, buyers).

Tool 2: The Yardstick

Just as market research is essential to planning an AARC, research also provides the basis for measuring the success of an AARC's marketing plan. For example, research enables the developer to set benchmark standards (such as "How many people recognize and understand the brand name?") that can be reassessed over time to measure the effectiveness of each aspect of the marketing strategy.

A beautiful clubhouse, such as this one at Heritage Highlands Golf and Country Club in Arizona, functions as a key marketing tool.

Before spending money on anything else, a developer must do research. Understanding that people over age 50 are not a homogeneous demographic group and that their wants and needs differ is essential to the success of the community. Research highlights differences, reveals untapped potential, and uncovers truths that are not self-evident when the project concept is first being developed. To address "active adults" as though they were a single group would be a marketing disaster.

A marketing department needs three kinds of research to make accurate and useful decisions:

- Market research: includes an analysis of market demand by price segment and an analysis of competitive developments.
- Product research: includes an analysis of similar kinds of homes and communities that are for sale in the market, and consumer focus groups to test interest in potential products. Focus groups can also be used to evaluate marketing strategies and techniques—for example, to test model-home or merchandising options.
- Consumer research: includes demographic profiles, psychographic profiles (attitudinal profiles of specific market segments within the active adult age group), exit surveys, and follow-up surveys of sales prospects and buyers.

122

As noted in chapter 2, this research must be undertaken initially as part of the development planning process. However, it must also be updated continuously throughout the marketing period. Current information obtained on a regular basis is especially important in large-scale, multiphase developments that are marketed and sold over a number of years.

Although it is an expensive undertaking, market research creates a foundation of fact that can prevent developers from making subjective—and avoidable—marketing errors. Its benefits can range from the complex (assisting developers to design homes and to develop advertising copy that will attract prospects with particular psychographic profiles) to the simple (giving developers a healthy understanding of the competition). Regardless of the eventual use made of the findings, the world of marketing active adult communities is too competitive to enter without the kind of safety net that only research can provide.

Tool 3: The Glue

Marketers of active adult communities need to create and use a community's unique selling propositions (USPs). USPs are the attributes of a community that are uniquely defensible or special. For example, a development's USP might be a water feature, or the only home priced at less than $200,000 that includes a first-floor master bedroom suite. The USPs are the glue that holds together the entire marketing and communications platform.

Among the attributes that could constitute a community's USPs are location, amenities, programming, and value. The creation of USPs should start as early in the development process as possible, though it is never too late to begin. USPs should be incorporated into everything—from advertising to sales-center displays, and from collateral materials (such as brochures, flyers, and other printed information) to sales presentations. The USPs make a community memorable during the shopping process, help to guarantee that it will have a "share of mind," and may ultimately help persuade active adult buyers that this community is the place that they should call home.

A prominently placed bulletin board announcing community events and activities not only informs residents but also shows sales prospects the kinds of clubs, parties, and programs that the community offers.

One way to understand how USPs work is through examples of USPs that have been created for other products. In the realm of automobiles, for example, the USP for Volvo is safety. Certainly, most cars are safe, but as a result of the company's marketing campaign, when consumers think of the word "safety," they think Volvo; when they think Volvo, they think "safety." When it comes to overnight delivery, people think FedEx; when they think FedEx, they think "overnight." In short, the USP is the defining characteristic of the brand—the one that sets it apart from its competitors.

Tool 4: Nuts And Bolts

To create a defensible position in the marketplace, innovation is essential, especially in marketing AARCs. How to innovate is a matter of imagination and budget.

Seasonal decorations invite visitors into the sales center at Continental Properties' Cedar Village community at Brick in New Jersey.

Advertising. Many developers confuse advertising and marketing. Advertising is one component of the marketing strategy, and its purpose is to create an image of the community to the outside world. It is a vital element in the creation of a brand, in corporate image-building and public relations, and in attracting potential purchasers.

Never is the ego of the buyer more vulnerable than it is in response to an advertising campaign. There is wide agreement in the industry that active adult buyers purchase lifestyle, not houses, and understanding how older adults think of themselves during this time of their life is key to creating a successful advertising campaign. For this reason, advertising for AARCs must be resplendent with images of the enriching life that awaits potential purchasers.

Much of a developer's marketing budget will go for advertising. A foundation of appropriate research that makes possible the careful assessment of the demographic and psychographic profile of the targeted consumer will help ensure that the money allocated to advertising will be well spent.

As discussed in chapter 6, all advertising for AARCs falls under the guidelines of the Fair Housing Act. Ads must contain the equal-housing disclaimers, and any relevant legal language required by individual states. It would be prudent to have all advertising reviewed by local counsel before publication to ensure that it contains nothing remotely illegal or discriminatory. Photographs should depict people from a wide range of ethnic and racial backgrounds.

There are some key points to remember in designing an advertising campaign:

- Create a look and feel that is unique to the community. Push the agency to create a defining image.
- Incorporate USPs as the main points in the advertising copy.
- Choose models who are age-appropriate yet youthful.

- Showcase the amenities.
- Use larger type for collateral and print ads for an AARC than would be used in ads for an intergenerational community.

All print advertising should include a phone number for prospects to call for more information. Telephone responses create a telecommunications databank that will be the core of the relationship-marketing effort.

Technology. The Internet is a vital tool of modern marketing. The marketing budget for an AARC should include an allocation for creating and maintaining a Web site, and the marketing team must understand how to process and fulfill requests from e-mail correspondence.

Baby boomers—and many more mature adults—are highly computer literate. Every year, more people use the Internet to "shop" for communities. In the old days, it was "let your fingers do the walking"; now it's "let your mouse do the walking." On today's Web sites, some developers offer interactive media, downloadable videos, and 360° views of properties.

A display of technological capabilities belongs in the sales center, and it should be personalized to demonstrate the how's and why's of the community's technology program—for example, a computer terminal that allows a user to experience the speed of Internet access or allows the visitor a glimpse of the community's social programming via the community's own Internet site. All advertising and collateral materials should include the developer's Web address. With the new, easily accessible digital cameras, developers can show prospects a community's new amenities simply by e-mailing them photographic images. Digital photography can also allow buyers to watch the progress as their new homes are being built.

People buy books, compact disks, computers, even cars over the Internet. A beautifully designed and informative Web site is a valuable—and increasingly essential—addition to a company's marketing platform. If ever there was an area to use innovation, this is it.

Public Relations and Promotional Events. A fully integrated public relations and publicity program should be part of a developer's marketing efforts. If the local newspaper allows it, make use of "advertorial" space to tell the community's story. Cultivate a relationship with a real estate editor. Active adults are regular newspaper readers and will likely read stories about local communities and developers.

Promotional events are an essential part of the marketing budget. At first, events must be seeded with developer dollars; later, the developer can turn over control to residents. Developer-sponsored events should reinforce the community's USPs.

Special events involving both residents and prospective buyers are a way to give a community a unique position in the marketplace and to afford guests a taste of what life could be like

Standard Elements of an Active Adult Community Advertising Campaign
• Print advertising
• Radio advertising
• Billboards
• Television (a very persuasive vehicle, if budget allows)
• The Internet

Bonita Bay Properties, Inc., and Technology

Bonita Bay Properties, Inc. (BBPI), uses technology in various ways to market its communities. One of the most important efforts along these lines was to provide fiber DSL (digital subscriber line) service to residents of The Brooks, an active adult retirement community in Bonita Springs, Florida. Fiber DSL, coupled with a community-wide intranet and a closed-circuit television channel, has created a unique selling proposition for The Brooks; similar technologies are planned for Mediterra, another active adult retirement community in Naples, Florida, and for future communities.

BBPI also uses technology to market its projects via the Internet. BBPI's Web site—a dynamic, interactive, and convenient place to gain information—features each of its projects. The "hosting reports" indicate that the BBPI site receives over 2,300 visitors per week, with the average visitor staying on the site for over nine minutes. Moreover, two out of three visitors return to the site on a regular basis to receive updated information about the communities.

BBPI's Web site reflects its current marketing programs while presenting information about the features of each community, including homesites and homes for sale, technology, amenities, and lifestyle. The target market for BBPI's Web site includes business partners, prospects, and realtors. The site's objective is to tell the BBPI audience as much as possible about the lifestyle and home options available within each of the communities.

To use technology to market the Web site itself, the company uses search-engine optimization techniques: for example, by using keywords on its site, the company ensures a prominent position on all search result lists. (Web designers embed keywords into a site, which a search engine will pick up when it reports the results of a search inquiry.) The company also advertises on many real estate–related Web sites. Perhaps the most

effective form of marketing for the Web site is a permission-based, opt-in, e-mail marketing program, through which visitors to the company's Web site agree to allow BBPI to send them e-mail information about its communities.

It is important for developers to use both their in-house community channels and their Web sites to cross-market to residents of and visitors to some of their other communities. For example, on the community channel, BBPI keeps residents and visitors up-to-date on new product offerings both within the community and in the company's other communities. On the Web, BBPI employs an interactive home search that asks visitors a series of questions, much as a realtor would, to help prospects determine which homes and neighborhoods fit their lifestyle. This database is "intelligent"—meaning that it will never bring back zero results. For example, if a prospect is looking for a single-family villa in the Shadow Wood community, a neighborhood in The Brooks, for under $200,000, the database would tell the customer that nothing is available in Shadow Wood but that results have been found in Spring Run, another neighborhood in The Brooks, that fit their criteria. Once users of the database have finished selecting a home, they can e-mail the information directly to a sales representative and schedule an appointment to see the model in person.

This "Find Your Home" database saves the information entered by each prospect so that BBPI can send out targeted marketing information. The database is invaluable to sales agents because it enables them to categorize prospects on the basis of interests. For example, the golf enthusiast who is looking for a villa under $200,000 might be interested in learning whether a new golf course is proposed or whether the community has released additional villa products that fit his or her lifestyle or price requirements.

Source: Based on information provided by Dennis E. Gilkey and members of the marketing team at Bonita Bay Properties, Inc., Bonita Springs, Florida.

At Sun City at Huntley, a small, staffed café located at the edge of the model-home park offers residents and visitors free refreshments and a place to sit and chat. Current residents are the community's best salespeople, and the café encourages informal interaction between homeowners and prospective purchasers.

there. By creating traditions that are unique to a community—a Shakespeare festival, an ice cream social, a moonlight harvest and dance—such events can, over time, become part of the community's character and identity. Holidays are natural times for festive gatherings. The opening of an important amenity—such as the clubhouse, the remaining nine holes of the golf course, or a major phase of development—can also be cause for celebration. Such events have the added advantage of providing prospective buyers with an opportunity to mingle freely with and talk to existing residents, who—if the developer has done a good job—are among the community's best salespeople.

Referrals. There is no more ideal sale than one that comes from a referral. Cultivating a referral base is an essential part of a well-balanced marketing program, and referrals from current homeowners mean that the developer and the marketing team have done their jobs and done them well. Communities built through referrals are usually highly functioning and well-run developments. A high referral rate is an excellent indication to the developer of the level of customer satisfaction.

Referrals can be encouraged in a number of ways. The most obvious is to treat customers with respect and professionalism throughout their homebuying experience so that they will voluntarily refer the community to their friends. Even so, referrals may not be forthcoming, so developers need to know how to ask for them:

- Create a formal homeowner referral program through which residents are rewarded in some way for helping to build the community. Local real estate laws govern this practice and must be researched before any real or perceived compensation is afforded to a homeowner.

- Conduct a survey of buyers that asks the simple question, "Would you refer us to a friend?" If the respondent answers yes, follow up with a phone call and ask for a referral.
- Thirty days after each closing, have the sales associate follow up with a request for a referral from the buyer (if the experience was a smooth one).

Never be heavy-handed when asking for referrals. Residents will find it distasteful to think that the developer is trying to "buy" friends' names from them; make certain that all referral names are treated with the utmost respect and consideration. Referrals are a direct link to the existing homeowner base and, as such, should be carefully guarded. Referrals can not only save time and money but also make the community a more pleasant place to be.

At The Fairways at Lake Ridge, in New Jersey, the clubhouse and model-home complex are located near each other, just inside the project's entrance.

Signage. Signage is an integral part of an identity program, and good signage is especially important in an active adult community because vision becomes less acute as one ages. All signage within the community should be clear and easy to read. Signs directing automobile drivers to existing and future amenities are particularly important. Especially during the early stages of community development, the developer should install "coming soon" signs for retail, medical, and commercial facilities to lessen the "pioneer" feeling among new residents. Interior signage in the welcome center is also important. Research indicates that members of the Eisenhower generation and older baby boomers are particularly likely to respond positively to directional signage, such as a request to "please sign in" at the welcome center.

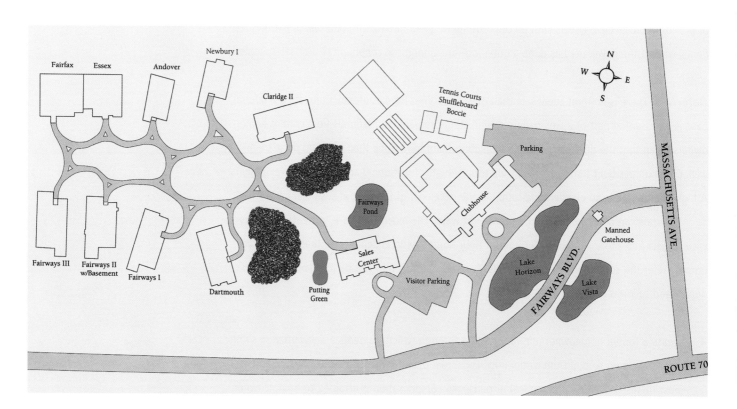

Tool 5: The Laser

If advertising is a shotgun, database marketing is a laser. It is accurate, precise, and relationship-driven. And, it is potentially the most important tool in the box. In a database marketing effort, the developer relies on lists, created in-house or acquired from an outside source, to make direct, one-on-one contact with a potential buyer. The simplest form of database marketing is a hand-written note from a member of the sales team to a prospect. In its more sophisticated form, database marketing could, for example, tap lists of people who match the desired demographic and psychographic profiles and have purchased sport utility vehicles within the past eighteen months. How a developer creates database targets is an individual decision.

A community's proprietary database includes all the people who have shown an interest in the development: everyone who has indicated even the slightest interest must be religiously logged into the database. If a call comes in from a prospect, it should be used as an opportunity to add to the database. If prospects write for information, register them. If they visit the Web site, register them.

Be aware, however, that members of the Eisenhower generation and older baby boomers typically hate to register: they don't want to take the time to do it, they don't want to be "sold stuff," and they don't want their privacy violated. But every time a prospect slips away without registering, valuable marketing dollars are wasted. One way to encourage people to register is to attach registration to a drawing of some sort, with prizes. Simple truth-telling works well, too. "Would you like to be on our mailing list to be informed of new product offerings?"

Whatever the method, it is essential to get each and every name. Active adult buyers remain in the buying cycle longer than traditional buyers. Keeping them informed by mail of what's new and what's happening in the community is critical to maintaining their interest. Developers who are not communicating with sales prospects consistently can be sure that someone else is.

Some developers include follow-up telephone calls in their database marketing effort. However, because of the prospects' age and attitudes (they may consider such calls intrusive), many developers no longer consider telemarketing a good idea. To avoid provoking negative reactions, those who do use telemarketing time their calls carefully to show sensitivity to buyers' lifestyles and habits.

The marketing database can be used to maintain a historical perspective on each prospect: to track how many times each prospect has visited, the individual's or couple's interests, and the likely time frame for buying. A sophisticated database can create individual customer information files that can help a developer avoid dependence on mass media. The marketing database must be updated and maintained regularly to ensure that it is accurate at all times.

Attractively displayed photos of the community's homebuyers offer an appealing way to show sales prospects that many people just like them have chosen to live in this community. This display is in Village Greenes, which was developed by Kevin Scarborough Homes in Ocean County, New Jersey.

The walkway from the sales center to the model homes at Indian Ridge Country Club, in Palm Desert, California, features golf course views. The models' rear windows also look out onto the golf course.

THE SALES EXPERIENCE

Developers must ensure that the sales experience—from the time visitors arrive at the site, through registration and the sales presentation—is tailored to the characteristics and preferences of the active adult market.

The Sales Center

Whether it is a temporary or permanent structure, a sales center need not be extravagant to be effective. It does have to be exquisitely planned and designed, however, because it also serves to welcome visitors and sales prospects to the community, and should communicate a feeling of warmth, hospitality, and graciousness. Most consultants advise allowing three months for the planning of a successful sales center, but a full six months is preferable: remember that the sales center gives prospective buyers their first impression of the community. Once a prospect has crossed the threshold of the sales center, a developer will never be able to undo that first impression.

The first step in planning the center is to establish its purpose. What is the building to do? Will it function only as a sales center, or will it house administrative offices as well? Will the building be turned over to the community association at some point, or will it function as a sales pavilion until sellout? As a rule, one of the sales center's purposes is to reinforce the brand identity. The following questions will help guide the design of the sales center:

- How can the sales center help to establish a theme?
- Which of the community's USPs will the center focus on, and how?

- How will the center draw visitors into the vision of the community that the developer wants to project?
- How will visitors "live the brand experience" during their visit?

Above all, the sales center should be perceived as welcoming and helpful. At Leisure World of Virginia, the developer hosts free monthly luncheon seminars for prospective buyers on topics such as "How to Prepare for Moving" and "How to Retire Actively."

Registration

Registration—obtaining the names, addresses, and telephone numbers of visitors—is the lifeblood of an AARC. No entries in a database are as valuable as those that come from sales-center registrations. People who walk through the door of the sales center are self-selected: they are already interested in this particular location and type of development. It is essential to seize this opportunity to maintain contact with them.

Whether registration information can be obtained depends largely on the quality of the sales staff. The sales center hosts are the human face of the developer's brand, and a mistake on the hosts' part can ruin any feeling of goodwill that prospects have developed about the brand.

The sales center at Leisure World of Virginia, in Lansdowne, Virginia, features a registration area, displays, a comfortable lounge and, not shown in this photograph, classroom areas, a design center, a kitchen area, and model condominiums. As part of its ongoing marketing program, the developer offers prospective buyers periodic luncheon discussions on topics related to moving to an active adult community.

Market Strategy Planning during the Life Cycle of an Active Adult Retirement Community

Life Cycle Stage	Product	Pricing	Inventory	Promotion
Introduction	Offer mature and tested product; keep product line and mix small, based on the size of the community	"Skim the cream" by value introductory pricing; keep out price-sensitive innovators	Build the pipeline to the consumer or end-user by employing fast delivery and sales methods to create urgency	Create primary demand for product; spend generously on extensive "flight" advertising
Growth	Improve product; keep mix limited; weed out bad sellers or unsaleable space	Adjust price to meet competition as needed	Increase market presence and market penetration	Spend substantially on expansion of sales volume
Maturity	Distinguish your product from the competition; expand product offerings to satisfy different market segments	Capitalize on price-sensitive demand by adjusting prices	Control the inventory by establishing planned sales programs to sell what you build or need to lease	Emphasize community/ builder/product appeal; differentiate the product or space in the minds of buyers or renters
Decline	Proliferate your mix and diversity into a new or different market segment	Keep the pricing stable to avoid close-outs	Intensify the sale of your existing or phased inventory	Maintain the status quo; support your market position
Phaseout	Prune your mix radically	Carefully increase price to increase urgency through added value	Do not increase inventory: consolidate, and build only on order	Reduce advertising activity to reminders to sales prospects or to generate urgency to purchase limited inventory

Source: William E. Becker, managing director/president, The William E. Becker Organization, Teaneck, New Jersey.

Successful hosts identify with the culture and values of the company and understand the major effect they have on sales. A gracious, warm, and hospitable environment will help put visitors at ease and encourage them to linger for the sales presentation. If visitors hesitate to register at first, a sales associate should offer them something to drink, ask if they have any questions, then gently guide them to register during or after the sales presentation.

Interior design that encourages prospects to envision living in the homes is a key component of a developer's merchandising effort. This home is at SaddleBrooke.

The Sales Presentation

Selling an AARC differs from selling an intergenerational community in a number of ways. No one shopping for an active adult community has a child getting ready to go to school. Few are being transferred to a new job. In short, all the things that create a sense of urgency to buy a home in a traditional intergenerational community are absent from the AARC sales process.

Perhaps most important, the nature of the purchase is different. Generally speaking, AARC buyers are seeking to buy a lifestyle rather than a housing product, and the home purchase is the price of entry into that lifestyle. It is by integrating the lifestyle elements of the community into the sales process that the developer articulates the value of the community. The developer needs to ensure that the USPs are a fundamental part of the sales process.

Essential Elements to Include in an AARC Sales Center

- Visual displays of the lifestyle offered
- Photographs of people who are 10 to 15 years younger than those in the target market doing active things
- A history of the development company and a list of its accomplishments
- A topographic table with a model of the community
- A map indicating the time and distance to medical care, shopping, services, the airport, and houses of worship
- A "hometown map" showing where current residents come from
- A display demonstrating the community's use of "smart" features or computer connections
- A site plan showing which homes are available and which have been sold
- Displays of collateral materials.

Compared with a young couple buying their first home, older adult buyers are sophisticated, savvy, and experienced. This is not their first home purchase, and mature adults have the time and inclination to shop carefully. As a result, every well-trained AARC sales agent must understand the following about active adult sales prospects:

- The purchase is purely discretionary: buyers have no sense of urgency.
- They will shop at many places before they make a decision.
- They will not be pressured or rushed.
- They are eager to talk about their lives.
- They are seasoned, skeptical, and want to know the facts. No facts, no sale.
- They want to be assured that they are doing the right thing.
- They will not tolerate condescension. Never "talk down" to an active adult sales prospect.
- They want to hear the truth. A buyer who is told a falsehood of any kind will never be regained.

In summary, active adults may *buy*, but they cannot be *sold*. Training programs for sales staff must make this distinction clear.

The sales staff should represent a cross-section of the target market. The staff should include men and women of all ages—well-trained, with a professional appearance, and ready to go. The Eisenhower generation and older baby boomers that make up the market today want to deal with salespeople who look and act like professionals. And remember that since all people tend to think of themselves as younger than their chronological ages, a 60-year-old male prospect will enjoy discussing his golf game with a 50-year-old sales associate whom he considers his peer.

The entrance to the sales office and model-home park and the model home itself must be inviting and attractively landscaped. The example shown here is at Mirage at Holiday City Barnegat, in Ocean County, New Jersey.

Most important, the salespeople and the sales center should embody a culture of positive energy. For the buyer, purchasing a home in an AARC represents a positive experience: the gateway to new opportunities, new friends, and a new life.

Model Homes

Privacy is a crucial part of the AARC sales process, and prospects should be allowed to visit model homes unattended if they wish. As the visitors walk through the model park, they can share their opinions openly with one another, which sets the stage for a more honest and direct conversation with the salesperson on their return. Model homes should be merchandised (finished and furnished) to create a sense of value and to evoke a positive emotional response—including a sense of belonging. Can visitors see themselves drinking wine on the patio? Playing bridge in the kitchen? To gracefully de-emphasize the accommodations made to residents' advancing age (bathtub rails and ledge seats in showers, for example), the model homes should include furnishings that suggest residents' lifestyle and that are of the highest caliber.

Although well-conceived model homes are important, ultimately it is the presentation of the community's lifestyle amenities that will make the purchase decision for the buyer. Sales associates must guide prospects around the site and walk them through all the clubs, community buildings, and common areas. The key is to paint a picture of how wonderful life could be at this community. These are fit and active people. Lifestyle means everything to them, and how that lifestyle is demonstrated will determine a community's sales success.

A design center offers buyers the opportunity to customize their homes and can be a significant profit center. At Sun City at Huntley, outside of Chicago, the design center is located within the Prairie Lodge clubhouse.

Mini-Vacations

Guest programs—"mini-vacations," "guest getaways," "fly and buys"—are a popular means of immersing the buyer in the lifestyle of a community. Many developers regard such programs as a secret weapon in the sales wars. To offer such paid-for or discounted vacation experiences, the developer must have a cottage or condominium product dedicated to this purpose. Vacationing guests are registered at check-in and required to take a sales tour of the community before using any of the amenities. The sales experience should be designed to make the remainder of the stay informative, smooth, and enjoyable.

Vacation getaways tend to be most successful in vacation-destination locations such as Arizona, Florida, and the Carolinas. Most developers promote mini-vacations through classified advertising in magazines and use database marketing and telephone contact to communicate with potential buyers who respond to their ads.

Guest programs work especially well when they include contact with satisfied residents. Talking with residents allows guests to see firsthand what it is like to live and play within the community. Homeowners are a very effective team of ambassadors, and can really increase the conversion rate of visiting guests into satisfied purchasers.

LOOKING TO THE FUTURE

We have all heard that as the baby boomers age, the market for AARCs will undergo many changes. One change that will affect the market is the largest transfer of wealth that has ever taken place in this country: the baby boomers' inheritance of their parents' wealth. Combined with the increasing emphasis on health and exercise, the transfer of wealth means that fitter, younger-thinking, better-financed 55-year-olds who want to fulfill their dreams will be visiting active adult communities.

And their dreams are as varied as the psychographics and demographics of the customers themselves. One person's dream is to return to the college town that evokes some of the best memories of his life. Another's idea of early retirement is golf, golf, and more golf in a Sunbelt climate. Yet another wants to retire near her grandchildren, the dentist she's been going to for twenty years, and the familiarity of a hometown. Yet others seek a fantasy retirement in Idaho, Montana, Key West, or other escapist destinations that offer particular kinds of recreation.

Looking ahead, the only certainty is change. When it comes to marketing and thinking about the future of an ARRC, here's something to consider: Mick Jagger is age-qualified to live in an active adult retirement community. You can't rely on the marketing techniques of your grandfather's era.

6

Legal Considerations

Wayne S. Hyatt, Chairman, Hyatt & Stubblefield, P.C., Atlanta, Georgia

In the context of creating communities for active adults, a discussion of the legal considerations is essential to avoid exposing the developer and all who subsequently become the housing providers to substantial risk.

There are both direct and indirect legal considerations in structuring—and, perhaps more important, in operating—a planned community for active adults. This is so because the standards for structuring and operating such communities arise from a civil rights statute that is to be, in legal parlance, "strictly construed." Because of the requirements of federal law, many of the operational aspects of an active adult community have subtle but substantial differences from the operational aspects of a traditional master-planned community. As a result, this chapter has several objectives.

First, the chapter seeks to impart an understanding of the requirements and the impact of the Fair Housing Act, the applicable federal

Homes in Robson Communities's SaddleBrooke development, outside of Tucson, offer luxurious details such as high ceilings, archways, and wall-sized windows.

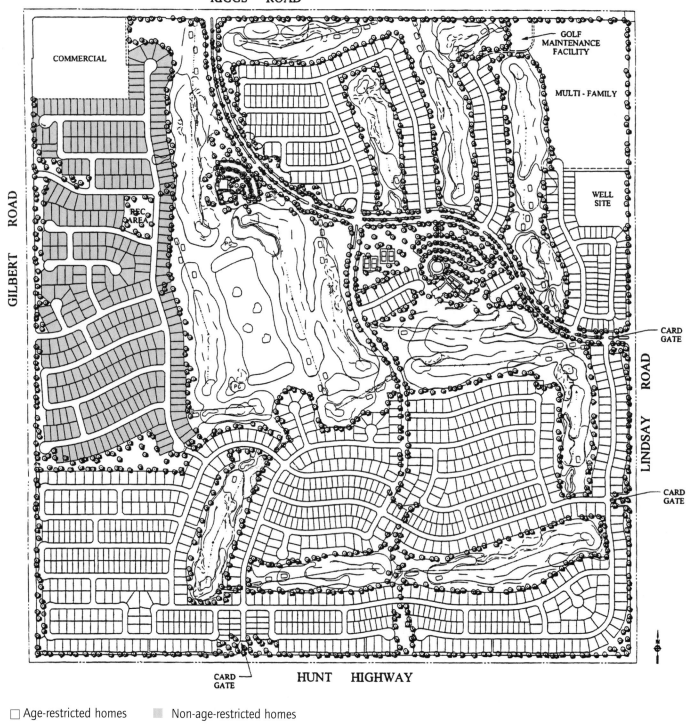

RIGGS ROAD

GILBERT ROAD

LINDSAY ROAD

HUNT HIGHWAY

COMMERCIAL

REC AREA

GOLF MAINTENANCE FACILITY

MULTI - FAMILY

WELL SITE

CARD GATE

CARD GATE

CARD GATE

☐ Age-restricted homes ▦ Non-age-restricted homes

statute, upon the creation and operation of an active adult community. Second, the chapter seeks to help readers understand that the statute essentially allows discrimination against younger persons, rather than providing for discrimination in favor of older persons. This is a subtle but real difference, and it can affect the perceptions of those involved in the creation and operation of an active adult community. As will be discussed later, understanding how the statute is designed to work becomes especially significant in the operation of the community. Finally, the chapter seeks to explain the importance of the Fair Housing Act as a civil rights statute and to clarify what that means for operations.

The chapter assumes (1) that the developer has already determined to create an active adult community as a common-interest community utilizing a community association format and (2) that the developer understands the basic legal considerations in structuring sound community governance for a common-interest community. Accordingly, the emphasis and focus here will be on the legal and operational considerations that differ from those that apply to a "normal" master-planned community. To further this understanding, the chapter contains a section on "pure" operational issues that seeks to illustrate the legal principles discussed throughout the chapter.[1]

The chapter will emphasize how to make the community work and point out some of the problems, cauldrons of discord, and special challenges in creating and operating a community for active adults. At the same time, it will seek to signal some unique characteristics and opportunities. Too often, a developer seeks to borrow someone else's formula or approach without realizing that the far better approach is to master the essentials and then to build upon these basics to create the community and governance structures that work best for the project at hand. In an active adult community, the legal issues are rigid and clear-cut. Thus, once a developer understands what they are and how they might be applied in practice, there is considerable opportunity to create a community that meets the various needs of the individual market and other local conditions.

The preliminary site plan (opposite) for Pulte Corporation's Springfield Lakes community, in Chandler, Arizona, calls for a mixed-use development that integrates age-restricted single-family and multifamily residential uses; non-age-restricted residential uses; commercial uses; and a golf course and other recreational amenities.

STATUTORY BASIS
Fair Housing and Federal Law

In 1968, Congress adopted Title VIII of the Civil Rights Act. This statute prevented discrimination in the provision of housing on the basis of race, color, religion, sex, or national origin. Twenty years later, Congress adopted the Fair Housing Act of 1988, which became effective in February 1989. This Fair Housing Act, as it was initially called, added "familial status" and "handicapped" to the list of protected classifications. Familial status included the fact that a family had children. This provision was added largely in response to a growing trend, particularly in rental housing, to restrict housing to those who did not have children. Congress, therefore, sought through the Fair Housing Act amendments to protect families with children in their search for available, affordable housing.

In prohibiting discrimination against persons based upon familial status, Congress was nevertheless mindful of the desire and need for housing that *did* exclude children and, perhaps, was created solely for persons above a minimum age threshold. As a result, the Fair Housing Act of 1988 provided exceptions from the prohibition of discrimination for three types of communities designed for older persons.

The fitness center at Del Webb's Sun City Hilton Head is an inviting structure off the town square.

The first type is a community specifically designed and operated for the elderly under state or federal programs. The second is for communities intended for and occupied *solely* by persons who are at least 62 years of age. These two exceptions are not generally involved in the private sector's efforts to create active adult communities and will therefore not be discussed in this chapter. However, the third exception is, and was intended to be, directly applicable to our subject. That exception is for communities that meet specific criteria and that are intended for and occupied by households in which at least one person is 55 years of age or older.

At the time of the original amendments to the Fair Housing Act, one of the criteria was "the existence of significant facilities and services specifically designed to meet physical and social

needs of older persons." This provision caused considerable consternation among many. In a nutshell, one could not be sure exactly what constituted "significant facilities and services specifically designed to meet physical and social needs of older persons," and if one could, one was certainly confident that it was extremely expensive and difficult to provide and administer them.

In response to the problems arising from difficulties in interpreting and applying the specified criteria for the third exemption, the Housing for Older Persons Act of 1995 eliminated the requirement for significant facilities and services. As of this writing, in order to qualify for this third exemption, a community need only meet three distinct criteria, described in the three sections that follow. It is important for readers to pay close attention to these criteria: it is quite common for developers, managers, and particularly marketing persons to misunderstand and to misapply them, and doing so can have substantial negative consequences.

Criterion 1. At least 80 percent of the occupied units in the "housing facility or community" must be occupied by at least one person 55 years of age or older.

Note that this requirement relates to *occupancy* and not to ownership. Note further that it says "at least 80 percent," not 100 percent and not 79 percent.

There is a great deal of complexity in determining whether the 80 percent requirement has been met because certain types of units can be excluded from the total number of units from which the 80 percent figure is calculated. (The exclusion of units from the total increases the possibility that associations will meet the 80 percent requirement.) To calculate correctly, associations must determine when the project was constructed, when it was first occupied by current occupants who are aged 55 or older, and who currently occupies the units.

The following guidelines explain which units must be included in the total number of units from which to calculate the 80 percent occupancy requirement. (Note that these guidelines address new construction or renovation when the entire project was unoccupied for at least 90 days before reoccupancy.)

- For housing that was constructed (or renovated to the extent that the entire project was unoccupied for at least 90 days before reoccupancy) after March 12, 1989, the 80 percent requirement does not apply until at least 25 percent of the units are occupied.
- If less than 80 percent of the occupied units were occupied by a person aged 55 or older on September 13, 1988, the association may still qualify under the exception, provided that at least 80 percent of the units occupied by new occupants after September 13, 1988, are occupied by at least one person 55 years of age or older.
- Unoccupied units are not included in the total.
- Units occupied by association employees who perform substantial duties and are under 55 years of age are not included in the total.
- Units occupied by family members or assistants whose occupancy is necessary to assist a disabled person are excluded from the total. (Permitting such assistants to live in the association is considered a reasonable accommodation of a disability, which is also required under the Fair Housing Act.)
- If, in calculating 80 percent of a total number of units, a fraction of a unit is included, then that unit must also be occupied by a person aged 55 or older. For example, if 80 percent of the total number of included units is 25.6 units, 26 units must actually be occupied by a person aged 55 or older.

Making creative use of the clubhouse rooftop, developers of Leisure World of Virginia, in Lansdowne, Virginia, constructed tennis courts with sweeping views of the surrounding countryside.

Finally, note that the requirement says "at least one person 55 years of age or older" and that it does not say "occupied solely by persons 55 years of age or older." Each word in the requirement is significant and needs to be observed and met.

There is no room for variation, even though there is considerable flexibility within the requirement itself. The lesson that the development team must immediately embrace is that one may legitimately use authorized flexibility, whereas one may not vary the requirements themselves.

Criterion 2. The facility or community must publish and must adhere to policies and procedures that demonstrate an intent to comply with the requirements of the Fair Housing Act.

This requirement does not mandate that there be covenants, conditions, and restrictions (CC&Rs) but that the basic policies and procedures demonstrating an intent to comply and requiring compliance will be in the CC&Rs. There may be, in addition, policies and procedures in the nature of rules, handbooks, and other devices. The key words in this requirement are *publish, adhere to,* and *intent to comply.* The regulations state that any of the following may be used to show the necessary intent:

* Descriptions of the association as a "55-or-older" community to prospective residents
* Advertisements of the association as a 55-or-older community
* Public posting in the association's common property or statements indicating that the association is designed for persons aged 55 or older
* CC&Rs and other association rules and restrictions that include 55-or-older language
* Any lease provisions containing 55-or-older language
* Development of and adherence to any age-screening processes
* Actual practices of the association

- Documented, good-faith attempts to amend association restrictions and rules to create a 55-or-older community, even if such attempts fail.

When communities run afoul of the Fair Housing Act, it may be because there was insufficient initial publication of the policies and procedures. But it is also often the case that policies and procedures are in place but not adhered to. The developer needs to keep in mind that the legal considerations in an active adult community may not be satisfied initially and then laid aside; instead, they constitute an ongoing obligation.

Criterion 3. The community or facility must meet the rules for verification of occupancy.

This criterion illustrates the challenges of effectuating these policies and procedures on an ongoing basis. It is worth noting several key concepts in this requirement. Verification of compliance must be proved by *reliable* surveys and affidavits. This means that the person or entity responsible for verification must have a system that is, on its face, reliable. Merely asking prospective residents their age is, to most people, not a reliable survey.

While the Department of Housing and Urban Development appears to allow flexibility in the type of procedures developed, the regulations refer to the use of resident surveys to determine the occupants' ages and update the information. Surveys can collect the following information: whether units are occupied by persons aged 55 or older; whether there are any occupants aged 55 or older who moved into the association after September 13, 1988; whether association employees live in any units; and whether any units are occupied by persons who are there to assist a disabled occupant.

Collecting such information provides associations and developers with a more complete defense if they are challenged with violations of the Fair Housing Act. The regulations also permit the incorporation of age verification into any purchase or lease documents.

The regulations state that any of the following may be used as proof of age:

- Driver's license.
- Birth certificate.
- Passport.
- Immigration card.
- Military identification card.
- Any other official government document that shows a birth date.
- A document (such as an affidavit, certification in a lease or purchase agreement, etc.) signed by any member of the household aged 18 or older that asserts that at least one person in the unit is 55 or older. This document does not have to be signed under oath.

Even if a resident refuses to provide evidence of age, an association may still consider that the unit is occupied by a person aged 55 or older if the association has

- Government documents such as a local government household census (not the national census) that show that the unit is occupied by a person aged 55 or older.
- Prior forms, applications, or other information verifying the ages of unit occupants.
- Affidavits from persons not in the household who have personal knowledge that an occupant is 55 or older. The affidavit must state how the individuals have personal knowledge of the age of the occupant and be signed under penalty of perjury.

Landscaping and natural construction materials enhance the entrance to the Coralina model in the Bellasera community in Scottsdale, Arizona.

Note also that these verification procedures must be done not just once but on an ongoing basis. Obviously, the occupants of units can change as times and circumstances change. Consequently, merely verifying the occupants' age at the time of initial sale or lease of a unit will not satisfy the requirement. At least every two years, associations must re-verify the informa-

John Ormond/Courtesy of IBZ Architecture + Planning

tion generated by the original survey or other procedures. Associations do not have to regather information that has already been collected, but they must reconfirm that residents counted as occupying units for the purposes of meeting the 80 percent requirement still reside in the association. If new occupants move into the association, the association should collect information from those residents before or upon their arrival.

The requirements also address a difficult operational issue: the necessity of requiring occupant compliance and having a back-up plan to respond when residents resist the verification. There are many reasons that residents might resist the verification requirement, ranging from vanity about their age to a more sinister motive—namely, a desire to occupy when one is clearly not within the permitted age band. (More information about how this circumstance may arise is offered later in the chapter.) For whatever reason, however, the association rules need to include a provision to require—and indeed to compel—compliance with the verification procedures. Finally, it is essential to understand that the information produced through these procedures is not proprietary or protected from access: instead, the facility or community must make the occupancy surveys available for inspection upon reasonable notice by any person.

Fortunately, the Housing for Older Persons Act created a defense to a claim of familial status housing discrimination for people who believed, in good faith, that an association qualified for the 55-and-older exemption. The defense only applies to people, not to corporations. To qualify to claim the defense, individuals must have actual knowledge, prior to the date upon which the discrimination is alleged to have occurred, that the association's authorized representative (board or manager) certified in writing and under oath that the association qualified for the 55-or-older exemption. If those claiming the defense have actual knowledge that the association does not qualify for the exemption, however, they cannot claim the defense, even if they received the written certification.

Fair Housing and Local Law

Two sections of the Fair Housing Act (42 USC 3601 et seq.) address preemption issues with regard to discriminatory housing practices. *Preemption* is the legal term used to describe instances in which federal law supersedes state or local law. It does not do so in all instances. In this case, the federal statute does not preempt the field but allows state and local regulation as well. For example, Section 3615 provides states with the power to impose additional laws in this area unless such laws allow discriminatory housing practices.[2]

Finally, a comment from the *Code of Federal Regulations* that accompanies the new regulations pertaining to housing for the elderly states that though states and localities may impose requirements in addition to, but not inconsistent with, those in the act, the act's provisions must still be met to qualify for the exemption. In other words, one must consider applicable state and local laws in this context, and they may impose higher requirements.

An inviting conversation area within the clubhouse of Rancho Resort, a manufactured-home community outside of Tucson.

LESSONS FROM EXPERIENCE

It is not easy to do an age-restricted community. There is a temptation to look at successful, smoothly functioning developments, such as Del Webb's Sun City communities, and say, "Oh, that looks easy. I think I can do that, too." However, looks are deceiving, and a great deal of talent, experience, and commitment go into making the difficult appear easy. There are a number of reasons for these difficulties, and it is appropriate to take a look at several of them.

Strict Compliance. The first source of difficulty is the previously discussed requirement of strict compliance. Because the Fair Housing Act is a civil rights statute, it is strictly construed, and there is no "wiggle room" in its provisions or applications. When the statute says 80 percent it means 80 percent. Simply stated, it requires strict compliance.

Emotional Issues. On a different level, but of no less significance, are the emotions involved in an age-restricted community. One can easily imagine the discord that can arise when, much to the consternation of some residents, a gentleman of some years marries a younger wife (what some might call a "trophy wife"). This is a common source of friction. Of course, the same reaction may occur when a senior woman takes a much younger husband. While both younger spouses would be permitted under the standard that only one occupant must be 55 years old or over, the emotional discord can be substantial even if, strictly speaking, the legal requirements have been observed.

Record-Keeping and Information-Gathering. As noted earlier, the obligation for age disclosures may trigger emotional reactions, and procedures need to be in place not only to acquire the information but also to do so in as nonconfrontational a manner as possible. For example, taking an annual age census at the time that activity cards are renewed or as part of other preconditions for the use and enjoyment of the facilities may well smooth the process and increase the likelihood of veracity and willing compliance.

Diversity of Interests within the Community. Another serious potential disruption within the age-restricted community is the potential for substantial diversity of interests among residents. This diversity can arise as a consequence of age, background, economic level, health, and a wide variety of other considerations. Just because the community is denominated as one for active adults or as one that is age-restricted in accordance with the Fair Housing Act does not mean, for example, that all of the residents will be in the same age bracket. While the average age may remain fairly constant, the range of ages and the "clustering" of ages will vary significantly over time.

Because of the age span, disparities in health are also likely to arise, thus producing another whole range of variables: for example, some residents may have professional care providers residing in the home; others may have children under the age of 55 residing with them in order to provide care. Both of these scenarios are permitted; however, there is a potential for substantial difficulty when the "underage" children desire to remain in the unit after the death of a parent. Most likely, such an arrangement would not be permitted, either under the community's procedures and practices or under the requirements of the Fair Housing Act, if it would jeopardize the 20 percent limit. Accordingly, clear procedures must be in place to address such an issue and to ensure that the regulations are consistently followed.

For each type of diversity of interest, subsidiary issues produce further challenges, both for the drafting of covenants and procedures and for those in charge of operations.

Matching Expectations with Reality. Quality assurance and the expectations of purchasers present another array of issues that contribute to the difficulty of undertaking a successful age-restricted community. These purchasers have high expectations, have generally had enough experience to investigate to ensure that these expectations are met, and have time on their hands. Many of them also have the wherewithal to sue to realize the expectations—which sometimes, regrettably, are artificially inflated and unrealistic. The builder and the marketing team must be constantly vigilant that expectations are not unrealistically elevated and that promises are met.

High Levels of Community Involvement. It has been said that there are at least two categories of residents in communities for the over-55 age group. One is made up of residents affected by the "power loss stress syndrome"—people who once had substantial power and authority in their business lives, who now feel the loss of that power and authority, and who thus seek to realize it once again through involvement in their community association. Another group is made up of those who are affected by the "power never had syndrome": members of this category are retired from positions that were never truly satisfying, and they therefore seek to realize that satisfaction by virtue of their involvement in the community association. Accordingly, it is vital that extreme care be given to the planning and structure of governance, to areas of potential interpersonal dispute, and to customer service. In an age-restricted community, each of these areas is fraught with a variety of legal consequences—much like those seen in "ordinary" master-planned communities, but taken to greater heights.

Referrals. All of these issues affect one other significant marketing consideration: the role and importance of referrals. It is important to successfully address emotional and operational issues not only because it is necessary for the smooth operation of the community but because the smooth operation of the community directly affects the marketing of the community.

DRAFTING CONSIDERATIONS: DEALING WITH AGE ISSUES

There are a number of important but often overlooked considerations inherent in drafting documentation for any master-planned community. Because other texts and sources address these issues in detail, they will be covered only briefly here.[3] The reader is advised to consult these other sources and to remember that in addition to understanding the legal considerations unique to the creation of an active adult community, developers must thoroughly comprehend the legal considerations applicable to master-planned communities generally.

As in all master-planned communities, preserving a degree of flexibility is advisable and can prove most beneficial. For example, the development team should consider reserving the right to change marketing plans should it become necessary to do so. However, once a significant portion of the units have been sold, it will be very difficult to "unrestrict" the community. Therefore, the developer should give serious thought to the long-term viability of the chosen format before creating the documentation and initiating the marketing process.

There are a number of specific considerations that must be addressed in dealing with age issues.

Definition of a "Housing Facility or Community." There are specific document provisions and drafting considerations applicable to the age issues. The first such issue concerns the definition of a "housing facility or community." Generally, this definition may include any dwelling or group of dwelling units that are governed by a common set of rules or restrictions. However, a portion or portions of a single building cannot constitute a housing facility or housing community. This does not mean, however, that a portion or portions of a larger master-

Each neighborhood in the Bonita Bay community, in Bonita Springs, Florida, is designed with a distinctive entrance. The award-winning landscaping showcases the community's emphasis on preserving natural areas.

With the acquisition of Spruce Creek Communities, Del Webb Corporation has entered the Florida active adult market.

planned community could not make up the housing facility or community; however, the developer should consider carefully the governance issues that may arise if the federally mandated restrictions are imposed on one portion of a community and not on others. The Fair Housing Act says that one cannot advertise a project as an adult community unless the entire community meets the requirements (that is, one cannot advertise Condo X as an adult community and then allow noncomplying units on three out of the four floors).

By the same token, one cannot advertise a project as an adult community if the whole community is not age-restricted. However, as long as a project's advertising does not discriminate, there is no reason that the developer cannot conduct a separate advertising campaign for one neighborhood within the project as an adult community, if that neighborhood meets the requirements and there is an association to monitor and enforce the requirements for that neighborhood. The question is whether a separate neighborhood association is needed or whether the master association could be required (and relied upon) to do the monitoring and enforcing for one neighborhood. It is not the author's intent to indicate that such a structure could not or should not be created. In the appropriate circumstance, the age-restricted component could easily be developed utilizing the neighborhood structure that is often employed in larger master-planned communities.[4] The point is that it should be done thoughtfully and not simply automatically.

The definition of housing facility or community specifically includes condominiums, homeowners' associations, and cooperative projects. The property may be leased or under private ownership, and may, in addition, include mobile-home parks.

Identification of Exempt Units. A second issue unique to the age-restricted community concerns the details of exemptions applicable to certain units. The reader will recall that the basic requirement calls for at least 80 percent of the units to be occupied by at least one person who is 55 or older. The 80 percent factor is applied to "occupied" units. Therefore, should 20 units out of 100 be totally unoccupied, the 80 percent factor would be applied to the 80 that are occupied: thus, in this case, 64 units would have to be occupied by at least one person over the age of 55. However, there are additional units that may be exempt from the requirement, and these units may be subtracted from the total before the 80 percent factor is calculated.

The exemptions for certain units fall into three categories. The first, the category of unoccupied units, has already been mentioned. It is important to note that units rendered temporarily vacant because the occupant resides there only periodically do not qualify as "unoccupied." Such units would be included in the inventory that is subject to the occupancy percentages, and the occupants of that unit would be subject to the periodic verification of occupancy and age.

The second category of units that may be subtracted from the total are those occupied by employees of the housing provider. Occupancy in this case extends to the families of employees, which, obviously, might include children. If an employee performs substantial duties directly related to the management or maintenance of the housing and resides within the community, the unit may be declared exempt. Finally, units occupied by persons who are needed in order to provide reasonable accommodation to disabled persons do not count in the total against which the 80 percent factor is applied.

Definition of a "Qualifying Occupant." To demonstrate its intent to operate as housing for persons 55 years of age or older, a community must include appropriate occupancy restrictions in an enforceable document that is binding on all occupants of dwellings in the community. In the case of rental housing, such documents would most likely be the leases, and in the case of "for sale" housing, recorded covenants.

In order to be in a position to ensure compliance with the Fair Housing Act, such occupancy restrictions should include a requirement that, unless the landlord or homeowners' association grants an exception in accordance with the act, every occupied dwelling shall have at all times at least one permanent occupant who is 55 years of age or older. This person would be the "qualifying occupant" for that dwelling—in other words, the person whose occupancy ensures that the dwelling is in compliance with this requirement.

Although the act does not specifically define occupancy in terms of a number of days or months that the qualifying occupant must live in the dwelling in order for the dwelling to be considered "occupied" by such a person, the community needs to be in a position to demonstrate its intent to comply with the spirit and letter of the act. To do so, it must be able to ensure that the person recognized as the qualifying occupant for a particular dwelling does, in

The MountainView Clubhouse in the SaddleBrooke community, outside Tucson.

fact, reside in the dwelling (as opposed, for example, to maintaining his or her primary residence elsewhere and just visiting the grandchildren for a month or two every summer). Thus, the occupancy restriction should include a measurable, enforceable standard for what is meant by a "permanent occupant." For example, the provision might require that such person consider the dwelling to be his or her legal residence and actually reside in the dwelling for at least six months during every calendar year.

Demonstration of Intent to Comply. Provisions for demonstrating the housing provider's intent to comply with the requirements of the Fair Housing Act include those that would impose the obvious limitations on occupancy, those that would obligate residents to comply with verification, and other related procedures to ensure compliance and notification. Included in the notification requirements would be notification upon first occupancy and upon any and all subsequent changes in occupancy.

These provisions need to be drafted carefully and thoughtfully, with sufficient "teeth" to ensure that the association or the developer has the ability to compel the necessary information to be provided in a timely manner and to be verified in a way that provides the necessary degree of certainty that it is accurate. Remember that requiring this information is not simply a matter of compliance with a CC&Rs provision. It is a matter of federal law.

Monitoring and Enforcement. Part of demonstrating the intent to comply means including provisions for monitoring compliance and provisions for enforcing compliance.

OPERATIONAL CONSIDERATIONS

As discussed, there are documentary provisions addressing operations that are tailored for the age-restricted community, and they should be reviewed as part of the legal considerations. For the purposes of this section, these provisions will be merely highlighted, as they become more obvious in the subsequent discussion of actual operations.

The first provision that requires consideration is reducing responsibility for maintenance to reflect the age and desires of residents. That such a reduction should occur is only common sense, but it is important not to overlook it: the documents and the management plan, which will later become part of the marketing plan, need to be drafted to reflect this specific change rather than simply carried forward from plans for a more traditional master-planned community.

There needs to be the capacity to provide and to charge for specific services for owners or occupants who desire to receive them. This might include on-site health care, dining at different stages or levels, housekeeping and maintenance within the interior portions of the unit, a transportation service, and programs and activities to fill residents' leisure time and interests. Successful age-restricted communities acknowledge that time is a major amenity, and they provide ways and means of using that time in a highly efficient, customer-satisfying manner.

The powers and duties of the community association in an age-restricted community need to be broader to permit it to function as a housing provider with respect to all meanings of that term. At the same time, the provisions dealing with the board members and officers need to be well tailored in order to (1) avoid power struggles and (2) avoid the creation of cliques that may seek to exercise control to the benefit of some and the detriment of others. As part of this tailoring, the documents need to institutionalize regular communication within the association to ensure that everyone is fully informed of what is being done and why.

All of these contingencies result in a greater need for and a higher level of demand upon professional management. As part of the legal considerations—and in the drafting undertaken in response to those considerations—the development team must focus upon management issues, including how management is to be undertaken and what powers will be afforded the third-party manager. In the traditional governance structure, for example, the documentation will identify the owners of units as the members of the association and note that they are the individuals who are entitled to serve on the board as officers of the association.

In active adult communities, a child of the occupant is often the actual owner of the unit, for tax or other reasons. Whereas traditional documentation would empower the nonresident owner to be involved in the governance while excluding the experienced, time-available occupant who has a greater interest in the day-to-day operation of the community, the documents for an AARC need to permit residents as well as owners to serve on the board; moreover, the drafter needs to thoroughly consider the differing interests and needs of tenants, resident owners, nonresident owners, and other such when drafting governance documents.

Reserve funds offer an illustration of how the different needs of different segments of the community might be played out. While most would agree that some level of reserve fund is needed, an older population is less likely to set aside today's dollars for tomorrow's repairs. Accordingly, the drafting team may conclude after due consideration that mandating a reserve is in the best interest of the overall community. Mandating that there be a reserve, however, does not solve the issue of the level at which that reserve should be funded. Therefore, this issue of funding levels must also be studied and a decision made regarding a minimum funding level.

KEYS TO SUCCESS

To survive and flourish in today's society, successful active adult communities require successful management. A successful community is much more than the value of its "hard goods"—the sticks and bricks and facilities. Although they are necessary and important to developers, once the hard goods are complete, they give way to the importance of managing lifestyle as the development matures and secures its identity.

Successful communities are measured in the long run according to the value of the "soft goods." Soft goods include relationships between neighbors, respect for the diversity of the community, participation of owners as stakeholders in building and maintaining community unity, and the value placed on leadership within the community.

How does the developer get from the hard goods to the soft goods? The industry has proven that the most significant single item a developer has to sell is service. After the purchase is made, the community that exemplifies success is the one built by service.

The model of a successful community is based on the premise that developers establish a sound development plan, work that plan from the very beginning, retain control throughout the entire development process, and eventually turn the development over to community management when the development phase is completed.

The critical element of that model is service. Service can be broken down into people, timing, product, responsiveness, follow-up, assistance, smiles, and attitude. It is so critical to the success of the soft goods that it cannot be emphasized enough or initiated too early in the development process.

The list that follows highlights the most critical aspects of service that the developer should address in the community-building process:

The Oak Ridge Fitness Center, at The Landings in Skidaway Island, Georgia, houses an indoor Olympic pool, locker rooms, an aerobics room, a fully equipped exercise facility, and a small juice bar.

Prepare and Maintain Good Records. There is nothing more critical for a community than to know it holds all the pieces of the puzzle as leadership is transferred from a developer to the community. Land deeds, board decisions, and corporate records are the most critical records, but any record that enables the community to continue and grow uninterrupted strengthens the relationship between the developer and the association.

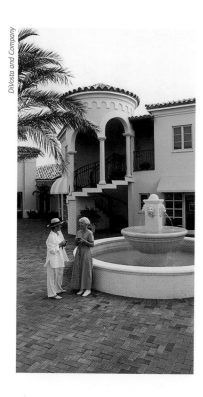

A fountain accentuates the Mediterranean architecture of the "deconstructed" town center of the Village Walk community in Naples, Florida.

Encourage the Building of Community. The development of "community" is not a new concept; however, it has reached a new and exciting emphasis in today's marketplace. The Community Associations Institute Research Foundation, in coordination with the Urban Land Institute, has developed a community success survey to be conducted nationwide. The purpose of the survey is to measure the success of "community" in community associations.

Community is a lot more than sticks, bricks, and amenities. It is the glue that encourages people to stay in their homes. Developers who want to build successful communities would do well to embrace a number of new perspectives—which, collectively, represent a paradigm shift in the world of development.

- Use "neighborhood guidelines" instead of "rules and restrictions."
- Refer to "homes" instead of to "units."
- Promote the concept of stakeholders instead of that of property owners.
- Emphasize the concept of "the village" instead of "the "compound."
- Include all residents in programs instead of isolating certain segments (e.g., renters).
- Create a focus on the positive aspects of "community."
- Create neighborhood and community-wide programs and events to bring people together and encourage participation in building community. Choose a community charity to support.
- Develop the theme that all meetings of the community are to be considered celebrations, opportunities to share in the governance process and to praise accomplishments.
- Build fun into the development programs. Create opportunity for residents to have input into the process and use their varied talents.
- Establish courtesy in customer-related programs, covenant enforcement, and notifications. Use alternative dispute resolution as the backbone of appeals and enforcement.
- Show appreciation to volunteers on a regular basis. There are communities that form a committee to oversee their annual volunteer-recognition program.
- Create opportunity for communication using all available techniques and technological advances.
- Encourage civility in all activities and meetings.
- Develop welcome packages and hold orientation sessions for new residents.

Evaluate Residents' Perspectives Regularly. Understanding the client and updating that understanding over time is particularly critical to increasing the longevity of the relationship between the developer and the association and the success of the community. There are several reasons that it is important not only to communicate with residents but also to listen to them.

In active adult communities, physical, emotional, and financial needs invariably change as the community ages in place, creating challenges for management and residents alike. Unless they have a consistent monitoring program in place, the developer and management are often placed in a reactive posture—and are more likely to be surprised by shifting concerns and needs.

Because they change, grow, and develop in a variety of ways, the expectations of community members are difficult to get a grip on; nevertheless, doing so is one of the most important tasks for a developer. Remembering that perception is reality, developers may need to ask themselves what the expectations of the community members are, where they come from, and what will fulfill them.

In fact, expectations are developed long before potential buyers reach the front door. They are drawn from their own personal history and environment, from others' comments about the development, from what they have seen in the form of advertising, and probably from what they have read. Expectations also come from older adults' perceptions of what retirement is supposed to be, how hard they have worked to achieve it, and what they think the world owes them.

Develop Strong Relationships. Programs, neighborhood events, and community-wide social events that bring people together and encourage participation in community building are the engine for successful community building. Activities that enable the members of the active adult community to interact with residents of the surrounding area provide even greater opportunity to strengthen ties both within and outside the community and to ensure that there continues to be a focus upon these community issues and involvements.

Creating opportunity for residents to use their varied talents in participating in the governance process is challenging, but it is necessary for successful service development.

A Management Checklist

A developer should consider the following questions when establishing the proper level and type of management to fit the service needs of the community:

- What are the key aspects of the leadership model between the developer and the community that I want to capture and secure in the future?
- How do I define successful community management?
- What do I hope to accomplish through management of the community?
- What issues do I plan on handling through management?
- How can I build community value through management and community leadership?
- What level of service do I expect to perform through management?
- What are the hard and soft goods of the development?

Source: Rob Felix, manager, Sun City Vistoso, Tucson, Arizona.

Looking outside the community, developers should also establish lasting positive local and municipal relationships. Leave a legacy for the community by developing strong working relationships with local governments, trade organizations, and contractors. Be a part of the greater community by encouraging residents to serve on councils, committees, and task forces and by donating to local charities and community groups.

CONCLUSION

In creating any master-planned community, the developer and her team need to follow certain immutable principles. Team members must understand the community association concepts, appreciate the roles and functions that the community association will play, and be aware of the needs and expectations the community association will be called upon to meet, both in ordinary and extraordinary circumstances. The team must understand the particular project and realize that "one size does not fit all." Understanding the project means having an appreciation for its unique geography, demographics, amenities, and other aspects. All these factors are made even more acute—and the team must be even more sensitive to them—in the age-restricted community.

Any successful project reflects, in its documentation and governance structure, three basic strategies: a governance strategy, an amenity strategy, and an exit strategy. In the active adult community, the governance strategy has an overlay not found in the more traditional project—namely, a compliance strategy that addresses all the requirements of the Fair Housing Act as well as the specialized operational considerations that flow from the demographic makeup of the community.

Understanding the project also means that the team will comprehend what the community association will do and own, and how it will function. Once again, the unique aspects of the age-restricted community add substantial burdens to what the association will do and how it is to do it. Finally, understanding the project means recognizing the level of participation to be anticipated from the residents of the community. Generally speaking, in an active adult community the level of participation dramatically increases, but the tolerance level of group members may well decrease. Accordingly, the documentation and planning for legal considerations must reflect all of the foregoing factors and situations.

As in any project, the governing documents must dispense information and delineate responsibility. The active adult community may need an even greater sensitivity to this requirement because of residents' high degree of inquisitiveness and demands about such issues.

As always, the development team must anticipate that things can, may, and probably will go wrong at some point in the evolution of the community. As a result, the documents need to be drafted with sufficient flexibility and resilience to meet the changes in times and circumstances.

Finally, a lesson hard-learned from many years of experience is that the developer and the development team must take the process of community structure and governance as seriously as they take the product they are creating. Too frequently, there is a great commitment of time, money, and intellectual capital to the design, construction, and marketing of the product, while not enough of these important assets are devoted to what can set a development above the ordinary and move it into the realm of the highly successful—or, regrettably, from the ordinary to the unsuccessful, litigation-prone. The development team must invest intellectual capital, time, and commitment in the creation of a process to match the product. Doing so requires an appreciation for the legal considerations and all of their ramifications.

---

1. Rob Felix, manager for Sun City Vistoso, in Tucson, Arizona, provided the original draft of the operations section, and it reflects considerable operational experience and wisdom. It should be read carefully as a basic primer in line with the Urban Land Institute maxim on focusing upon mistakes made and lessons learned.

2. Specifically, the law states that "Nothing in this title shall be construed to invalidate or limit any law of a State or a political subdivision of a State, or any other jurisdiction in which this title shall be effective, that grants, guarantees, or protects the same rights as are granted by this title; but any law of a State, a political subdivision, or other jurisdiction that purports to require or permit any action that would be a discriminatory housing practice under this title shall to that extent be invalid."

3. See generally, Wayne S. Hyatt, *Condominium and Homeowners Associations: Community Association Law*, 2nd ed. (ALI-ABA, 1988); Wayne S. Hyatt, *Condominium and Homeowners Associations: A Guide to the Development Process* (WestGroup, 1985); Wayne S. Hyatt, *Community Association Law: Cases and Materials on Common Interest Communities*; and Lloyd Bookout, *Residential Development Handbook*, 2nd ed. (Washington, D.C.: ULI–The Urban Land Institute, 1990).

4. See Hyatt, *Condominium and Homeowners Associations*, sec. 7.12; and Bookout, *Residential Development Handbook*, 294–96.

Case Studies

The term *active adult retirement community* (AARC) can refer to communities that include a wide range of product types and development sizes, that are built in a variety of locations, and that are created by different types of project developers. This chapter features ten developments in diverse geographic locations (two are outside the United States) that illustrate the range of different approaches and features that characterizes AARCs.

Each case study provides an overall view of the project; indicates its location and its developer; describes the project planning process; notes important design features; and details purchase arrangements and pricing, sales and marketing, management and operations, and lessons learned. Project data, photographs, site plans, unit plans, and clubhouse plans are also included.

St. James Plantation's full-service marina on the Atlantic Intracoastal Waterway.

This chapter includes the following projects:

SaddleBrooke: Tucson, Arizona

Village by the Arboretum:
Guelph, Ontario, Canada

Leisure World of Virginia: Lansdowne, Virginia

St. James Plantation:
Southport, North Carolina

Clover Commons: Pittsburgh, Pennsylvania

Indian Ridge Country Club:
Palm Desert, California

Sun City at Huntley: Huntley, Illinois

Village Walk: Naples, Florida

Dee Why Gardens: New South Wales, Australia

Heritage in the Hills: Detroit, Michigan

SaddleBrooke

Tucson, Arizona

Situated 3,285 feet above sea level in the foothills of the Santa Catalina Mountains just north of Tucson, SaddleBrooke is a well-executed, traditional, age-restricted Sunbelt AARC. Planned for up to 4,200 units, it offers a leisure-oriented lifestyle centered around golf, recreation, and a wealth of social activities. Work on SaddleBrooke began in 1987. The development is being built in two overlapping phases of approximately equal size. About 1,900 homes have been built in Phase I (approximately 200 more are planned), and Phase II now contains 800 homes. The development features 45 holes of golf, two clubhouses, 13 lighted tennis courts, swimming pools, and a retail center.

The developer, Robson Communities, Inc., and its affiliated companies (doing business as SunLakes Marketing, Inc.) are private, family-owned businesses. Its founder, Edward Robson, purchased a tract of land just outside of Phoenix in 1972, intending to build an active adult community. Despite the energy crisis and economic

The Santa Catalina Mountains provide a dramatic backdrop for the SaddleBrooke community.

downturn of the mid-1970s and the high-interest-rate environment of the early 1980s, Robson stuck to his vision. The result was Sun Lakes, one of the largest and most successful AARCs in the nation. Since then, in addition to Sun Lakes, the company has built three other successful adult communities, all of which have won industry awards.

Robson Communities and its affiliated companies include a home mortgage company, a resale company, and a property management company. Every Robson community is built by its own development and construction companies. Scott Homes, a subdivision of Robson Communities, and Santa Clara Development (the developer's California operation), which are headed by Ed Robson's sons, build intergenerational homes and apartments. Together, Robson Communities and its affiliated companies constitute the largest privately owned retirement development company in Arizona, employing more than 1,000 people. In all, the company has built and sold more than 15,000 homes.

Until recently, Robson Communities had developed exclusively in the state of Arizona, a location that appeals to the "snowbird" market. About 79 percent of its buyers overall are from out of state; most of the others relocated to Arizona at an earlier time. The company has just initiated development of a 2,725-acre site in Denton, Texas, near the Dallas–Fort Worth metroplex, an area of five million people.

SaddleBrooke is the company's second AARC. The Tucson area is a popular retirement destination, and, according to Michael Osborn, Robson Communities' senior vice president, "We just fell in love with the site." The rolling terrain, the native vegetation, and the beautiful views afforded by the backdrop of the mountains seemed a perfect retirement setting. In 1986, Robson created the SaddleBrooke Development Company to purchase and develop the property.

The specifics of the site-selection process focused primarily on size, price, and location. The size of the property had to be at least 700 acres—enough to accommodate at least 2,000 homes. According to Osborn, 2,000 homes is the "target base," or minimum community size that makes possible the economies of scale and sufficient revenue to provide a private 18-hole golf course. The company also wanted to be able to expand the development through the purchase of additional land. Location considerations included a time-distance of less than one-half hour to an airport, and proximity to a hospital and other medical facilities. The site is 14 miles from the edge of Tucson and 17 miles from a major shopping mall.

Robson's first land purchase for SaddleBrooke was 1,100 acres. The company now owns 2,100 acres and may buy more in the future. In addition, it has bought an additional 2,200-acre site six miles away, which it may one day develop as another AARC.

At the time of purchase, the SaddleBrooke property was zoned for development as a master-planned community, and a small number of homes had been built near the center of the site. Some changes were made to the original plan, which required public meetings and resulting accommodations, such as drainage channels to manage runoff near the existing homes.

Pinal County was a cooperative development partner. Osborn explained that in its negotiations with local governments, the firm demonstrates that AARCs contribute to the local economy by providing tax income while requiring few public services, primarily because there are no school-children. Robson Communities installs its own roads, sewer, water, cable access television, and other infrastructure, and it created its own utility company. SaddleBrooke also has its own fire station, which is paid for through taxes from its residents; and it maintains its own security patrols, though crime is not a problem. Streetlights are prohibited because of nearby observatories.

To the extent possible, the company wanted to preserve the native vegetation, especially the beautiful paloverde trees; mesquite; and barrel, prickly pear, and cholla cactuses. Not only are these plants more characteristic and attractive in this setting than alternative choices, they also thrive in the desert climate with little care. To preserve the paloverde trees, each one that had to be moved during construction was tagged and put into a nursery until it could be put back in place.

The 26,000-square-foot MountainView Country Club is the heart of SaddleBrooke's active lifestyle.

To conserve water, the golf courses consist of Bermuda grass, which is dormant during the winter and requires no water. Only the greens are seeded with rye grass. To provide the community's water supply and maintain the landscaping, the company uses groundwater, drills its own wells, and uses recycled water for irrigation.

In SaddleBrooke the company is building its most expensive products, primarily because homes are more expensive to build on this site. Grading in this rolling, rocky area has been challenging, and development was dogged by environmental issues, especially in Phase II.

Project design was driven by the dictates of the site and a desire to maximize views. The community is designed along a loop road approached through a three-mile, county-owned entry road. The first structures seen upon entry are the shopping center and fire station, then the homes and clubhouses. Most of the homes are oriented to the mountains.

As in its other developments, Robson Communities offers three different categories, or "series," of homes at SaddleBrooke: Villa, Premiere, and Luxury. The categories represent groupings of homes of different sizes, prices, and levels of luxury. Overall, homebuyers can choose from more than 20 floor plans, nearly 100 exterior designs, and hundreds of optional design features. To the extent possible, the company will also customize home designs to meet buyers' needs.

The interior of the MountainView Clubhouse, with its soaring ceilings, stone fireplace, and generous use of wood finishings, is warm and luxurious.

The Villa series consists of duplex homes that range in size from 1,452 to 2,165 square feet. Villas have been especially popular with "snowbirds" and single people. The Villa homes are sold as condominiums, with all landscaping, exterior maintenance, common area and street maintenance, and building insurance included in the residents' monthly Villa Homeowner Association assessment. Because of this arrangement, the Villas are all located together, whereas homes from the other two series can be built on lots anywhere in the community. Villa features include dual-pane windows, volume ceilings, concrete tile roofs, stucco patio columns, two-car garages, and a covered patio.

Homes in the Premiere series range from 1,827 to 2,360 square feet. Standard features in this series, depending on the home selected, include tile roofs, dual-glazed aluminum windows and sliding-glass doors, volume ceilings, sculptured plant shelves, storage cabinets in the laundry/hobby room, and rounded corners on interior walls. Among the standard bathroom features are ceramic tile surrounds, elongated water closets, and double lavatories in the master bath. All homes have a vented two- or three-car garage and a covered patio and entry.

The homes in the Luxury series, which range from 2,120 to 3,484 square feet in size, offer standard features such as a grand Roman tub in certain models, a walk-in closet, more built-in storage cabinets, clerestory windows, electric cooktops, and microwave ovens.

The price of added optional features ranges from $1,000 to $30,000 and averages around $15,000. The company is studying the requirements and demand for high-tech wiring for all homes and may include it in the future.

The SaddleBrooke Country Club clubhouse was completed in early 1989, along with the first 18 holes of golf. The clubhouse, furnished in a Southwestern design theme, includes meeting rooms, a library, a dining area, a large lounge with a two-sided fireplace, barbecue grills, and a café.

The second clubhouse—MountainView—was designed to provide more flexible space all on one floor. Completed in 1998, it complements the first clubhouse by providing 26,000 square feet of additional space, along with a number of amenities: a large but divisible auditorium/grand ballroom, a library, a variety of indoor and outdoor gathering spaces, a catering kitchen, and a bar and lounge area. Inside the clubhouse, natural materials such as wood, stone, stucco, and tile create a rugged yet elegant ambience.

The MountainView Clubhouse is one building within the MountainView Country Club complex, a three-building campus that includes the clubhouse, an arts and crafts facility, and a fitness facility with a health club, lounge, restaurant, and pro shop for golfers. The health club features BodyMasters equipment, which Robson had specially designed for use by older people. The restaurant is run for and by the community. As Osborn explained, "It's part of the lifestyle, just like the swimming pool. If it doesn't make money, that's okay." Robson operates the pro shop, though it is more for residents' convenience than for profit. Five tennis courts and golf cart storage complete the complex. A whirlpool spa and two swimming pools—one for socializing and one for swimming laps—adjoin the health club building. Near the pool is a parking area for golf carts, but it is recessed so that only the roofs of the golf carts are visible from the pool. An area for the storage of recreational vehicles is located off site.

Both the SaddleBrooke Country Club and MountainView Clubhouse include office space. The sales center is in a separate building. In Phase I, the developer has turned over the sales center to the homeowners' association.

The community also includes a small strip commercial center, owned by Robson Communities, with a gas station, a convenience store, a dry cleaner, a restaurant, a barber shop and beauty salon, a resale shop, and a bank. Initially, the company leased space in the center at special rates to attract retail operators; it now charges lease rates that are closer to market rents.

SaddleBrooke has its own newspaper, the *SaddleBrooke Progress,* published by Robson Communities' publishing company. Homeowners also publish a newsletter, *SaddleBag Notes.* Soon, SaddleBrooke, like Sun Lakes, will feature its own homeowner newscast station on cable television.

Though only about 50 percent of the residents play, golf is the major amenity offered. Phase I includes 27 holes of golf in three nine-hole segments, and Phase II contains an 18-hole course. Each course is challenging and has at least four tees to accommodate different levels of play. The nine-hole segments enable players to choose different combinations for 18 holes of play. (And, not incidentally, it makes golf course maintenance easier to schedule.) Starter facilities are located at various points in the courses to make different combinations of play possible. The fairways are interspersed among the homes to maximize views of open space.

So that the golf courses can be built early in the development of a project, the company initially makes them semiprivate. Later, it eliminates public play.

Social life is active at SaddleBrooke and centers around clubs, events, and the recreational facilities. The guiding principle, according to Osborn, is "allowing homeowners to do the things they want to do most." Residents have formed clubs to enjoy a wide range of common interests, from bridge to pottery to bicycling. A group consisting primarily of women has organized a putters' league that plays at scheduled times. The University of Arizona in Tucson generates cultural offerings. Volunteer work has been a particularly popular activity.

SaddleBrooke is marketed through referrals, through advertisements in local media, and through advertisements in national periodicals that are targeted to older people. Potential buyers who respond to national advertising receive a video that describes SaddleBrooke and Robson Communities and are contacted by the firm's Preferred Guest department, which offers prospects an opportunity to participate in the Preferred Guest program. Through this program, prospects can, for a small charge, sample the community's lifestyle by staying for several days in one of the dozen or so homes within the community that were built for this purpose. The stay includes dinner with homeowners, a round of golf, and access to all community facilities, amenities, and activities. Many of the Preferred Guest program coordinators are people who live in a Robson community. Because their earnings are tied to results, they screen potential buyers carefully before inviting them to participate. About 12 percent of Preferred Guests purchase a home; this represents 40 percent of all sales.

The community's primary appeal is the lifestyle it offers. Its remote location is presented as a benefit, offering a fantastic setting, clean air, and an uncluttered environment. As Art Vaughan, SaddleBrooke's sales manager, explained, the approach is, "We sell the mountains and give you the house." He added that the sales staff, most of whom have been with the company for a long time, understand that older buyers are knowledgeable and will not accept high-pressure tactics. "We see our role as counseling rather than selling. If the community is not right for them, we don't push them."

Approximately 6 percent of the people who walk into the sales office buy a home, compared with an average of 2 percent for typical tract housing. In part, this is because people who come to SaddleBrooke are there because they are interested. "No one drives *by* SaddleBrooke; they drive *to* us," noted Vaughan.

People have come to SaddleBrooke from throughout the nation, but, besides Arizona, the largest number of buyers are from California, New York, and Washington state. The average buyer is 58 years old, but the average age is decreasing over time. Fair Housing Act restrictions require that 80 percent of the homes be occupied by at least one person who is 55 or older. Because the community has been underway for some time, the average age within the community is 68. Eighty-five percent of residents are retired. About half of all buyers live in SaddleBrooke on a seasonal basis. Relatively few single people have bought homes there: Osborn feels that this is primarily because its location is somewhat remote and because its large size makes it more difficult for individuals to integrate easily into the community's social life. Moreover, Saddlebrook appeals more to seasonal buyers, and few singles can afford second homes.

The community's major amenity is golf. Like all of the landscaping in SaddleBrooke, the golf courses are designed to reflect the Southwestern climate and setting through the use of natural features and vegetation.

According to Osborn, the community's primary competition is the family home and other areas of the country. Within Arizona, he believes that the primary competition is Quail Creek, another Robson community near Tucson.

Sales were slow during the first three years of Phase I but picked up rapidly after the clubhouse and golf course opened. With sales of 350 homes last year, SaddleBrooke was the number-one subdivision in Tucson in terms of annual sales. This sales pace is as rapid as the company is structured to manage.

Because the hilly site affords many gorgeous views, depending on the location, lot premiums may be attached to the home sales prices. Premiums also apply to lots with golf course views, lots on corners, and lots on culs-de-sac. Premiums range from $10,000 to $150,000, and average around $40,000. Approximately 80 percent of the lots command a premium.

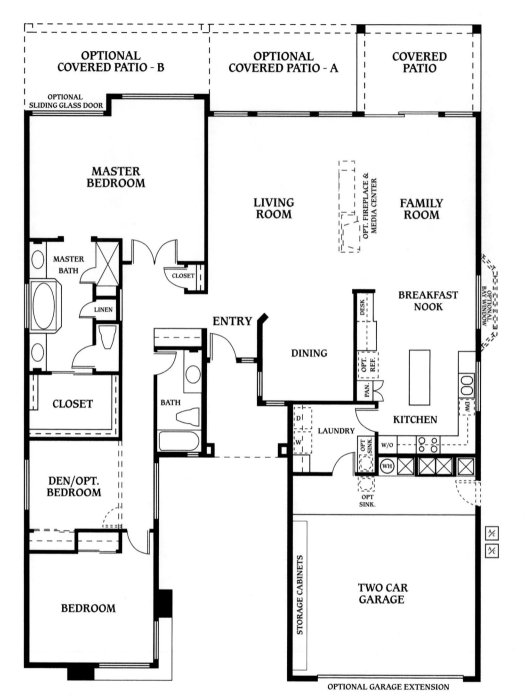

OPTIONAL
COVERED PATIO - B

OPTIONAL
COVERED PATIO - A

COVERED
PATIO

OPTIONAL
SLIDING GLASS DOOR

MASTER
BEDROOM

MASTER
BATH

LINEN

CLOSET

CLOSET

BATH

DEN/OPT.
BEDROOM

BEDROOM

ENTRY

DINING

LIVING
ROOM

OPT. FIREPLACE &
MEDIA CENTER

FAMILY
ROOM

OPTIONAL
BAY WINDOW

DESK

BREAKFAST
NOOK

OPT. REF.

PAN.

KITCHEN

DW

LAUNDRY

D

W

OPT
SINK.

W/O

WH

OPT
SINK.

STORAGE CABINETS

TWO CAR
GARAGE

OPTIONAL GARAGE EXTENSION

The popular 2,289-square-foot Ponderosa model, one of the homes in the Luxury series, features two bedrooms and a den.

About half of all buyers pay cash. Among those that finance their purchases, down payments average 50 percent of the purchase price. Osborn notes that money is not an issue for most sales prospects. "This is something they planned for; it's not an emotional decision." "However," he added, "if you don't have an emotional moment during the buying process, you will not make a sale."

Each of the two phases has its own homeowners' association, which maintains all common areas and amenities. Phase I is owned by the homeowners' association. Phase II is still developer controlled and, according to its covenants, conditions, and restrictions, control will be transferred

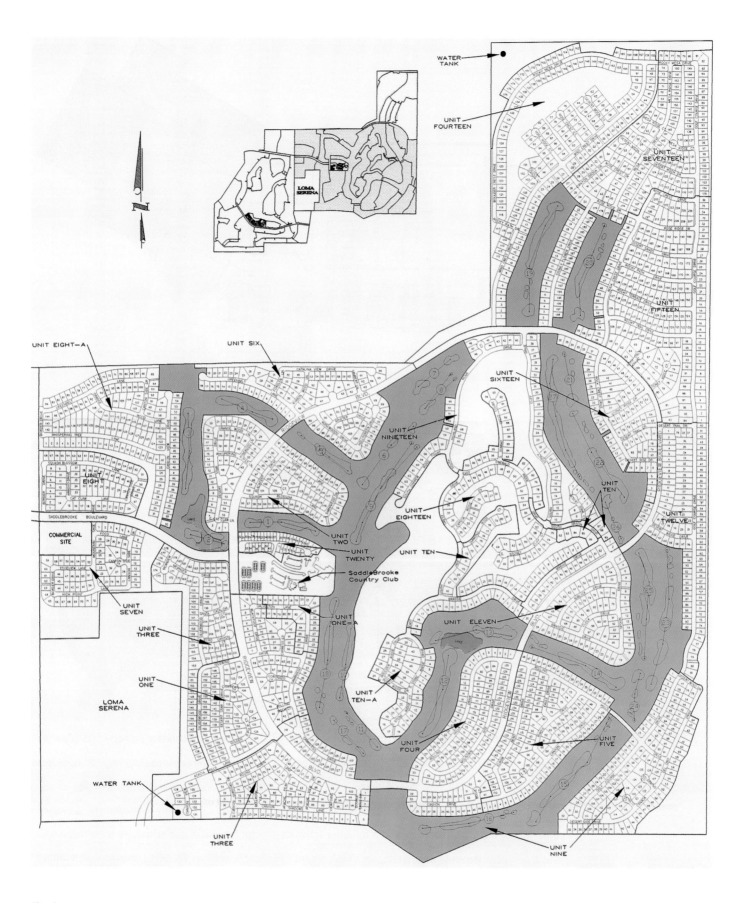

Site plan.

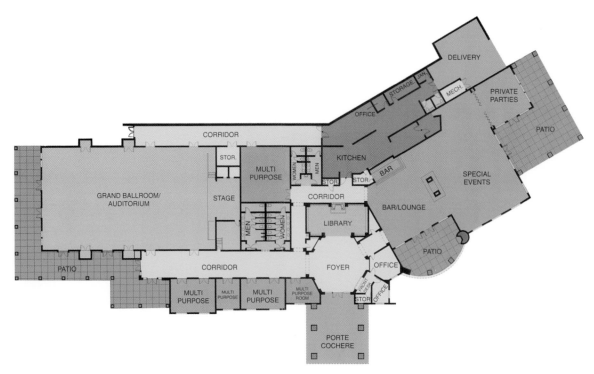

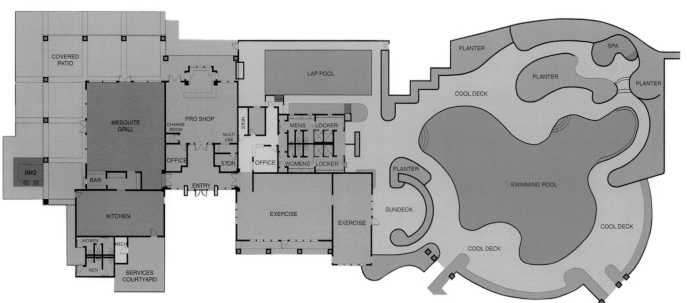

The clubhouses of MountainView
Country Club.

to the homeowners when the last home is closed. In addition, a secondary homeowners' association has been established to manage the additional exterior maintenance (and levy the additional maintenance fees) associated with the duplex homes. A reciprocal-use agreement enables all residents to enjoy all the development's facilities and amenities. Community management is overseen by a general manager, and a full-time activities director facilitates and schedules social activities.

Like all of its projects, the development of SaddleBrooke has added to Robson Communities' fund of knowledge and experience. For example, according to Osborn, SaddleBrooke was built in two phases because of the market strength and the development opportunity; in the future, however, because of this experience, the company will avoid the complexity and "turf issues" associated with building in phases that have separate homeowners' associations.

The range of offerings at SaddleBrooke has grown out of the company's 28 years in business and is continually being refined in response to changing consumer tastes. The company keeps careful track of the interests expressed by prospects during the sales process and by participants in the Preferred Guest program. As a result, for example, home sizes have been increasing over time, and the company has learned that customers are looking for higher levels of quality as well. Prices, too, undergo continuous adjustment. Home prices at SaddleBrooke have increased by approximately 6 to 8 percent each year.

On the basis of what it learns about how residents use them, the company is constantly refining the recreational facilities it provides. For example, the first clubhouse in SaddleBrooke did not have large card rooms. Playing cards has proved to be a major pastime, so more space will be designated for that activity in the future. To appeal to its increasingly well educated and demanding customers, the firm has also upgraded the quality of the finishes and furnishings in its clubhouses to give them a more elegant look. This change is reflected in the feeling of "western elegance" that characterizes the design and furnishings of the MountainView Clubhouse.

In response to homeowners' expressed desire for on-site, care-oriented housing, Robson is developing a congregate care facility, Renaissance Luxury Residential Suites, at its Sun Lakes development. This facility will offer meals and housekeeping (but not medical care) in a condominium environment. The initial development will consist of 180 units, though the zoning allows up to 400 units, with an option to add an assisted-living component later. If this new product line proves successful, Robson will include it in its other communities.

PROJECT DATA

Land Use

Site area	2,095 acres
Clubhouse and other common buildings	73,000 square feet
Golf course	500 acres
Other open space and outdoor amenities	300 acres
Streets and parking	130 acres
Number of single-family detached units	3,800+
Number of attached/multifamily units	250+
Gross density	2 units per acre

(continued on page 176)

Single-Family Unit Information

Unit type	Lot size (minimum)	Unit size (square feet)	No. of units (planned/built)	Price range
Premiere	65' x 112'	1,827–2,360	1,976/1,318	$170,400–$187,400
Luxury	65' x 112'	2,120–3,484	1,828/1,216	$200,400–$287,400
Villas	55' x 90'	1,452–2,165	253/88	$132,900–$184,400

Golf Course/Club Information

Total number of holes	45
SaddleBrooke	Three 9-hole courses
Average course length (per 18-hole course)	6,500 yards
MountainView	18 holes
Course length	6,728 yards
Clubhouse, Phase I	22,054 square feet
Other facilities, Phase I	12,295 square feet
Clubhouse, Phase II	26,130 square feet
Other facilities, Phase II	12,539 square feet

Golf membership type	Fees
Annual	$150/month; no initiation fee
Daily	$23–$46 (varies by season): no initiation fee

Development Cost Information

Site acquisition cost	$30,000,000
Hard and soft costs	$125,000,000
Total development costs	$155,000,000

Operating Cost Information

Homeowners' association fees (per unit per month)	$86.25
Monthly homeowners' association operating expenses	$250,000 net

Development Schedule

Site purchased	1986
Planning started	1986
Site work started	1987

	Phase I	Phase II
Number of units	2,062	1,995
Planning started	1986	1993
Construction started	1987	1994
Construction completed	1999	2003 (estimated)
Sales started	1987	1995
Sales completed	1999	2005 (estimated)

Development Team

Developer

SaddleBrooke Development
  Company
40001 South Ridgeview
Tucson, Arizona 85739
(520) 818-0968

Land Planner

B & R Engineering
Sun Lakes, Arizona
(480) 895-0799

Architect

Architecture Plus Ltd.
Phoenix, Arizona
(602) 264-7500

Golf Course Architect

MountainView Course

Gary Panks Associates
Scottsdale, Arizona
(480) 563-7175

SaddleBrooke Course

Keith Foster & Associates
Phoenix, Arizona
(602) 279-4232

Project Address

63395 East Flower Ridge Road
Tucson, Arizona 85739

Contact Information

Michael Osborn, senior vice president, Robson Communities
(480) 895-4332

Date of site visit: February 8, 2000

All project data are current as of February 25, 2000.

Report author: Diane R. Suchman

Village by the Arboretum

Guelph, Ontario, Canada

The Village by the Arboretum is an age-targeted development of single-family detached and attached homes built on a 112-acre site leased from the University of Guelph. Located adjacent to the university's 500-acre arboretum, the development offers a retirement lifestyle in a village atmosphere near the cultural offerings of a large university. The Village by the Arboretum is just down the street from shopping centers and golf clubs. Two major hospitals and two medical centers are located in the city. As of December 1999, 375 homes had been sold. At buildout, which is anticipated in 2002, the development will include a total of 570 homes and a 43,000-square-foot clubhouse.

Plans are underway for construction of an extended-care facility on a corner of the property. Though the concept is still being developed, it is intended to provide optional, fee-based services and facilities that will enable residents to age in place. The Arboretum will develop, own, and operate the new facility separately from the Village.

The Village Centre clubhouse at the Village by the Arboretum, with its distinctive clock tower, as seen from the landscaped entry garden.

This streetscape exhibits the developer's attention to detail in exterior design and landscaping.

According to Orin Reid, president of Reid's Heritage Homes, Inc., the Village by the Arboretum is the only AARC in the city, though others are located in the outskirts. None of the others provide medical or custodial care on site.

The arboretum, which was founded in 1970, includes a 50-acre nature center, interpretive trails, and wildlife gardens where visitors can enjoy more than 3,000 species of plants, shrubs, and flowers. This gardenlike setting is also the locus of a variety of special activities throughout the year.

Guelph, known as The Royal City because it is named for the British royal family, is located near Toronto in the province of Ontario. The city draws its unique physical character from its architecturally distinctive downtown buildings, which are constructed of brick and local limestone, and from landmarks such as the statue and fountain in St. George's Square. The farmers' market, Riverside Park (with its floral clock), the Kortright Waterfowl Park, and seasonal events such as the Guelph Spring Festival also contribute to a strong sense of community.

During the 1960s, the University of Guelph acquired a number of real estate properties through donation or purchase. In 1986, the university's newly established real estate division, seeking an economic use for these lands, designated a number of university-owned properties to be developed in ways that would generate income for the Heritage Fund, the university's endowment. Among the properties was a 110-acre site adjacent to the arboretum, which the university set aside for an adult lifestyle community—the Village by the Arboretum—for a period of 99 years. The university commissioned market studies, which included focus groups with potential future residents; obtained a rezoning of the property as a residential retirement zone; and selected Reid's Heritage Homes to be the project developer. The university entered into a 50-year "head lease," or master-lease arrangement, with Reid's Heritage Homes, which agreed to assume responsibility for project management, construction, sales, and property management. Should the relationship founder, the university would assume the developer's role.

Founded in 1947, Reid's Heritage Homes, Ltd., is primarily a land development and residential construction company, though it has been a partner in commercial developments. The company builds approximately 1,200 homes per year throughout southern Ontario, and does all its architectural and interior design work in house.

Before construction began, the university sold 80 lots at the property's border to individual purchasers. This sale had several purposes: to establish the development's boundary; to populate the boundary with residents who understood what sort of further development was planned and who would therefore be unlikely to oppose it; and to bring the university some initial income.

The property's zoning enabled the developer to design the project to accommodate the market. No registered subdivision plan was required, and no individual lot lines were drawn. Apart from the requirements generated by utility services, the placement of homes was completely flexible, which made adjustments to the initial development plan possible. For example, plans called at first for 616 units rather than 570. Once the marketing process was underway, the developer realized that prospective buyers preferred larger homes than those that had been planned. As a result, the development plan was changed to include fewer but larger units.

Despite the university's precautions, neighboring residents did initially object to the development plan. Reid met with the opponents one at a time to find ways to overcome their objections, which was primarily a matter of increasing the density of tree plantings and other vegetative buffers. He advises that neighborhood objections will always be part of the process, and that developers should plan to "give something" in return for the neighbors' support or acquiescence.

Reid's Heritage Homes did its own market studies in addition to those undertaken by the university and did not accept deposits on homes until the property was ready for construction. By that time, the university had amassed a 1,000-person list of sales prospects, and 40 homes had been presold.

Construction began in 1994 and will proceed in a total of six phases of approximately 100 homes each. As of December 1999, Phase III was being completed and Phase IV had begun. The clubhouse was built when 125 homes had sold. (The developer had originally planned to construct the clubhouse when 225 homes had sold, but market pressure moved the trigger point.) All buildings are constructed to conform to guidelines set forth by the university.

Reid's Heritage Homes was responsible for obtaining financing for the development of the project. However, because Reid's Heritage Homes does not own the land, the company cannot encumber the land or assign leases as part of a financing arrangement. To finance construction, Reid's Heritage Homes relied on its own resources and on loans obtained through the use of other collateral. In addition, the developer had to post a C$2 million letter of credit to the university to guarantee the development of the project's infrastructure.

The first two phases of the community are arranged in concentric circles around a central recreational facility. The other four phases extend to the north and to the east of this core area.

Visitors enter the community through a stone gatehouse. A wide, landscaped boulevard leads past a pond to the clubhouse, known as the Village Centre.

The 14 detached models range in size from 1,161 to 1,874 square feet. The six attached models range from 1,045 to 1,489 square feet. Once the development is complete, approximately 390 units will be single-family detached houses, and 179 will be attached homes arranged in groups of three or four to create a townhome configuration.

All homes include front porches; a garage (11 feet 6 inches wide); sodded and landscaped lawns; wheelchair-accessible doors; and unfinished, full-height basements. Among the optional features are fireplaces, whirlpool tubs, vaulted ceilings, skylights, sunrooms, decks, and finished basements. Because there are no load-bearing walls inside the homes, buyers can change the design of the homes' interiors at will, and customizing is common. Residents can augment the landscaping at the walls of their homes but cannot make changes to the homes' exteriors. Home designs are continuously being adapted to customer preferences. For example, stair treads have been made wider, and the rise is now less steep. Electrical outlets have been moved somewhat higher on the walls.

Readily identified by its clock tower, the C$4 million Village Centre, which opened in 1998, is the focal point of the community. Like the homes, it reflects the brick-and-stone colonial architecture of the city of Guelph. In designing the center, the developer solicited suggestions from community residents to ensure that it met their needs. The center has a total of 43,000 square feet, of which 28,000 are on the main floor and have been finished for various uses. The remaining 15,000 square feet are located on the lower level and can be finished at a later date, as additional uses are identified. The center includes a large, furnished, two-story entry foyer; a multipurpose room with gymnasium flooring that can accommodate 450 people for a sit-down dinner (or be used as a 650-seat auditorium); a 76-foot-long indoor lap pool with a deck and whirlpool spa; an exercise room that overlooks a garden; a billiards room; a "boardroom" for meetings; an arts and crafts room; a large, comfortable television lounge that shares a two-sided fireplace with a book-lined library; a catering kitchen; and community management offices.

The Village Centre features 12-foot ceilings, decorative moldings, deep windows in all rooms, interior French doors, bay windows, and bright, light colors. The carpeting looks all-of-a-piece but is in fact composed of squares that can easily be replaced if a spot is damaged or discolored. Outdoor amenities include ponds and landscaped waterfalls, which are part of the stormwater management system; two tennis courts; barbecue areas; and extensive walkways.

The university set forth guidelines for landscaping as well as for structures to be developed on the property. In 1986, it established a nursery so that 1,000 mature trees would be available for transplanting onto the property during its construction. As one might expect, the development is beautifully landscaped.

Homes are purchased through a 20-year renewable land-lease agreement, which is binding on the purchasers' heirs. From the purchasers' viewpoint, the lease arrangement ensures that the

Unique detailing on the ceiling adds interest to this comfortable living room.

current design and maintenance standards will be maintained over time. Because home purchase prices do not include land, they are slightly lower than the prices of homes of comparable quality in a fee-simple community. As of December 1999, prices for detached brick bungalows ranged from C$182,800 to C$242,400, and bungalow townhomes cost C$184,500; prices include a C$8,500 contribution to the recreation center and the goods and services tax. (C$ denotes Canadian dollars.) The developer also offers purchasers a number of incentives—the inclusion of a dishwasher, a lower cost for an added sunroom in a single-family home, and reductions in land-lease costs for the first year.

In Canada, land can be leased for a maximum of 21 years less one day, and communities that lease land generally do so for 20-year periods.[1] If they wish, homebuyers at the Village by the Arboretum can renew their 20-year leases each year, giving them a "usage horizon" of 20 years, though no one has yet done so. Residents seem to feel comfortable with the lease arrangement. According to Judy Phillips, administrator of the Village by the Arboretum, "the university's involvement gives buyers confidence in the long-term viability of the project, and they are also reassured by the developer's respected reputation in the area."

Among the many amenities in the Village Centre, the indoor swimming pool is one of the most popular.

The rate that residents pay for the leased land is controlled by the Ontario Rent Review Act. Land-lease rates for single-family homes average between C$265 and C$400 per month, beginning in year two; for townhouses, between C$175 and C$220 per month. (As a buyer incentive, the land rent is reduced by half for the first year.) Increases in land-lease rates are tied to increases in the cost of living, but the university guarantees in writing that land-lease rates will not increase by more than 3 percent per year. Because homes are not sited on individual lots, land-lease rates are determined by the home's frontage, which varies from 35 feet for townhomes to 40, 50, or 60 feet for detached homes.

In addition to the one-time fee to join the Village Centre (included in the sales price and transferable upon resale), residents also contribute approximately C$30 per month to the capital reserve fund, pay monthly fees for the maintenance of the grounds and the operation of the clubhouse, and pay taxes on their homes. The monthly fees, which are also based on the home's frontage, range from C$576 to C$820 per home.

Homes may be resold through Reid's Heritage Homes or through an outside agent, but all new buyers must be approved by the university. At the time a home is resold, the new buyer must sign a new 20-year lease.

The project was initially marketed from a trailer in the University of Guelph's parking lot. Marketing vehicles include print ads in the *Toronto Star* and in magazines targeted to seniors, contact with the university's prospect list, and referrals from residents. Follow-up is through postcards, project videos, and phone calls. The developer has held many functions and events for homeowners—who are the primary marketers of the project—and for sales prospects. To encourage and reward referrals, Reid pays residents $500 for each prospect they refer who buys a home. Reid has held luncheons at his main office for prospective buyers, to help them feel comfortable with and confident about the company as the project developer. Most already felt reassured by the fact that the university owns the land.

Reid's Heritage Homes uses its own salespeople rather than real estate agents to sell the homes. Reid feels that real estate agents are often too aggressive to work well with older prospects and do not understand the land-lease concept. He pointed out that the sales process for an active adult community is much more difficult and time-consuming than for a more typical residential development, and "it takes a huge market area to do one of these."

Reid's Heritage Homes builds 100 homes per year at the Village by the Arboretum. On average, the company closes ten homes each month, and most homes are constructed after they are sold; few are built speculatively. Resales have been snapped up quickly.

The project's market area is greater Toronto and southern Ontario. In the first phase of development, most purchasers were aged 70 and older. In subsequent phases, the average age of buyers has decreased. In Phase III, a large proportion of the buyers were in their 50s. Eighty to 90 percent of homebuyers pay cash.

Though the development is not age-restricted (age-restricting is not legal in Canada), by agreement between the university and the city of Guelph, no more than two people can reside in a home at the Village by the Arboretum unless the developer specifically approves a third person in the home. This arrangement is intended to prevent children from residing in the village full-time and university students from living in the homes with their grandparents. There is no limit to the number or age of visitors allowed.

The Ontario New Home Warranties Plan Act protects the buyers of new homes in Ontario. According to the act, a builder must warrant that a new house will be free of defects in workmanship and materials for one year. The builder must guarantee for two years the electrical, plumbing, and heating systems; cladding, caulking, windows, and doors; and the resistance of the building envelope and basement to water penetration. The act protects buyers from major structural defects for seven years. Reid's Heritage Homes has maintained the highest ratings possible under the act.

Reid's Heritage Homes is responsible for managing and maintaining the community and maintains a full-time staff to do so. It does not employ subcontractors. The fact that the developer is in charge of community management lessens the likelihood of conflict between neighbors and makes it easier for the manager to resolve problems and disagreements.

Community management includes the maintenance of common facilities and grounds: for example, sprinkling and cutting grass, shoveling snow (to residents' front doors), and maintaining both individual lawns and community landscaping. In addition, a customer service office makes home repairs and takes care of homes while residents are away; these services are pro-

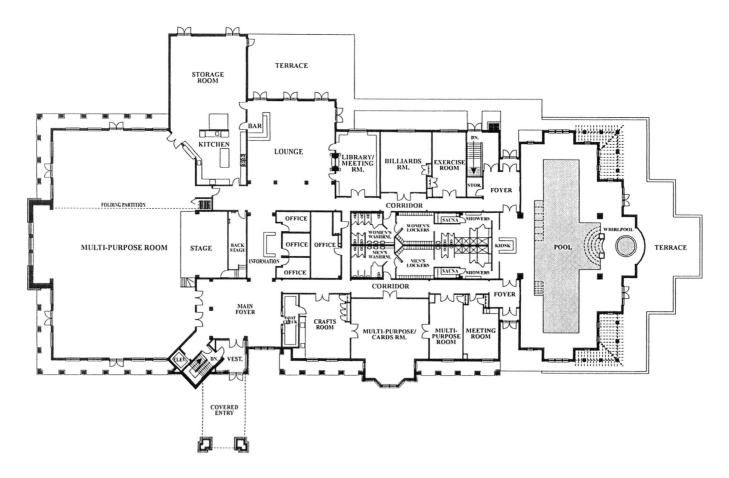

Village Centre floor plan, main floor.

vided on a fee basis at the resident's request. For "snowbirds," the customer service office will handle incoming mail, water plants, and check inside and outside the home.

The community is gated but not fenced. To minimize costs, the gate is not staffed. Instead, access is permitted by an electronic card, which also admits residents to the clubhouse and to the men's or women's locker rooms within the Village Centre.

A residents' association, formed in 1994, develops programs and activities and publishes a monthly newsletter. Because the residents' association does not own any property, it has no legal authority, and its function is social and advisory. The more than 40 activity groups that have been formed through the association represent a wide range of interests and pursuits. All residents automatically belong to the residents' association and pay dues of C$15 per household per year.

Though there is no formal relationship between community residents and the university, the university operates a "third age learning program" which offers, for a fee, special courses geared to older adults. In addition, residents of Canada who are aged 65 and over can participate in the university's regular schedule of classes at no charge.

There are risks and rewards to both the university and the developer in undertaking a development of this type. Though its ownership of the land puts its reputation on the line, the university is somewhat protected by the fact that it retains control of all major decisions by reserving the right to final approvals. At the same time, the project benefits the university in a number of

ACTIVE ADULT RETIREMENT COMMUNITIES

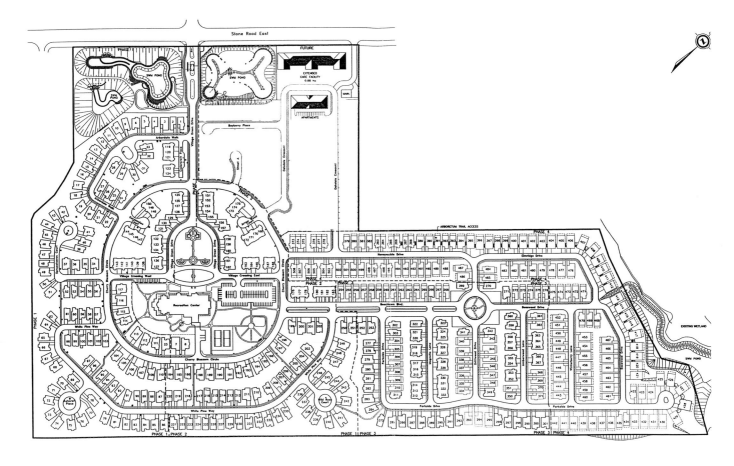

Site plan.

ways. As the landowner, the university receives income from land-lease payments—both from the developer, through the head-lease arrangement, and from the land-lease payments made by homebuyers. The university also gets a small percentage of the gross sales price of each home. And, as intended, the development serves as a buffer strip at the institution's perimeter.

The developer assumes the financial risk and the largest share of market risk, but profits from the development in several ways and can control the long-term viability of the project through good management. The developer garners income from the sale of homes and from property management fees, and is also entitled to a percentage of the homebuyers' land-lease payments.

According to Reid, a project such as the Village by the Arboretum requires a developer's full commitment. He explained that "when you do a project like this, you have to put your whole heart, soul, and life into it." He attributes the project's success to two factors: first, ensuring that there was a market for the intended development and that the community was designed to satisfy the needs and preferences of that market; and second, paying thorough attention to detail throughout the process.

---

1. "Head leases," or leases to a development entity, can be for a maximum of 50 years. The 21-years-less-a-day restriction applies to "subleases," or leases between the developer and the homebuyer.

PROJECT DATA

Land Use

Site area	112 acres
Clubhouse and other common buildings	43,000 square feet
Streets and parking	3 acres
Number of single-family detached units	391 (proposed)
Number of attached/multifamily units	179
Total number of units	570
Gross density	5.2 units/acre

Single-Family Unit and Townhome Information

Lot size (frontage)	Unit size (square feet)	No. of units (planned/built)	Price range	Lease rate (per month)
Single-family units				
40'	1,161–1,496	185/104	C$182,800–C$205,400	C$265
50'	1,553–1,924	186/127	C$218,800–C$242,400	C$330
60'	1,553–1,924	7/6	C$218,800–C$242,400	C$400
Townhome units				
35'	900–1,389	179/73	C$162,800–C$184,500	C$175 (inside unit); C$220 (end unit)

Development Schedule

Site leased	March 1993
Planning started	September 1987
Site work started	March 1994
Project completion	December 2002 (estimated)

	Phase I	Phase II	Phase III
Number of units	141	99	121
Construction started	May 1994	October 1995	June 1998
Sales started	March 1994	June 1994	Ongoing
First closing	October 1994		

Development Team

Developer
Reid's Heritage Homes, Ltd.
Rural Route #22
Cambridge, Ontario
N3C 2V4
(519) 658-6656

Land Planner
Patrick Sweet & Associates
Mississauga, Ontario
(905) 274-1047

Architect
Viljoen Architects, Inc.
Downsview, Ontario
(416) 630-2255

Project Address

221 Stone Road East
Guelph, Ontario N1G 4X3

Contact Information

Judy Phillips, administrator, Village by the Arboretum
(519) 767-5000

Date of site visit: December 10, 1999

All project data are current as of January 6, 2000.

Report author: Diane R. Suchman

Leisure World of Virginia

Lansdowne, Virginia

According to conventional wisdom, the active adult retirement market prefers single-family homes. But since 1980, The IDI Group Companies, headed by Guiseppi Cecchi, has successfully defied that view; it continues to do so in its most recent development for active adults, Leisure World of Virginia, an age-restricted multifamily condominium development in Loudoun County, in suburban Washington, D.C. At buildout, which is expected to occur in 2010, the development will be the largest AARC in Virginia, containing 2,122 residential units, two clubhouses with an array of amenities, and extensive landscaped open space laced with nature trails. Plans call for seven 11-story high-rise and five four-story low-rise residential buildings. The project will be built in 12 phases. As of this writing, the developers are midway through the construction of Phase II.

IDI has been developing planned condominium communities for over 20 years, and before undertaking the Loudoun County project had built more than 9,000 units in more than 18 communities in

Riverbend, the first condominium building constructed at Leisure World of Virginia, offers both underground and surface parking. The community's unobtrusive security fence and entry gate are visible in the foreground.

One of the most popular features of Leisure World's Clubhouse West is the 15-meter heated indoor pool. The pool's windowed walls open in the spring and summer onto two outdoor terraces where residents can relax in the sun.

the Washington, D.C., market; it has an additional 3,000 under construction. The firm has also developed office buildings, hotels, residential subdivisions, and urban mixed-use products.

IDI's first AARC was the final portion of the Leisure World of Maryland development, which was begun in 1980. Also a multifamily condominium project, Leisure World of Maryland today consists of more than 2,100 high-rise and low-rise units located within an otherwise low-density age-restricted, master-planned community. The firm plans approximately 800 more units there.

The first of the Leisure World recreation-oriented adult communities was built in California some 30 years ago by the Cortese family, and was followed by successful communities in Arizona, Florida, New Jersey, and, again, in California. The Cortese's company, RCC, Inc., is a partner in both Leisure World of Maryland and Leisure World of Virginia. Leisure World of Virginia is the eighth Leisure World community in the United States.

IDI's Virginia project is located on 91 acres within Lansdowne, a 2,300-acre master-planned community. As a planned community within a planned community, Leisure World can offer residents some assurance about future development within and around its borders.

Lansdowne, which is owned by Xerox Corporation, was originally planned for office park and office-related development. In the early 1990s, when the local market for office development collapsed, Xerox sought rezoning to increase the amount of residential development that could be built. At around the same time, IDI was looking for a site in Virginia for its second AARC in the Washington, D.C., area.

In its traditional condominium product, IDI typically sells about half the units to empty-nesters. When it created its first senior housing development within Leisure World of Maryland, the company surveyed current Leisure World residents to determine what modifications would be needed to tailor the product to an age-restricted market. (Essentially, the company learned that the market buys lifestyle rather than product and is keenly interested in security and freedom from maintenance.)

The developer felt that Lansdowne, located 45 minutes from Washington, D.C., in a developing low-density residential corridor, would be an excellent location for its Virginia retirement project. The location is convenient to Dulles International Airport, regional and local shopping centers, golf courses, satellite college campuses, and the historic town of Leesburg, Virginia. The community offered adequate acreage for the intended development, the infrastructure was in place, and the surroundings would enable IDI to created the desired ambience.

In addition to office parks, Lansdowne will include residential neighborhoods featuring a variety of housing types and extensive nature trails for walking and biking. Within the community is the Lansdowne Resort, which offers an 18-hole golf course designed by Robert Trent Jones Sr., a conference center, restaurants, and a variety of recreational amenities, which Leisure World residents can use on a fee basis. Lansdowne has enough land to develop two more golf courses. Loudoun County Hospital, which provides outreach services in addition to traditional hospital care, is located on a nearby site within the Lansdowne community. Because of the hospital's proximity, no health care facilities are planned on site at Leisure World. IDI also owns a parcel of adjoining land outside the Leisure World gates, for which development plans have not been made final.

Located on a wooded ridge overlooking the Potomac River, the project's 12 residential buildings will be positioned to encircle the recreational amenities and landscaped open space. The project's density makes possible extensive open space for nature trails and landscaped areas; most of the site will be preserved as open space.

The development is being built in phases, which mitigates the developer's market risk and makes it possible to adjust the product in response to market demand. The first phase of construction consisted of the project's entrance and gatehouse, and the first residential building, Riverbend, which was occupied in 1998. Phase II consists of the second residential building, Blue Ridge, which IDI is now constructing and marketing. Phase III will be a low-rise building containing 64 residential units.

The Riverbend building was built in two stages. The entire shell of the 11-story building was constructed in the first stage, but only half of the units were built out. When the first stage of construction was 50 percent sold, the remainder of the building was completed. Blue Ridge, located adjacent to Riverbend, is also being constructed in two stages. IDI expected to complete the first stage of construction on the Blue Ridge building in March of 2000. (The building was more than 50 percent sold as of December 31, 1999.)

A $4.5 million clubhouse, known as Clubhouse West, is also being built in phases. Because IDI recognized the importance of providing most of the project's amenities early in the development process, the first part of the clubhouse was completed and opened for use in October 1999.

All the condominium buildings are constructed of reinforced concrete frame with masonry exterior walls, sound-insulated interior walls, and double-pane glass windows. Each building includes a party room, a large lobby with conversational seating, and high-speed elevators.

Twelve different floor plans are currently offered, ranging in size from 874 to 1,534 square feet, with prices that range from $130,000 to more than $290,000. Because the buildings are located just across the golf course from the Potomac River, upper-floor units have beautiful views of the river to the east and of the Sugarloaf Mountains to the west. Units feature elegant foyers, separate dining rooms, oversized windows, eat-in kitchens with pantries, walk-in closets, baths with tubs and separate shower stalls, and lots of storage space. Buyers can select from a variety of finishings, options, and upgrades in the sales office's design center, including modifications to accommodate the needs of handicapped residents. One of the most popular options is an enclosed balcony, which functions as a year-round sunroom.

Secured by wrought-iron perimeter fencing, a 24-hour guarded entry gate, controlled-access buildings, and video surveillance of individual entrances, the development is an exclusive community with a variety of on-site facilities for residents' use. The first phase of Clubhouse West features a fully equipped health club, rooftop tennis courts, a magnificent indoor pool with a pool deck that extends outdoors, a whirlpool spa, saunas, and men's and women's locker rooms. The clubhouse also includes a lobby, meeting rooms, a library/computer room, an art studio, craft and hobby rooms, a woodworking shop filled with power tools and equipment, a hair salon, a newsstand, a nurse's office, a bank, and a convenience store with a deli that provides carryout service. The second phase of Clubhouse West will add a large auditorium with a stage, a restaurant, a billiards room, a chapel, an area for washing cars, and offices. Individual garden plots are available.

Residents can participate in numerous activities offered within the community, including social events, clubs, classes, trips, and special programs. A shuttle bus transports residents to shopping and other destinations. A range of personal services, including home repairs and help with moving in, selling a home, and receiving service calls are available on a fee basis. In terms of services, as Norman Dreyfuss, executive vice president of IDI, explained, "Everything is geared to reduce the need for purchasers to have to do anything that is inconvenient."

A second clubhouse (Clubhouse East) will be built in a future phase. So that the developer can respond to market preferences at the time that it is built, the design of the clubhouse will remain flexible.

Just outside the development, Lansdowne Resort offers residents, in addition to golf and restaurants, tennis facilities, indoor and outdoor pools, a fitness center, a seasonal day camp for grandchildren, and hotel accommodations for visitors. The nearby riverfront provides opportunities for boating and fishing.

To facilitate the development of Leisure World of Virginia, Xerox Realty Corporation obtained a special zoning designation—PDAAR, for "planned development, active adult/age-restricted"—from Loudoun County. Private investors provided funding for the project's upfront expenses, such as land acquisition, initiation of the clubhouse, and startup marketing. Proceeds from presales and a construction loan from a local lender, Mercantile Mortgage, financed the first phase of construction. Mercantile is also funding construction of the second phase.

Each building is managed by its own condominium association, and residents are also members of the Leisure World of Virginia Community Association. The building associations cover everything from the bricks inward, and the community association manages common areas and security. Residents elect members of the condominium boards, but IDI controls each building's interim board between the time of first settlement until the building is 75 percent sold; IDI

Clubhouse West is a two-level health, fitness, and recreational facility for the enjoyment of Leisure World's residents and their guests. A second phase of construction, which will be undertaken as the community's population grows, will expand the clubhouse's offerings.

Among the features in this 1,251-square-foot, two-bedroom, two-bathroom model condominium are a luxurious open living area, a fireplace, and ample storage space.

then relinquishes all but one seat on the board. Owners are assessed a monthly fee, which includes both associations and a small amount for the Lansdowne Conservancy, which governs the rest of the Lansdowne community. The monthly assessment varies with the size of the unit, but averages $350 per month. The fee covers professional management services, maintenance of common areas, insurance, common utilities, use of all clubhouse and recreational facilities, security, and bus transportation. There is a small additional charge for garage parking.

From its Maryland experience, IDI learned that between 80 and 85 percent of the buyers came from within a 10-mile radius of the site. They were generally looking for a more secure, maintenance-free lifestyle, but in the same geographic area as their current home. Suburban Virginia did not have an AARC like Leisure World, but the senior population's demographic and economic characteristics resembled those of the Maryland market. Specifically, in Maryland, the potential market of 30,000 income- and age-qualified homeowners yielded 150 new sales each year. In Virginia, the potential market totaled 35,000, so the expected capture rate would likely be similar.

The biggest question was whether the condominium theme that had worked so well in Maryland would carry over to a young, growing area of Virginia. Sales in Maryland come largely from referrals, where IDI initiated its development within an established, large-scale retirement community. In Virginia, IDI is breaking new ground.

IDI's marketing strategy appeals to retirees' desire for a maintenance-free lifestyle and a fresh start in life. The company relies on broadcast media, print ads, and referrals. It hired an activities director to initiate social activities for residents and to maintain close relationships with buyers. As part of its marketing effort, IDI also hosts an ongoing luncheon seminar program for prospective buyers that features speakers on topics such as "How to Retire Actively" and "The Art of Moving"; the seminars attract 30 to 40 people each. To date, 80 percent of the sales prospects have come from within a 15- to 20-mile radius of the development.

The project has little competition. It is the only high-rise residential building in Loudoun County, and people who want to be in an AARC in the Washington, D.C., area do not have many choices. According to Dreyfuss, the development's primary competition comes from high-rise condominiums elsewhere in the area, whether age-restricted or not. A few care-oriented housing developments for seniors elsewhere in the metropolitan area nip the market at the older end, and a planned retirement community in an outlying town nips the younger end of the market, but essentially the project faces little real competition because there are no similar products offered. Potential purchasers often think that they would prefer a single-family home, but once they have bought, they find that multifamily is actually preferable because it requires less maintenance.

The sales process is slow, with buyers visiting the project an average of two to three times over a six-month period before making a purchase. Some prospects have been visiting for three years. According to Patrick Rhodes, project manager, "They want to see developer commitment and performance. It takes a lot of planning and front money to get off the ground and gain the confidence of the market."

In addition, the sales pace is often uneven and unpredictable. Many sales involve adult children, who have their own ideas regarding whether the family home should be sold. Dreyfuss observed that prospects worry about whether they will have sufficient funds as they get older, do not want to carry debt, are "not looking for trouble," and have no sense of urgency in making a buying decision. As a result, "you have to entice them with the kind of excitement that makes them want to buy."

According to Dreyfuss, the typical buyer earns between $45,000 and $60,000 per year, has assets of $400,000, and owns a home. Rhodes noted that 70 percent of the purchasers pay cash, and that those who do borrow, borrow only a small amount. For most people, it's a lateral move.

Under federal law, 80 percent of households in the project must have one resident who is over 55 years old. In this development, residents range in age from their 40s to their 80s; the average age is around 65. The core market is between 60 and 69 (buyers at Leisure World of Virginia tend to be somewhat younger than buyers at Leisure World of Maryland). To increase the pool of potential purchasers, the company would like to position its products to attract more buyers between the ages of 55 and 60.

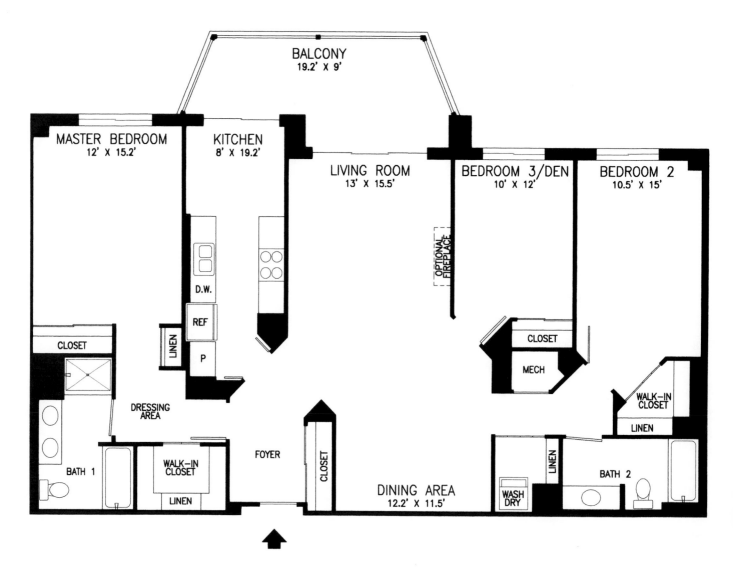

BALCONY
19.2' X 9'

MASTER BEDROOM
12' X 15.2'

KITCHEN
8' X 19.2'

LIVING ROOM
13' X 15.5'

BEDROOM 3/DEN
10' X 12'

BEDROOM 2
10.5' X 15'

OPTIONAL FIREPLACE

D.W.

REF

P

LINEN

CLOSET

CLOSET

MECH

WALK-IN CLOSET

LINEN

DRESSING AREA

FOYER

CLOSET

BATH 1

WALK-IN CLOSET

WASH DRY

LINEN

BATH 2

LINEN

DINING AREA
12.2' X 11.5'

This 1,475-square-foot, three bedroom, two-bath condominium was one of the many models offered in the Riverbend building.

IDI does focus groups of owners and prospects to learn about its market. Rhodes notes that as a result of this research, IDI is offering larger units, more luxurious options, and more design choices in Phase II of the project. For example, the design center was created to enable buyers to make choices among the standard and optional finishings available with which to customize their homes, ceiling heights have increased from eight feet to nine, and the company now offers fireplaces. In addition, Rhodes expects that the target market will become younger because people are retiring earlier.

Because older buyers want the lifestyle-creating amenities in place when they buy, AARCs require a tremendous upfront investment, which exposes the developer to significant risks. To mitigate those costs and risks in Leisure World of Virginia, the clubhouses are phased with the residential construction—but carefully—so that, according to Dreyfuss, "the first phase contains almost every essential amenity."

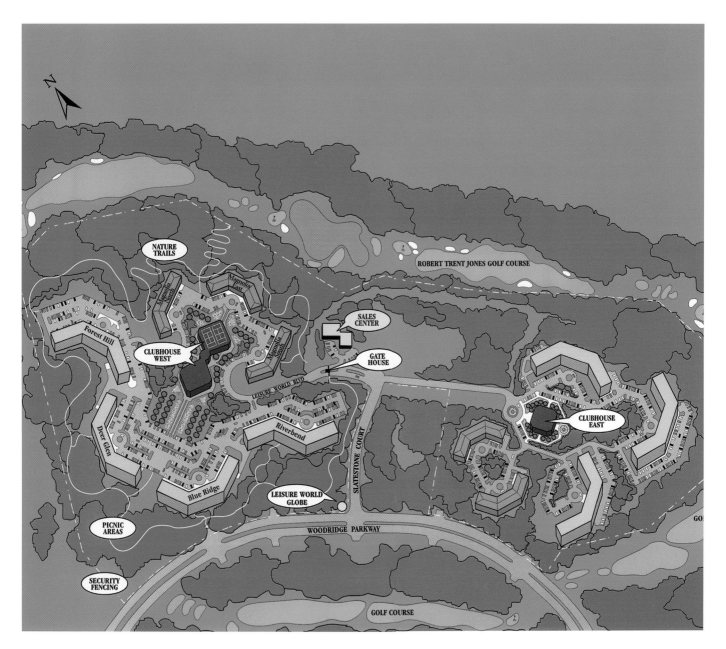

Site plan.

PROJECT DATA

Land Use

Site area	91 acres
Clubhouse and other common buildings	60,000+ square feet*
Other open space and outdoor amenities	70 acres
Streets and parking	15 acres
Total number of units planned	2,122

(continued on page 200)

High-rise units	1,683
Low-rise units	439
Gross density	30 units/acre
Number of parking spaces	
Off-street	2,653
Underground	1,058
Surface	1,595

---

* Construction of approximately half this square footage has been completed. The remainder will be built during later phases of the project.

Residential Unit Information

Unit type	Unit size (square feet)	No. of units	Price range	Condo fee (per unit per month)
Riverbend I	874–1,509	121	$125,000–$277,000	$262–$371
Riverbend II	1,246–1,475	110	$325,000–$365,000	$262–$371
Blue Ridge I	874–1,534	132	$139,500–$292,800	$287–$391
Blue Ridge II	To be determined	110	To be determined	

Development Cost Information

Site acquisition cost	$9.8 million
Hard costs	$56.50/square feet
Soft costs	$111.78/square feet
Total development costs	$168.28/square feet

Development Schedule

Planning started	October 1994
Site purchased	March 1995
Site work started	July 1996
Project completion	2010 (estimated)

Phase I: Riverbend Building (1)

Number of units	121
Planning started	October 1994
Construction started	October 1996
Construction completed	March 1998
Sales started	July 1996
First closing	March 1998
Sales completed	August 1999
Sales completed	December 1999

Phase II: Riverbend Building (2)

Number of units	110
Planning started	October 1994
Construction started	September 1997
Construction completed	June 1998
Sales started	October 1996
Sales completed	December 1999

Phase III: Blue Ridge Building (1)

Number of units	132
Planning started	October 1996
Construction started	October 1998
Construction completed	March 2000 (estimated)
Sales started	September 1998

Phase IV: Blue Ridge Building (2)

Number of units	110
Planning started	October 1996

Development Team

Developers

IDI Group Companies
1700 North Moore Street
Suite 2020
Rosslyn, Virginia 22209
(703) 558-7300

RCC, Inc.
218 Marigold Avenue
Corona del Mar, California
92625
(714) 723-4844

Land Planner

Smith-Williams
Harmony, California
(805) 927-1673

Architect

Holle & Lin
Washington, D.C.
(202) 266-1190

Project Address

Leisure World
Lansdowne, Virginia 20176

Contact Information

Patrick Rhodes Jr., project manager

(703) 724-0100

Date of site visit: October 26, 1999

All project data are current as of October 26, 1999.

Report author: Diane R. Suchman

St. James Plantation

Southport, North Carolina

Meeting the housing and recreational needs of retirees and second-home buyers was the objective of St. James Plantation, a 3,500-acre master-planned community located just south of Wilmington, North Carolina, on the Atlantic Intracoastal Waterway and only a ten-minute drive from the Atlantic Ocean. An additional 2,500 acres can be developed over the next eight to ten years. Recreational amenities include three 18-hole golf courses and a private beach with clubhouse, showers, changing facilities, and a pool. An additional nine holes are being built at an existing course, and another 18-hole course is planned.

Homesite sales are the main focus at St. James. Most lots are sold to families and individuals who will be contracting with a builder of their choice; however, some sites have been sold to builders for speculative development. While the primary business is land sales, St. James Plantation also offers a limited number of townhomes, condominiums, and patio homes in a home/lot package.

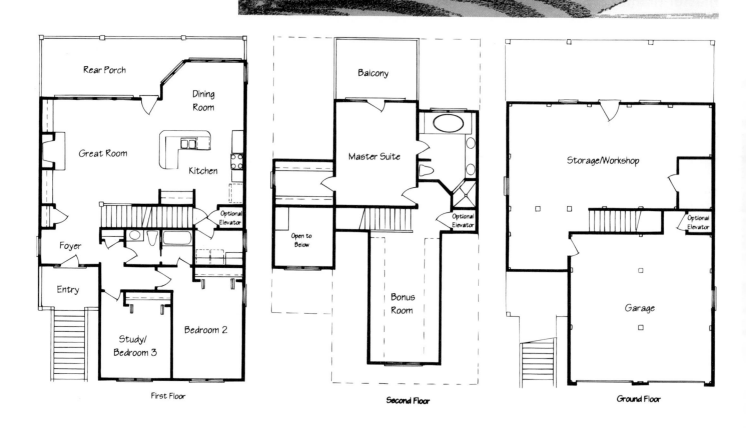

A low-country-style house with porches and wood siding (floor plan below) is typical of the homes at St. James Plantation.

St. James Plantation

First Floor

Rear Porch

Dining Room

Great Room

Kitchen

Optional Elevator

Foyer

Entry

Study/ Bedroom 3

Bedroom 2

Second Floor

Balcony

Master Suite

Optional Elevator

Open to Below

Bonus Room

Ground Floor

Storage/Workshop

Optional Elevator

Garage

To date, most of the homes are primary residences; however, a small but growing number of buyers are purchasing property for second homes. In particular, families who live in the Raleigh-Durham–Research Triangle Park area (which is less than a three-hour drive from St. James) are flocking to the community as a weekend getaway.

John Atkinson, Homer Wright, and Claude Smith, the developers, had been developing residential properties in North Carolina, primarily in the Piedmont area, for nearly 30 years before coming to the North Carolina coast in the early 1980s. Vast tracts of relatively low-cost land graced by beautiful flora and fauna attracted them to the coast. The tracts available along Highway 211 North were large enough to develop a master-planned community for the growing number of retirees, particularly from the Northeast, who would be the project's primary market. The land was largely rural, and despite the many competing developments whose signs dot the landscape along the highway, it remains largely rural in all directions.

In 1984–1985, the developers purchased the heavily wooded, 6,000-acre site. The property is laced with saltwater marshes and wetlands; in fact, the cattail, a plant indigenous to wetlands and marshes, is the community's logo. The Atlantic Intracoastal Waterway lies to the south, providing a water view for many homesites in St. James Plantation. Because of its marshes, wetlands, and proximity to the intracoastal waterway, the development was subject to a host of environmental regulations emanating from the Clean Water Act, the Endangered Species Act, and the Coastal Area Management Act (CAMA).

The developers learned that it is necessary to be patient when developing sites that include wetlands and other protected habitats. For example, the regulatory process was particularly cumbersome in the development of the marina, with the North Carolina Department of Environmental Management, as required by CAMA, acting as a clearinghouse for the comments and approvals of more than 21 agencies. Final approval, which came in 1997, was the result of nearly three years of negotiation. However, few objections were raised because an environmental consultant had been involved in every step in the development process and had already addressed all environmentally sensitive issues.

Some areas of the site are very low-lying and have a high water table, which made it easy to create water features, such as lakes and ponds, and was particularly advantageous in the development of the golf courses. But because the site is so low and can drain into the intracoastal waterway, stormwater runoff is an important issue. Thus, the development of St. James was regulated by the Army Corps of Engineers as well as the North Carolina Department of Environmental Management. According to the developer, the major challenge that the development team faced was ensuring that the site was drained properly. The high water table also facilitated the development of the project's marina, which is now in operation. The marina connects to the intracoastal waterway via a small channel, and will eventually include some retail shops.

The site is just four miles west of Southport, a town of 4,000 permanent residents located where the Cape Fear River, the Atlantic Ocean, and the intracoastal waterway come together, and boating and fishing abound. Southport played a pivotal role in the Civil War, and, in addition to many examples of gingerbread architecture, its main street features many antique stores and year-round Christmas shops.

Wilmington lies to the north, within a 30-minute drive. With a population of nearly 100,000, Wilmington has cafés, galleries, music bars, and craft shops along the waterfront; a blues society and a ballet company for teenage dancers are new to the area. The city also boasts one of the largest movie studios east of Hollywood. About 40 minutes to the south of St. James is Myrtle Beach, South Carolina, which offers nightlife, abundant golf, and other amenities typical of a large vacation destination.

The guiding principle in designing St. James Plantation was to capitalize on the natural beauty of the site and the surrounding area, and to balance the conservation of the natural environment with the changes that are inevitable in a rapidly growing community. "Fortunately," says Jim Wright, who was in charge of protecting and preserving the ecology of the site, "these two goals have turned out to be largely complementary rather than conflicting, because we have found that providing our residents with the unspoiled natural environment they want almost invariably points us in the right direction development-wise."[1]

Upon entering the community, visitors are greeted by signs on St. James Drive, the loop road through St. James Plantation, identifying various types of flora: Indian hawthorn, yaupon (the name of a type of tree and its berry), yucca, Venus's flytrap, sweet gum, American holly, and African love grass. Egrets, herons, and deer roam freely. There are nature and fitness trails throughout the community. The three golf courses, which form the nucleus of the amenity package for residents, were designed to take advantage of the natural features of the site. The Gauntlet Club, designed by P. B. Dye; The Members Club, designed by Hale Irwin; and The Players Club, designed by local landscape architect Tim Cate, all maintain the character of the land; native trees and vegetation were used to the extent possible, and marshes, rather than being filled in, were preserved and spanned by low bridges that golfers can cross.

The Gauntlet Club was built right away because the developer believed that property sales would suffer unless prospective purchasers could see the actual facility rather than a rendering. The club includes a 7,050-yard, 18-hole golf course; a 12,000-square-foot clubhouse with restaurant, bar, golf shop, and lounge; tennis courts; and a swimming pool. Built in 1990, the club was refurbished in 1999. Most of the homesites surrounding the Gauntlet are developed.

The Members Club, which opened in 1996, includes a 6,887-yard, 18-hole golf course (with nine new holes opening in the fall of 2000) and a 16,000-square-foot clubhouse with a restaurant, bar/lounge, golf shop, locker rooms, and a fitness center. An indoor swim club and tennis complex were added in 1999. Many homesites and condominiums are still being developed in the area of The Members Club.

The Players Club, which opened in November 1997, includes a 7,042-yard, 18-hole golf course. The temporary clubhouse and snack bar will be replaced with permanent facilities in the future. Homesites are currently being developed in the area of The Players Club, and plans are being developed for a fourth 18-hole course.

Another amenity, the forested Waterway Park, takes advantage of the native vegetation and scenic beauty of the intracoastal waterway. The land on which the park is located is owned by the Army Corps of Engineers, a fact that is explicitly stated in disclosures required by the Department of Housing and Urban Development under the Interstate Land Sales Act. However, the corps granted the developer approval to use the land for a park, which includes nature and fitness trails, charcoal grills, picnic tables, and play equipment.

There are currently 20 neighborhoods within the community; lot sizes vary, ranging from one-quarter acre to one acre. Lot price depends on the location, with single-family interior lots being the least expensive and homesites with views of the intracoastal waterway commanding the highest prices. The minimum square footage of the homes to be constructed depends on the neighborhood and the lot size. Except for the minimum house size, which is neighborhood-specific, most of the other covenants apply to all neighborhoods.

In addition to the minimum home size, strictly enforced covenants, set by the Architectural Control Committee, dictate acceptable exterior construction materials and color. For example, vinyl siding is not allowed because the developers felt that the variations in vinyl quality made quality control too difficult. Wood siding and brick are the most popular exterior construction materials. While the committee encourages an architectural style that replicates some features of antebellum plantation houses, with their generous screened porches and wood facades, the property owner has some latitude with respect to style.

Although the sales staff does not recommend particular builders, the sales office maintains a list of builders and architects who are active in the community. Periodically, the St. James Plantation Property Owners' Association will offer a homebuilding seminar free of charge to property owners. Customer service extends to the homebuilding process: at an on-site design center, homebuyers can explore options for both exteriors and interiors.

As noted earlier, although St. James is designed primarily for the sale of homesites, home/lot packages are available. The developer has built 65 patio homes in the Georgetown neighborhood and offers them as home/lot packages to buyers who do not wish to build their own home. Another 30 patio homes are planned. The lot size of the patio homes is one-eighth of an acre, with units ranging in size from 1,300 to 1,600 square feet.

To appeal to the property owner who is not interested in maintaining a yard, the developers have built 150 condominium units of 1,100 square feet, with nearly 80 more planned. A limited number of townhomes have also been sold; these multifamily units are clustered in the central part of the site, about midway between the Members and the Gauntlet clubhouses.

Another natural feature of the site on which the developer capitalized is its proximity to Oak Island, which has south-facing beaches: Long Beach, Yaupon Beach, and Caswell Beach. Less than a 10-minute drive from St. James Plantation, Oak Island is separated from the site by the intracoastal waterway and is bordered to the south by the Atlantic Ocean. The developer

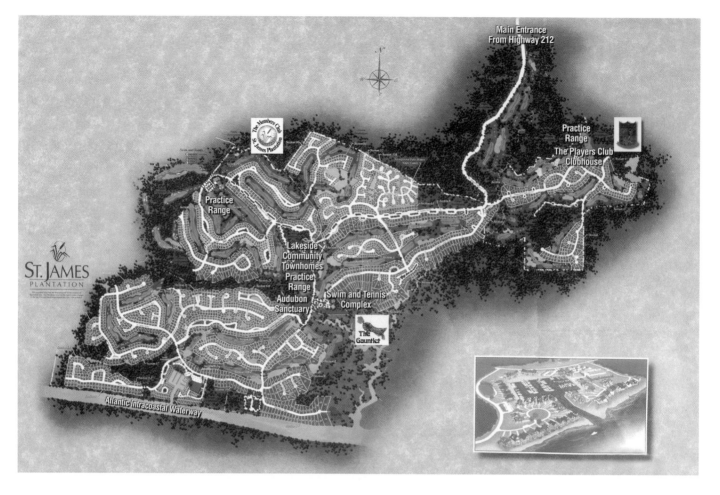

Site plan.   purchased a site on Oak Island and created a private beach club, St. James by the Sea, to appeal to all residents. Facilities include a clubhouse with showers, changing facilities, a pool, a gazebo, and a walkway to the beach.

St. James Plantation has a complicated ownership structure. The original tract of land is owned solely by Homer E. Wright Jr., but there are four different development companies: First St. James, Inc., owned by Wright; St. James Plantation, LLC, owned by John Atkinson and Wright's children; St. James Development Company, LLC, owned by Atkinson, Wright, and TriCity, Inc.; and Brunswick Harbor, Inc. Nevertheless, all of the developers are guided by the same philosophy, and covenants are the same for all properties.

A fourth legal entity, St. James Properties, LLC, manages the entire community and handles sales and marketing. The development companies pay prorated fees to St. James Properties for conducting all marketing and sales activities.

The maintenance and operation of the community is funded by annual fees paid by property owners to the St. James Property Owners' Association, Inc. Annual association fees are $512 for an undeveloped residential lot and $692 for a residence; they cover a 24-hour staffed entrance; sewer fees; and maintenance of common areas, open spaces, roadways, Waterway Park, and the beach club.

Though it is not age-restricted, the primary market for St. James Plantation is retirees. The developer's research suggested that individuals from the Northeast tend to seek the warm climate and year-round golf available in southern locations. The temperate climate of coastal Carolina makes it formidable competition for destinations farther south, like Florida. Moreover, the seasons change, which is not the case in many Florida locations.

In its initial project marketing, St. James Properties, LLC, cast a wide net, advertising in major newspapers such as the *Wall Street Journal*. A more targeted campaign included direct mailings to (1) prospective property owners who met certain age, income, and geographic criteria and (2) a database of prospective purchasers that included visitors to St. James and people who had contacted St. James to request further information. Promotions included a vacation package—for a modest rate, a three-day, two-night stay in one of the condominiums, a round of golf, and access to the other amenities of St. James Plantation—and a guided tour of the community conducted by a member of the sales staff.

Many of these vacation offerings coincide, by design, with an "event" at St. James, such as the opening of new homesites. Periodically, discounted prices are offered to visitors who purchase a homesite at the time of their visit. A getaway package offered in the spring of 1999, when many new homesites and slips at the marina became available, attracted over 200 visitors, 100 of whom purchased property during their visit. Since the first closing in 1991, more than 1,900 families and individuals have purchased homesites at St. James. Nearly one-half come from the Northeast, one of the major target markets for the project.

During the mid- to late-1980s, when private financial institutions were generally reluctant to lend, St. James Plantation easily secured financing for purchasers of individual lots. Projections of rapid growth in the number of affluent individuals seeking resort retirement homes made for impressive profit projections. Bank of America and BB & T (Branch Banking & Trust) are the project's primary lenders.

While residents have become acquainted at the golf courses, tennis courts, bridge tables, library, and chapel, the community would have benefited from a more active approach to community building through community events and programmed activities. The importance of open space cannot be underestimated. Though many property owners do not play golf, they do appreciate the nature and bike trails and the Audubon Society bird sanctuary at St. James.

The developers caution that knowing the market is critical to success. Recognizing which amenities would be required to attract buyers, they put in a golf course and the beach club early in the project's development. They believe that if they had not, sales would have languished. Another very important amenity is the small fishing village of Southport, which is free from the hustle and bustle that many residents want to leave behind.

---

1. *St. James Plantation Viewpoint Newsletter,* spring 1998

PROJECT DATA

Land Use

Total site area	6,000 acres
Total developed site area (all phases)	3,441 acres
Total undeveloped area	3,559 acres

Phase I: First St. James, Inc.	Acres used	Percentage of site
Detached residential	318	36.8
Attached/multifamily residential	9	1
Golf course/club	185	21.4
Roads	111	12.8
Common open space	169	19.6
Waterway park	11	1.3
Future	61	7.1
Total	864	100.0

Phase II: First St. James, Inc.		
Detached residential	226	35.6
Attached/multifamily residential	18	2.8
Golf course/club	187	29.4
Roads	64	10.1
Common open space	130	20.5
Future	10	1.6
Total	635	100.0

Phase III: St. James Plantation, LLC		
Detached residential	195	44.9
Attached/multifamily residential	12	2.8
Golf course/club	19	4.4
Roads	18	4.1
Common open space	10	2.3
Future	180	41.5
Total	434	100.0

The Players Club: St. James Development Company, LLC	Acres used	Percentage of site
Detached residential	130	16.4
Attached/multifamily residential	4	0.5
Golf course/club	184	23.1
Roads	25	3.0
Common open space	80	10.1
Future	372	46.9
Total	795	100.0

Residential Unit Information

Unit type	Lot size (acres)	Unit size (square feet)	No. of units (planned/built)	Price range
Patio home	1/8	1,300–1,600	90/55	$190,000–$210,000
Condominium	—	1,100	228/150	$148,000–$158,000
Townhome	—	2,200	18/3	$247,900

Lot type	Size (acres)	Price range
Single-family lot (golf course view)	1/3	$65,900–$100,000
Single-family interior lot	1/3	$45,900–$65,900
Marsh view lot	1/3	From $108,900
Intracoastal waterway (water view)	1/3	From $138,000
Intracoastal waterway (waterfront)	1/3–1/2	From $365,900

Golf Course/Club Information

The Gauntlet Club (18 holes)

Course length	7,050 yards
Clubhouse	12,000 square feet
Clubhouse facilities	Restaurant, bar, golf shop, meeting rooms
Additional facilities	Tennis, swimming pool

The Members Club (18 holes; 9 holes to be added)

Course length	6,887 yards
Clubhouse	16,000 square feet
Clubhouse facilities	Restaurant, golf shop, locker rooms, fitness center
Additional facilities	Indoor swim and tennis club

(continued on page 212)

The Players Club (18 holes)

Course length	7,042 yards
Clubhouse facilities	Temporary clubhouse with golf shop, snack bar; permanent clubhouse and amenities to be added

Development Cost Information (estimated)

Site acquisition cost (current 3,500 acres)	$ 4,200,000
Hard costs	$32,600,000
Soft costs	$18,000,000
Total development costs	$54,800,000

Development Schedule

Site purchased	1985	First closing	June 1991
Planning started	1986	Phase I completed	June 1996
Site work started	1987	Project completion	2004–2006 (estimated)
Sales started	May 1991		

Development Team

Developers

Homer E. Wright, Jr.

John A. Atkinson

St. James Plantation

Post Office Box 10879

Southport

North Carolina 28461

(910) 253-3001

(800) 245-3871

Site Planners

Tim Newell

Tim Cate

Sunset Beach

North Carolina

(910) 579-9163

Architects

Larry Zucchino

Patton & Zucchino

Raleigh, North Carolina

(919) 834-8620

Bernie Thursaum

Shoreline Design

Wilmington, North Carolina

(910) 395-0490

Scott Sullivan

Sullivan Design

Wilmington

North Carolina 28411

(910) 686-1223

Golf Course Consultants

The Gauntlet

P.B. Dye

Palm Beach, Florida

(561) 790-6733

The Members Club

Hale Irwin

Hale Irwin Designs

St. Louis, Missouri

(314) 567-0902

The Players Club

Tim Cate

Sunset Beach

North Carolina

(910) 579-9163

Engineering Consultants

Jay Houston

Houston & Associates

Shallotte, North Carolina

(910) 754-6324

Cape Fear Engineering

Wilmington, North Carolina

(910) 790-8584

Alan Lewis

East Coast Engineering

Shallotte, North Carolina

(910) 754-8209

Environmental Consultant

Steve Morrison

Land Management

Wilmington, North Carolina

(910) 452-0001

Project Address

4006 St. James Drive

Southport, North Carolina 28461

Contact Information

Julie A. Frazier, executive vice president, St. James Properties, LLC

(800) 245-3871

All project data are current as of February 2000.

Report authors: Mary B. Schwartz and Diane R. Suchman

Clover Commons

Pittsburgh, Pennsylvania

The clubhouse at Clover Commons serves as the focal point for the active adult lifestyle.

Middle-income households who seek an active adult lifestyle near Pittsburgh can find it at Clover Commons, an age-restricted, manufactured-home community on the eastern edge of the Pittsburgh metropolitan area, only 25 minutes from the city. With 170 home-sites organized around a clubhouse, swimming pool, and lawn games, Clover Commons offers residents a desirable lifestyle and an excellent value.

In many parts of the country, manufactured housing provides an affordable alternative to more expensive, stick-built homes; and historically, this type of housing has been especially popular with retirees and young married couples just starting out. Rimco Properties, the developer of Clover Commons, developed the site and associated community amenities and leases homesites for a monthly fee. Like other developers of manufactured-home, land-lease communities, Rimco retains ownership of the property and the amenities and manages the community's operations and maintenance. Rimco

Homebuyers can customize the exteriors of their homes with a variety of site-built accessories such as garages, decks, and planters.

also sells the homes to people who lease property at Clover Commons and permanently sets them on the homesites.

Although the 45-acre Clover Commons site is hilly and wooded, giving it a quiet, rural flavor, the site is surrounded by other residential uses, and shopping centers, grocery stores, and medical facilities are a short drive away. Of the community's 170 planned homesites, approximately 110 have been leased and have homes installed on them. Lots average 50 by 90 feet, and buyers can choose from a wide range of home layouts and configurations. Amenities include a 3,900-square-foot clubhouse, an outdoor pool with picnic area, a bocce court, and a free van service to nearby shops and medical facilities. The community's residents' association supplements these amenities by organizing a wide variety of social activities for the residents of Clover Commons.

This is the fourth age-restricted community that Rimco Properties has developed. Its first active adult community, Cloverleaf East, was developed in 1969, and was the first manufactured-home community in the Pittsburgh area targeting the senior market. Previously, Rimco (then known as Sampson Brothers) had a long history of developing housing in and around Pittsburgh. In fact, Sampson Brothers developed over 10,000 stick-built homes in the Pittsburgh area in the three decades following World War II.

Before developing Cloverleaf East, Rimco had no direct experience with AARCs. However, Orin Sampson, the father of Myles Sampson, the current owner of Rimco Properties, felt that AARCs presented a good opportunity because the market was not being well served by other builders. Moreover, he felt that manufactured housing and the land-lease model would offer an excellent return on investment and would let Rimco retain control of the property while offering a good value to its customers, even if the development did not offer the same quick profits that a stick-built community might.

As the long-term owner of its manufactured-home developments, Rimco's primary interest is less in obtaining quick profits than in creating communities that will have lasting value and return on investment. Moreover, the firm is highly attentive to its customers' needs, and focuses much of its energy on creating a high-quality lifestyle and a pleasant environment in its communities. Rimco's goal is to offer buyers a complete package that includes a home, site-built accessories (such as decks or porches), and the amenities that customers want.

Because Rimco had developed other properties in the area surrounding Clover Commons, the team at Rimco was very familiar with the site and its context. Based on its working knowledge of the market, the team felt that an active adult community would be the best use for the site and that there was sufficient demand for such a project in that location. In fact, because Rimco still had many prospective buyers from the Village at Clover Ridge, a completed community two miles away, the firm did not undertake any additional market studies for Clover Commons.

Rimco purchased the Clover Commons site from an estate in 1992. The site was characterized by rather hilly terrain, and at the time of purchase it was undeveloped and zoned for housing. So, after somewhat protracted negotiations with the estate, Rimco agreed to make a payment to a local religious institution to gain control of the site. Once the site had been obtained, Rimco had to deal with the steep slopes on the land, which ultimately required extensive (and expensive) grading, and also dictated a lower development density than would otherwise have been permitted under the zoning for the property. The concept for the site was to have each home terraced into the hillside, with curvilinear streets circling the community's clubhouse.

The development team planned the site to appeal to its target market. For example, knowing that security and safety were major concerns for most of their customers, the plan called for only one entrance to the community. Although this proposal initially generated some concerns with the approving jurisdiction regarding access for emergency vehicles, the configuration—which provides a clearly identifiable entryway into the community and enhances residents' feeling of security—was ultimately approved. Rimco also pays to have private security officers patrol the community on a regular basis.

Another planning consideration was the location of the community clubhouse and amenities. As a reflection of their importance to the social lives of residents, the clubhouse and the pool were located at the center of the community, where they serve as a focal point for the development and are easily accessible to all residents. Finally, to reinforce the sense of Clover Commons as a self-contained community and to differentiate it from the surrounding area, the developer took advantage of the site's natural topography, placing the homes in such a way as to enhance privacy and to offer views of the wooded hills nearby.

Compared with the intergenerational communities that Rimco has developed, some of which are also manufactured-home communities, Clover Commons has a more extensive amenity program. The company's non-age-restricted communities do not have a clubhouse or the extra security patrols and transportation services that Clover Commons offers. In addition, younger buyers tend to purchase fewer accessories like decks, porches, or enclosed garages for their homes.

Financing for the new homes differed as well, since the seniors who purchase homes at Clover Commons are inclined to put down more money for their homes than those in younger age categories. In fact, about one-fourth of buyers pay cash for their homes, and the rest make a down payment of at least 20 percent, sometimes much more. For buyers who do not pay cash, Rimco has a subsidiary to provide personal-property financing at competitive rates.

Finally, Rimco has found that family-oriented communities require much more intensive management than its active adult communities. In family-oriented developments, community managers sometimes have to deal with children riding their bikes through the flower beds or teenagers vandalizing community property, whereas at Clover Commons, because residents are mature and interested in the maintenance of the community, the environment is more sedate and largely self-regulating.

The approvals process for Clover Commons went fairly smoothly. There were no significant environmental, infrastructure, or utility concerns. Rimco Properties paid for all of the on-site improvements and paid fees for off-site improvements, and there was no public sector contribution to the development of the project. Rimco negotiated with the Borough of Plum, the approving jurisdiction for Clover Commons, to increase the developable density of the site by reducing the setbacks that would have been required under the borough's zoning ordinance. By effectively addressing regulators' concerns and by offering other concessions (such as brick skirting for the homes and full asphalt driveways) Rimco was able to obtain planning and zoning approval for the project. A further positive influence in this regard was a Pennsylvania law that makes it illegal to discriminate against manufactured homes in the public approval process.

Perhaps the most important barrier to the approval of the project was public opposition, which is not unique to manufactured-home communities. Most opponents of the project objected to development of any kind on the site. There were also concerns, typical of the responses to proposed manufactured-home communities, about the kind of people that such a community would attract. Rimco had to do substantial outreach to demonstrate the quality of the project it was proposing and the stability of these types of communities. Public meetings were a part of the development approval process, and Rimco went so far as to take local residents who were concerned about the proposed development to the firm's other established communities. Rimco was a well-known firm in the area with a long history of building homes; moreover, it could point to the continuing success of its nearby communities to show the neighbors of Clover Commons that they would have nothing to fear.

Once Rimco obtained development approvals, site preparation began. In addition to the extensive grading work mentioned earlier, the only major problem that Rimco encountered during site development was an incident in which a severe storm caused some soil-retention material to fail, thereby blocking the nearby storm drains and flooding three homes.

Home sales began as soon as construction did. There is no overall phasing plan for Clover Commons. Instead, the buildout of the site is proceeding one lot at a time as buyers lease

The warm, welcoming furnishings of the clubhouse create an attractive environment for the community's many activities.

homesites and move into the community. Rimco expects the final homesites to be leased by the end of 2002.

All project development costs were financed by cash derived from Rimco's other manufactured and stick-built properties. Given the firm's experience and knowledge of the local market, along with the income stream that other Rimco projects were generating, the developer felt that this approach would enable Rimco to control risks and costs and maximize return on investment.

Rimco handles all home sales itself, and most customers buy their homes through Rimco. Customers may buy a home from another manufacturer if they wish, but they must then pay Rimco additional fees to have the firm monitor the installation of the home and the construction of accessory structures. Rimco sells exclusively Marlette Homes by Schult, a manufacturer with a reputation for quality with whom Rimco has worked for 30 years.

Buyers may choose from a number of accessories, such as enclosed garages (rather than carports), decks, and sunrooms. Furthermore, buyers can customize the interiors of their homes through an extensive choice of options. Everything—from the appliances to the floor and wall coverings—is open to change.

Rimco handles all the home installations, securing the homes to their concrete pads with steel tie-down straps, a service that is included in the purchase price. Finishes included in the land-lease/home purchase package for the lot include brick-to-grade skirts, a starter lawn, a tree and shrubs, and a lamppost.

Buyers at Clover Commons can choose from dozens of floor plans, though most purchase one of the four models. The homes are all double-section, and the four models range in size from 1,120 square feet to 1,540 square feet, with prices ranging from $67,600 to $89,400.

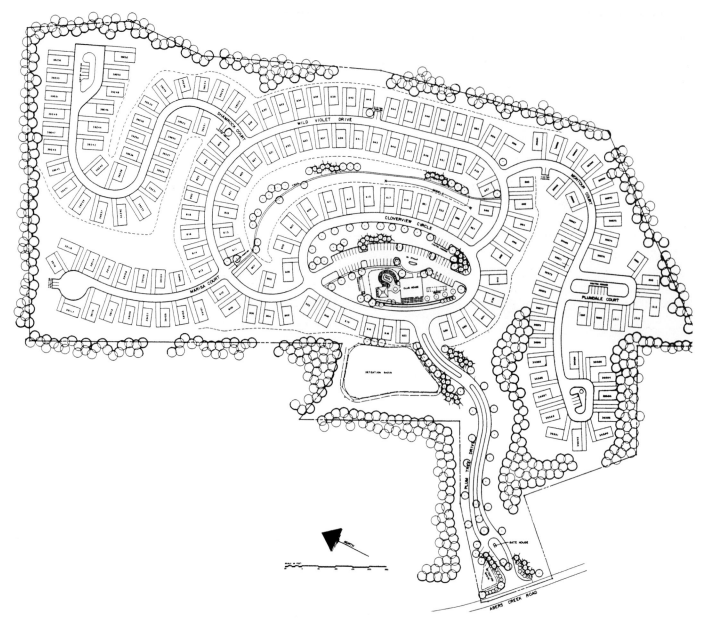

Site plan.

These prices make homes in Clover Commons very competitive for the area, and the purchase of a manufactured home saves buyers an estimated 30 percent over a comparable stick-built home. All of the homes have spacious living areas, and varied configurations are available for the bedrooms and bathrooms. All units have two or three bedrooms, and all have two baths.

Land-lease rates average around $270 per unit per month, and premiums are charged for homesites with the best locations within the community. The lease payment covers the cost of all community amenities, but residents must pay their own utilities, taxes, and insurance. The leases are lifetime leases, meaning that they run for as long as the resident remains in that home. Leases are renewed yearly, and rent increases are tied to the consumer price index for the Pittsburgh area, a feature that has had great appeal for residents concerned about their future housing costs.

At the clubhouse, which is the focal point for community activities, residents can find a fireplace and library, billiards, shuffleboard, and card tables. There is also a large banquet space with an adjoining kitchen, which the residents' association regularly uses for its activities, and which residents can reserve for their own functions free of charge. Next to the clubhouse is the outdoor pool, a covered picnic area, a bocce court, and horseshoe pit. In addition to all these community amenities, the residents' association, which receives a stipend of $10 per homesite per year from Rimco, offers a variety of social programs, including bingo and Bible-study sessions.

Rimco made a deliberate decision not to include any health or social services at Clover Commons. While seniors naturally have an increasing need for such facilities, Rimco felt that residents of an active adult community would be put off by on-site health care facilities that reminded them of their advancing age. However, residents of manufactured-home communities cannot easily relocate without incurring severe emotional and financial costs, so to address residents' health care needs, Rimco entered into an innovative partnership with Presbyterian SeniorCare to implement the "Cloverleaf Cares" program. Through this free program, a resident who needs health care or other assistance is visited by a caseworker from Presbyterian SeniorCare who assesses the resident's needs and then provides a referral for appropriate help. Rimco is considering the possibility of building an assisted-living facility in the future to meet the needs of the firm's current residents as they age.

The homes in Clover Commons are targeted to middle-income households whose members are older than 55 but who are still leading active lives and who do not currently need any medical care or assistance with daily living. Many residents in Clover Commons are still employed. Geographically, the community targets households who already live within a five-mile radius of the community.

Advertising is a central component of Rimco's marketing plan for Clover Commons. The firm has relied largely on advertisements in local newspapers, both small and large; on a direct-mail campaign; and on radio ads on local stations. Referrals actually generate a substantial number of leads for Clover Commons, and Rimco offers a $500 bonus to current residents who refer their friends to the community. Rimco puts substantial effort into following up on leads, which is particularly important given the fact that many buyers take a long time to make up their minds about moving. For example, Rimco holds open houses where prospective residents can meet with current ones, as well with local service providers and representatives from local businesses.

Like most new communities, Clover Commons has a sales center where prospective buyers can view floor plans, interior options, and a site plan. In addition to the regular sales staff, who are trained to understand the over-55 buyer, Rimco ensures that the receptionist for the sales center is someone who can relate well to prospective buyers. Rimco jointly markets Clover Commons with its other active adult, manufactured-home communities.

The marketing strategy for Clover Commons focuses on the value and the sense of community that the development affords. The marketing approach also tries to appeal to people who want to live in a community that has a wide variety of amenities, and who want their own home and yard but do not want to have the responsibilities that owning a larger home implies. So far, the typical buyer has been much as Rimco had anticipated. About two-thirds of the buyers move from homes within five miles of Clover Commons, and the rest come from elsewhere in the region. The age of the average buyer is in the early 60s, although Rimco has found that this average has been moving downward somewhat in recent years.

The main competition for Clover Commons comes from condominiums in the $100,000 to $150,000 range and from Rimco's other active adult communities. However, Rimco feels that the most serious competition comes from the prospective buyers' current homes. Generally speaking, people who buy at Clover Commons own their own homes free and clear, have been living in them for many years, and are in no rush to move. As a consequence, most buyers take months, or even years, to make a decision to buy in Clover Commons. In fact, it sometimes takes a major life event, such as the serious illness or death of a spouse, to trigger the decision to move. Rimco has learned from its experience with other communities that sales usually pick up as a development nears completion, when potential buyers realize that it's "now or never."

Rimco has found that buyers will almost never pay more for their new home than what they can get for their existing home. In markets where the average existing home sells for $250,000, a manufactured-home community may have difficulty achieving the desired level of sales, but in this particular Pittsburgh submarket, homes sell for substantially less than $250,000, and communities like Clover Commons are thus an attractive option for buyers and can be financially successful.

The active adult, manufactured-home market in Pittsburgh is quite stable, and competition is not very intense; Rimco believes that this situation will not change much over the next five years. In 1999, 28 new homes were sold at Clover Commons with an average price of $73,365 and additional accessories averaging $7,331. Rimco feels that this level of absorption is typical for the Pittsburgh area in general and for the active adult, manufactured-home market in particular.

The firm handles most of the resales in its manufactured-home communities, although residents do have the option of using an outside agency or selling on their own.

Rimco's strategy is to provide good value and an easy lifestyle to households who want to own their own homes, who do not want to live in multifamily dwellings, but who do not want to—or cannot continue to—live in their current homes. Rimco has succeeded because this market niche is not being well served by other development firms. People who move to Clover Commons appreciate the fact that it offers one-floor living, a professionally managed community, and an opportunity to make new friends in a secure and comfortable environment.

Given the opportunity to go back in time, Rimco would develop Clover Commons in the same way. Its experience in the local active adult, manufactured-housing market has given the firm a very good sense of what buyers want. Even though Clover Commons is Rimco's fourth active adult, manufactured-home community, it differs little from the earlier ones. Rimco continues to sell the same types of homes and to make use of the land-lease format. Perhaps the greatest change has been in the amenities offered. Rimco has seen a growing interest in community amenities, and it continues to research the kinds of amenities and services that its residents and prospective residents want.

The most important lesson that Rimco has learned from developing active adult, manufactured-home communities is the need to understand the market thoroughly. Because projects like Clover Commons serve a specific market niche, developers need to ensure that the necessary critical mass of potential buyers lives in the surrounding area. Communities like Clover Commons may simply not be possible in smaller markets.

Another major challenge is the high cost of developing and carrying an active adult, manufactured-home community until it is built out. Rimco staff feel that this is one of the major barriers to entry into this market and that it explains why there are so few competitors. The high initial costs are exacerbated by the extensive site preparation that manufactured-home communities require, as well as the need to have all the community amenities in place when the lease/sale process begins.

Perhaps the most significant barrier to developing projects like Clover Commons is simply gaining the approval to build them from regulatory agencies. Despite the best efforts of the industry, many people—including politicians and regulators—still have a negative view of manufactured homes. Though "trailer-park" stereotypes are persistent, they are not insurmountable, and Rimco has found that communities will accept manufactured housing once they see the design quality and durability of the homes that are currently being produced. Having other successful manufactured-home communities to point to has helped Rimco to educate people about what it means to live next to such a community. Rimco staff also note that in outlying suburban locations, community opposition is often focused more on whether to allow any type of development, rather than on whether to allow a manufactured-home community per se. Compared with other potential types of development, Rimco feels that active adult, manufactured-home communities are actually more readily accepted by neighboring residents.

Rimco will continue to own and operate its existing active adult, manufactured-home communities. While it has no specific plans for new developments, the firm feels that manufactured housing will continue to be a competitive option in the Pittsburgh market as the senior population continues to grow. It also recognizes that more seniors will need some level of medical or living assistance in the future and is therefore considering developing an assisted-living community near one of its existing active adult communities. But, for the moment, Rimco will continue to focus on delivering a satisfying home and lifestyle to the residents of its existing communities.

PROJECT DATA

Land Use

Site area	45 acres
Clubhouse and other common buildings	3,900 square feet
Open space, outdoor amenities, streets, and parking	19 acres
Number of multisection units (planned/built)	170/110
Gross density	3.8 units/acre
Number of off-street parking spaces	431

Single-Family Unit Information

Unit type	Unit size (square feet)	Price
Ashley (2 bedrooms, 2 baths)	1,120	$ 67,600
Classic (2 bedrooms, 2 baths)	1,188	$72,500
Wellington (2 bedrooms, 2 baths)	1,456	$89,400
Heritage (3 bedrooms, 3 baths)	1,540	$ 87,300
Average lot size		50' x 90'
Land-lease rates (per month for new homesites)		$280–$290

Development Cost Information (per lot)

Site acquisition cost	$ 3,000
Hard costs	$ 13,000
Soft costs	$ 4,000
Total development costs	$20,000

Operating Cost Information

Income (per unit per month)	As of April 13, 2000	At 100% occupancy
Land-lease income	$269	$275
Expenses (per unit per month)		
Management fees	$ 16	$ 16
Taxes	$ 25	$ 25
Monthly operating expenses	$ 146	$ 83
Debt service	$ 0	$ 0
Total monthly expenses	$ 187	$ 124

Development Schedule

Site purchased	October 1992
Planning started	October 1992
Site work started	September 1994
Construction started	July 1995
Project completion	December 2002 (estimated)
Sales started	June 1995
Sales completed	December 2002 (estimated)

Development Team

Developer

Rimco Properties, Inc.

772 Pine Valley Drive

Pittsburgh

Pennsylvania 15239

(724) 327-5755

Land Planner

Fahringer McCarty
& Grey, Inc.

Pittsburgh

Pennsylvania 15146

(724) 327-0599

Home Manufacturer

Marlette by Schult

Lewistown

Pennsylvania 17044

(717) 248-3947

Management Firm

Cloverleaf Communities

Pittsburgh

Pennsylvania 15239

(724) 327-5755

Project Address

660 Cloverview Drive

Pittsburgh, Pennsylvania 15239

Contact Information

Bill Cramer, president, Rimco Properties, Inc.

(724) 387-2555

Date of site visit: March 28, 2000

All project data are current as of April 13, 2000.

Report author: Oliver Jerschow

Indian Ridge Country Club

Palm Desert, California

Developed as a luxurious, country-club-style resort community, Indian Ridge Country Club attracts active adults who are purchasing either primary or second homes. Built in two phases—a condominium phase of duplexes and small-lot homes and a planned-unit-development phase of larger homes on large lots—the 640-acre, 1,069-unit gated community is centered, physically and socially, on its two golf courses.

Sunrise Colony Company, headed by William Bone, has been building this type of community in the Palm Springs resort area for over 30 years. Its first country-club community, built during the California real estate boom of the early 1970s, was Sunrise Country Club, followed shortly thereafter by Rancho Las Palmas Country Club, which also includes a Marriott resort hotel. These developments were followed by Monterey Country Club in 1979, which sold 548 homes on its opening day. Additional developments in California, Nevada, and Texas followed. Overall, the company has

As can be seen in this streetscape, the community's lush landscaping of palm trees, flowers, and plants creates a beautiful oasis within the desert landscape of Palm Desert.

built two resort hotels and ten master-planned resort communities that include more than 10,000 homes. Unlike most community developers, Sunrise Colony typically builds all the homes in its communities.

In addition to recreation and fitness facilities, the Sports Club offers opportunities for gathering out-of-doors in a garden setting.

Sunrise acquired the Indian Ridge site, along with another parcel to its south, as a result of a number of land purchases over a period of several years in the 1980s. In 1992, it began to develop the property with financing obtained from Japanese investment partners. In 1996, Sunrise joined Colony Capital, Inc., a Los Angeles-based private investment firm, to form the Sunrise Colony Company partnership. In 2000, it will begin construction on the parcel it owns south of Indian Ridge, as a similar development targeted to similar buyers.

Indian Ridge Country Club is located in Palm Desert, within the popular Coachella Valley resort area. The Coachella Valley consists of nine small cities, including Palm Springs and Palm Desert, that lie just north of the Santa Rosa and San Jacinto Mountains in southern California. Most of the development in the valley has been located between Interstate 10 and the mountains to the south, where the green, lushly landscaped developed areas contrast starkly with the arid brown desert landscape.

The city of Palm Desert is relatively prodevelopment, and there were no significant entitlement problems. The company's successful track record gave it excellent credibility in working with local government agencies. When development began, the site was virgin desert land and posed no unusual environmental issues. It included a small electric substation along an adjacent public street. (Landscaping screens the substation from the community.)

Homes are built as they are sold. Lots are released for sale on a phased basis, with about ten homes in a phase. When half the lots are sold, construction begins. Several phases are usually released for sale at any one time. Infrastructure construction is completed in corresponding phases. To minimize the intrusion of construction activity, active construction is separated from completed homes by fencing, and guards are posted to monitor construction traffic. Construction traffic enters the development at a separate access point.

A main spine road, Indian Ridge Drive, bisects the community. The homes are generally organized in quadrants around the golf courses, with the Sports Club, golf clubhouse, and club facilities located in the center of the property. The entire property is extensively landscaped. While many Palm Desert developments use landscaping to try to emulate a "Los Angeles look," the landscaping at Indian Ridge features native drought-tolerant plants. The results are not only aesthetically pleasing but have also been embraced by the market.

Visitors enter the property through a guarded gate, after which they may travel to the clubhouse and sales area. Access to the residential areas is by means of a separate gate and an electronic transponder system, which keeps a record of incoming and outgoing traffic. The perimeter of the property is fully walled.

The northern half of the community, which surrounds the Grove Course, one of the two Arnold Palmer–designed golf courses, consists of single-story duplexes and attached condominiums. The southern half of the property is a planned unit development with deeded lots. This change was made in response to market preference and because in California, construction-defect legislation has resulted in numerous situations in which condominium associations have sued developers. These suits have made it difficult for condominium builders and subcontractors to get insurance.

Current home offerings are grouped into three product lines. The three-bedroom Bougainvillea models sell for an average of $400,000. The Ocotillo models are priced at around $600,000. The two Jacaranda models—which, at approximately 4,500 square feet, sell in the $875,000 range—feature, among other things, clay tile roofs, granite countertops, and large, private courtyards with outdoor fireplaces. Sunrise Colony Company provides landscaping for all the homes.

The condominium area of the development, now sold out, includes both duplex homes and zero-lot-line single-family homes. The larger homes in the planned unit development section were introduced in 1997 in response to market demand for larger lots and larger homes.

Every home is located on the golf course, though a variety of orientations are offered. South-facing views are preferred; the quality of the view also affects the lot premiums, which can range from $10,000 to $100,000.

The popular "casita," or separate guest house, shown here separated from the rest of the home by an outdoor fireplace.

Designed in the Mediterranean mode, the homes' interiors have an open, light, airy style that is both casual and elegant. The feeling of openness is reinforced by volume ceilings and large windows that open onto lake and golf course views. All homes are single-story and include numerous luxury features such as courtyard entries, fully landscaped yards, fireplaces, security systems, solid interior doors, patio furniture, and two-car garages with a separate golf-cart garage. (The company experimented with two-story models at one time, but found that its market prefers a single-story lifestyle.)

Buyers can personalize their homes in a number of ways, including exterior designs, interior layout choices, and a wide range of optional features and finishes. A design center, built to facilitate the customizing of the homes, is located in the center of the community across from the clubhouse, and the company employs six interior designers to help buyers complete their homes. (At buildout, the design center and its parking lot will be converted to homes and sold.) Demand for options has been strong, and though the design center makes a good profit, balancing the customers' desire for a customized product with the company's need to complete construction on schedule has been a challenge.

The development includes two separate 18-hole, par-72 golf courses, the Grove Course and the Arroyo Course. The Grove Course, which features groves of date palms and citrus trees and is enhanced with lakes and waterfalls, has a green, stately, and traditional look. The Arroyo Course retains more of a desert flavor, with arroyos (deeply gorged-out areas) near the tees; canyons; dry creeks; streams and lakes; and boulders and indigenous vegetation, such as California fan palms, for landscaping.

Construction of the first 18 holes of golf accompanied the first phase of project development, and the course was completed at about the same time the first escrow was closed in 1993. The second golf course was built in two nine-hole segments. A key challenge was to create courses that would remain interesting for members who play frequently. To that end, multiple tees were constructed on each of the holes: this approach makes it possible to play the courses in a variety of ways; it also allows the courses to accommodate a range of playing abilities. In addition, the golf offerings include two putting greens and a driving range with tees at both ends.

Because the property is located in the desert, the land was flat, and more than three million cubic yards of dirt were moved to create undulations on the golf course. The excavated earth was used to elevate the housing pads to between six and ten feet above the level of the golf courses, both to create drama and to give residents views overlooking the golf courses. To enhance the "golf experience," landscaped berms shield street traffic from the golfers' view.

The opening of the first of the development's two clubhouses—the 21,000-square-foot Sports Club—coincided with the opening of the first golf course. The Sports Club includes a pro shop, a fitness center with an aerobics room and an active aerobics program, a health spa, locker rooms, a swimming pool complex, meeting rooms, a lounge, and an indoor-outdoor grill. The "Tot Stop" offers child care by appointment, primarily for visiting grandchildren. Other Sports Club facilities include 14 tennis courts (ten are lighted, and one is designed for exhibition play), two championship croquet lawns, and four paddle-tennis courts. In the swimming-pool area, members can choose from a lap pool, a social pool, a children's wading pool, and a whirlpool spa. The fitness center proved so popular that the company recently expanded it by 1,000 square feet.

In addition to the pools at the Sports Club, numerous small swimming pools are scattered in common areas throughout the development—approximately one pool for each 30 homes. In the newer sections, where residents tended to build their own pools, there are somewhat fewer.

The two-story, 40,000-square-foot Indian Ridge Country Club, which opened in 1997, is the heart of the community. The top floor of the building includes a service bar with a fireplace, a restaurant that serves dinner, and the informal, lunch-only Arroyo Grill. All dining areas flow together and are organized around a central kitchen. The club can handle sit-down dinners for 350 or stand-up receptions for 1,000. Downstairs are locker rooms and a pro shop targeted to golfers. About 70 percent of golf members have private carts, and there is a separate parking area and entrance to the club for people with golf carts.

The average age of Indian Ridge buyers has been in the mid-50s, which was typical of previous Sunrise golf communities. The target market is empty-nester households with a family income of over $200,000 and a net worth of over $1 million. About 70 percent of the community's buyers come from Los Angeles and Orange County, which are within easy driving distance.

Buyers include a mix of retired and preretired households. Historically, this type of community has appealed to second-home buyers, but in Indian Ridge, a greater percentage (an estimated 40 to 45 percent) are primary-home residents. According to Phillip Smith, president of Sunrise Colony Company's Coachella Valley Division, the typical pattern is that buyers first occupy their homes on weekends, then on long weekends, then for a season, then full-time.

The traditional Grove Course (facing page) and the more natural Arroyo Course (below) offer golfers distinctly different settings for the game.

ACTIVE ADULT RETIREMENT COMMUNITIES

Almost all residents are somewhat seasonal, however, because the summers are hot, and buyers are sufficiently affluent to travel at will and to own or rent other homes.

To date, just over 1,000 homes have been sold. The sales pace has been uneven because the sales period included the real estate downturn of the early 1990s, but in recent years, sales have been strong. In 1998, the company sold a record 181 homes in the community; 1999 topped that record with 204 sales. Qualifying buyers is not an issue. About half pay cash; those who finance typically put down between 20 and 25 percent.

The project is marketed through major media outlets such as the *Los Angeles Times,* the *Desert Sun* (a local newspaper); some magazines; outdoor billboards; and direct mail. The company experimented with advertising in national media but found that it was not cost-effective, given the number of people in its primary market. Sports events that take place at the community also bring the community media attention. About one-third of the homebuyers are referrals or purchasers of homes in earlier Sunrise developments.

The resale market is strong, and Sunrise Colony handles resales in competition with local brokers. The firm does about half the resale business at Indian Ridge. Homes that initially sold for $350,000 now command prices of $550,000.

According to Smith, the community's appeal is its active, social lifestyle, with the golf club, beautiful recreational facilities, and extensive social programming. The golf club features concierge services and a full-time social director to facilitate events and activities. No transportation, home

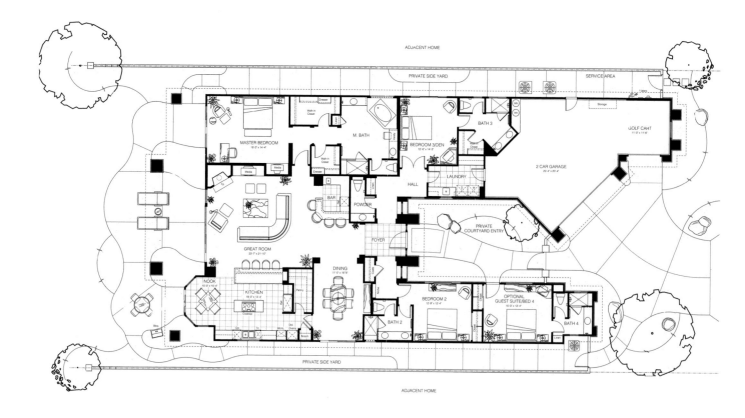

The popular 3,371-square-foot Ocotillo model offers three bedrooms and a den.

maintenance, or housekeeping services are offered. (The company experimented with such services in the past and found that their was little demand, in part because outside contractors are widely available.)

To use the golf courses, clubhouses, and other recreational amenities, residents must join the Indian Ridge Country Club. About 70 percent of the community's residents are golf members—the largest proportion of any of Sunrise Colony's communities. (Typically, about 50 percent of the residents in a country-club community play golf.) Membership, overseen by a membership director, is private, but members do not have ownership in the club. Golf members currently pay an initiation fee of $48,000 and monthly dues of $515. Sports Club, tennis, and social memberships are also available at much lower rates. A limited number of nonresidents may also join the Indian Ridge Country Club. The club has about 650 golf members and approximately 800 members in all categories combined. Overall, about 95 percent of residents join. To ensure that the golf courses, clubhouses, and other recreational amenities are maintained at the desired level of quality, Sunrise Colony owns and runs the country club and golf courses itself; there are no concessionaires.

Over time, the company expects the club to generate a modest profit. The company will retain ownership of the golf course and its associated amenities for the short term, but when development is completed, plans to dispose of them, either to the club members—who have the first right to negotiate a purchase—or to a third party.

The community is governed by two residents' associations. The condominium owners are organized into a condominium association, which maintains the homes' exteriors, including the

ACTIVE ADULT RETIREMENT COMMUNITIES

landscaping and streets. Its dues run approximately $540 per month. The planned unit development that makes up the southern half of the development is governed by a homeowners' association. For the monthly fee of about $240, the homeowners' association maintains the streets, which are all private, and the community's numerous swimming pools. Homeowners in the planned unit development are responsible for maintaining their own landscaping but must use an approved landscape company and maintain the landscaping to community standards. The two associations have entered into a formal agreement to fulfill common requirements, such as providing security and maintaining the community's main road.

According to Smith, the most challenging aspect of the active adult business is understanding the market, and, he says, "We do it by experience." In the course of years of developing this type of community, the project concept has evolved to its present form. Before developing the nearby PGA West community, the company had offered only one product line in a 1,000-unit development. Since then, it has begun to offer a range of products at different price points, sizes, quality levels, and levels of specification; the choices are similar to what would be available, through multiple builders, in a typical master-planned development. At Indian Ridge, for example, the company began by offering two kinds of home; it now offers three distinct product lines. This approach has broadened the market and increased absorption.

Also through its experience developing the nearby PGA West community, the company learned that really great golf does make a difference. Before, it had constructed "resort" courses, which were fine for the occasional player but did not attract serious golfers. At PGA West, including "great golf" not only broadened the market to include serious golfers but increased the size of the geographic market. Thus, Indian Ridge features two world-class, brand-name golf courses, which have proved to be a marketing plus. Three years of hosting the Bob Hope Chrysler Classic helped establish both the project's name and the credibility of its golf offerings.

Major challenges in developing Indian Ridge Country Club were, first, the need to create a salable product (which involved doing many things in a very short time, including constructing the golf courses in less than a year); and second, the necessity of keeping up with the market's changing needs and preferences.

In developing the community adjacent to Indian Ridge, Sunrise Colony Company plans to structure the golf club as an equity membership arrangement so that the residents know at the outset who will eventually assume ownership. Though the housing products will be of similar size, they will be designed somewhat differently to reflect changes in consumer tastes, and they will be built on larger lots. In response to the customers' increasing sophistication and desire to customize their homes, especially in this price range, the company will build into the architectural plans some standard options that offer more flexibility in the way rooms can be used. As Smith observed, "There's no limit to buyers' imaginations." One of the popular options (which was included in the Jacaranda models) that will be offered again is the "casita," or detached guest suite.

PROJECT DATA

Land Use

Site area	640 acres
Sports Club	21,000 square feet
Indian Ridge Country Club	40,000 square feet
Golf courses	312 acres
Clubhouse complex and golf course maintenance	20 acres
Total number of housing units	1,069
Number of single-family detached units	847
Number of duplexes*	222
Gross density	1.7 units/acre

* The condominium portion of the community is sold out.

Residential Unit Information

Unit type	Lot size (square feet)	Unit size (square feet)	No. of units (planned/built)	Price range
Planned unit development section				
Bougainvillea	8,000	2,217–2,742	290/158	$360,000–$455,000
Ocotillo	9,500	3,082–3,869	272/173	$540,000–$669,000
Jacaranda	13,000	4,575–4,580	49/14	$855,000–$960,000
Condominium section				
Acacia	5,200	1,706–2,368	222/222	$190,000–$319,000 (new)
				$309,000–$468,000 (resales)
Smoke Tree	6,500	2,392–3,562	103/103	$405,000–$590,000 (new)
				$899,000–$1,045,000 (resales)
Mesquite	6,200	1,948–2,368	19/19	$275,000–$340,000(new)
				$435,000–$440,000 (resales)
Palo Verde	7,000	2,482–3349	114/114	$379,000–$508,000 (new)
				$652,000–$670,000 (resales)

(continued on page 238)

Golf Course/Club Information

Grove Course

Number of holes	18
Course length	5,485–7,070 yards (depending on which tees are used)

Arroyo Course

Number of holes	18
Course length	5,395–6,926 yards

Indian Ridge Country Club

Membership type	Initiation fee	Monthly fee
Golf (transferable)	$48,000	$515
Sports Club	$4,000	$205
Tennis club	$2,000	$110
Social	$2,000	$75

Operating Cost Information

	Condo association	Planned unit development association
Homeowners' association fees (per unit per month)	$540	$240
Monthly homeowners' association operating expenses	$220,000	$80,000

Development Schedule

Site purchased	1986
Planning started	1990
Site work started	1992
Construction started	1992
Sales started	1992
Sales completed	June 2000 (estimated)
Project completion	March 2001 (estimated)

Development Team

Developer

Sunrise Colony Company

300 Eagle Dance Circle

Palm Desert

California 92211

(760) 772-7227

Land Planner

McLarand, Vasquez, Emsiek

Irvine, California

(949) 809-3300

Architects

McLarand, Vasquez, Emsiek

Irvine, California

(949) 809-3300

Robert Altevers Associates

San Diego, California

(858) 535-9777

Golf Course Architect

Arnold Palmer Course

Design

Ponte Verde Beach, Florida

(904) 285-3960

Landscape Architect

HSA Design Group

Palm Desert, California

(760) 341-1515

Project Address

76-375 Country Club Drive

Palm Desert, California 92211

Contact Information

Phillip K. Smith Jr., Coachella Valley president, Coachella Valley Division, Sunrise Colony
Company

(760) 772-7227

Date of site visit: February 11, 2000

All project data are current as of February 28, 2000.

Report author: Diane R. Suchman

Sun City at Huntley

Huntley, Illinois

Del Webb Corporation's first four-season retirement community, Sun City at Huntley, is a planned, age-restricted development that will contain approximately 6,000 homes on 2,150 acres. The project also includes an 18-hole golf course, a 94,000-square-foot recreation center, tennis courts, lakes, walkways, ball fields, and playgrounds. As of November 1999, 500 homes had been closed on, and there were about 900 residents. At buildout, anticipated within seven to ten years, the community's population will be approximately 10,000.

Del Webb Corporation, a national, publicly traded real estate company with corporate offices in Phoenix, is one of the country's largest builders of single-family homes, with revenues of $1.47 billion in fiscal year 1999. Since 1960, it has developed more than 80,000 homes in active adult communities in Arizona, California, Florida, Illinois, Nevada, South Carolina, and Texas. The company also builds family communities and country-club communities.

A streetscape at Sun City at Huntley, showing the homes' contextual architectural influences: covered entrances or porches, two-car garages, bay windows, brick-and-siding construction, and cedar shake accents.

Del Webb's Sun City developments, which are known for providing retirees with a rich array of amenities and activities in large-scale, lifestyle communities, have traditionally been built in warm-weather destinations. However, company research indicated that more than 80 percent of people prefer to retire close to home, near family, friends, and other longtime personal and professional ties. Sun City at Huntley is the company's test market for possible expansion into other four-season areas. Del Webb's strategy of geographic diversification was undertaken to enhance both its revenue base and its ability to weather regional housing recessions.

The location was selected on the basis of perceived market strength, land requirements (availability and cost), the local regulatory environment, and a long list of other criteria. According to David Schreiner, general manager of Sun City at Huntley, the key factors in the location decision were land and development costs, market prices for homes, and the propensity of age-targeted buyers to purchase in a lifestyle community. Before undertaking the development, the company spent five years conducting 17 studies evaluating the Chicago market.

Sun City at Huntley is located 45 miles northwest of Chicago in the Village of Huntley, a small (pop. 6,000) but growing town in what had been, until recently, a largely agricultural area. Situated on the border of McHenry and Kane Counties, northwest of Interstate 90 and Illinois's Route 47, the development is 30 miles from O'Hare International Airport and within 20 miles of the Schaumburg-Woodfield suburban activity center.

Residents can shop at nearby Spring Hill Mall and in the Village of Huntley, and can do their banking at one of Huntley's five banks. The development is one-quarter of a mile from Huntley Factory Shops, a 192,000-square-foot shopping center that includes more than 70 outlet stores for brand-name manufacturers. Huntley Park District offers outdoor sports and recreational facilities. Health care is available from doctors and dentists in the Village of Huntley and through an immediate-care facility five miles away. St. Joseph's Hospital, a 254-bed facility, is located 12 miles from the community; Sherman Hospital, with 418 beds, is 20 miles away. Nearby McHenry Community College offers a wide range of credit and noncredit classes and programs. Other nearby points of interest include Morraine Hill State Park, the Woodstock Opera House, the McHenry County Historical Museum, and the Railway Museum.

At the time Del Webb purchased the land, it was the residential portion of a larger property that had been zoned for a master-planned community and was already entitled for the proposed number of units. To build an age-restricted development, the company obtained an active adult community overlay zone for the property. The undeveloped land surrounding the development is either agricultural or entitled for commercial development.

The company has made a number of infrastructure improvements to serve the development. In addition to constructing internal roads, it has worked with the Illinois Department of Transportation to widen a section of Route 47 between its intersections with Del Webb Boulevard and Freeman Road.

Del Webb is well known for its environmentally sensitive approach to development. At Huntley, the company has conserved wetlands as parkland and passive recreational areas and built a large lake—now called Wildflower Lake—that will serve as a stormwater detention basin as well as a community amenity. The lake area will also include parking, a picnic area, and a small boat launch. To maximize the use of developable land, Del Webb also rebuilt an irrigation stream in a new location, creating new bends, turns, and riffles, and moving existing mollusk communities to the new streambed.

In addition, during the first phase of the project's development, Del Webb built the first phase of an off-site wastewater treatment plant to augment the existing public system. The company will also build the second phase of the plant; the Village of Huntley will build future phases. The plant now accepts flow from the development and will eventually accept flows from other parts of the Huntley area as well. Del Webb also drilled a 1,200-foot water well, which it deeded to the Village of Huntley as part of the village's domestic water supply network, and built a million-gallon elevated water storage tank to help meet the pressure and capacity needs of its new development.

Sun City at Huntley will be built in several phases, proceeding counterclockwise around the site, and is designed so that residents can enter and leave the development without passing construction sites. To ensure the separation of construction activity from completed homes, the company built a construction staging area in the southwest corner of the site (on the last parcel to be developed), and an access road, Sun City Boulevard, to control and redirect construction traffic during project development.

Neighborhoods are defined for the purpose of phasing construction. Phase I consists of approximately 900 units. As of November 1999, the developer was selling in Phase II, constructing Phase III, and planning Phase IV. Golf course development coincided with development of the first phases of the community. As of November 1999, the course had been completed and was scheduled to open in the spring of 2000. A recreational area with a ball field and a woodshop will be built in subsequent phases. So that it can continue to respond to changes in market preferences, the company is being flexible about the size and nature of future phases of development.

As a publicly traded corporation, Del Webb Corporation finances its developments through a combination of public debt and a line of credit from a consortium of banks. In addition, the company's existing project sales and activities generate a continuous stream of capital. Fairmount Mortgage, a broker subsidiary of Del Webb Corporation, offers consumer financing on site.

Currently, buyers of single-family homes at Sun City at Huntley can choose from 17 different floor plans, which include adaptations of designs that have proven successful in other Del Webb developments as well as designs that are specific to the demands of the local market. All exterior elevations are tailored to the local marketplace. The homes, which are classified by size, cost, and options, range in size from 1,130 to almost 2,700 square feet, with base price tags (on October 25, 1999) of between $166,450 and $300,000. The three categories of home are the Northwoods Classic, the Shoreline Premier, and the Great Lake Estate; the basic home includes, among other things, nine-foot ceilings (in Classics and Premiers; ten-foot ceilings in Estate homes), a two-car garage with a remote opener, and front- and rear-yard landscaping.

In The Clovers, Del Webb offers attached homes in a fourplex arrangement. The four home plans in The Clovers range from 1,014 to 1,559 square feet, include a two-car garage, and are priced from $136,450–$179,950. Among the standard features are nine-foot ceilings, pantries, ceramic tile foyers, and Thermopane windows.

Prairie Lodge, the community's recreation center and clubhouse.

Through its design center, the company offers homebuyers more than 2,000 upgrades and options to enable them to customize basic home plans to meet their needs, tastes, and desires. Selections range from upgraded carpeting, custom cabinetry, security systems, and skylights to sunrooms, outdoor decks, wine cellars, saunas, home theaters, and even a secret room (hidden behind a bookcase).

Subtle design features accommodate the needs of the target population. All the homes are ranch-style, though lower levels are available on some models. Doorways and light switches are wheelchair-accessible, and oversized windows maximize natural light. The company will incorporate additional accommodations for disabled residents.

Myriad amenities give residents of Sun City at Huntley an array of choices for the enjoyment of their leisure time. The community features the Del Webb–owned 18-hole Whisper Creek championship golf course, designed by Greg Nash and Casper/Nash & Associates. So that golfers of many different skill levels can play on the same course, the course includes more tee boxes than a traditional course, and greens are somewhat larger, though not necessarily easier to play. The course includes bent grass accented with bluegrass, areas of native fescue grasses, bunkers filled with white sand, rough, and water features that are enlivened with rock formations and waterfalls. Protected wetlands enrich the views, as do the newly planted and estab-

A view from the back of Prairie Lodge: the large, free-form outdoor swimming pool is visible, with the golf course beyond.

lished stands of trees. As is typical, the golf course is not only a recreational amenity but also serves to convey and store drainage. In addition to the course itself, golf facilities include a state-of-the-art, double-sided golf practice and teaching center with bent grass, bluegrass, and all-season hitting surfaces. The center includes two putting greens, a chipping green, and both green-side and fairway sand bunkers.

The 94,000-square-foot Prairie Lodge recreation center was built on the development's high ground, where it enjoys maximum visibility and overlooks the golf course and landscaped water features. Just outside the lodge, two towering historic trees remain on what was the once the Drendel family farm. Inside the lodge, residents can enjoy the Walleye Grill restaurant and bar; a sports pub; a golf pro shop; a six-lane, 25-yard indoor lap pool with a fountain and a whirlpool spa; a second-story walking track that overlooks the pool; a solarium; a large, well-equipped fitness center; an aerobics room; the Drendel Hall ballroom and theater; a ceramics room; a card room; a computer lab; and numerous other large and small gathering spaces. Also within the lodge is a wellness center, staffed by a local hospital, that provides health monitoring and referral counseling.

Decorated in reds, greens, blues, and golds, the casual yet elegant Prairie Lodge features stone fireplaces, floor-to-ceiling windows, and high-quality furnishings—including a piano, built-in bookcases, and art. In the 160-seat restaurant, which is open to the public, a large aquarium echoes the fish-and-water theme used throughout the lodge.

Because of ever-changing consumer needs, the company has found that it must maintain a balance of dedicated and nondedicated space within the recreation center. As long as this flexibility is retained, new interests can be easily accommodated. For example, a room that was once used for calligraphy might someday be used for leather-working instead, and no one interest group can claim "ownership" of the space.

Outdoor amenities include a free-form outdoor leisure pool, a lake pavilion and amphitheater, playgrounds, tennis courts, and bocce courts. In addition, the community's open space, which constitutes more than one-third of the land area, is enhanced by lakes, streams, walking trails, and extensive landscaping. Small park areas, with features such as gazebos, provide more private outdoor gathering spaces within neighborhoods. The impressive landscaping added includes, to date, more than 100,000 perennials, 30,000 annuals, and 5,000 trees.

According to Schreiner, a project of this size and cost must maintain a predictable sales pace to succeed. The development opened for sales in September of 1998 and had 206 new orders during its first month. During its first ten months of operation, the community generated a net of 700 new orders.

The marketing strategy relies on traditional advertising vehicles, augmented by general media attention. According to Schreiner, the project's size alone makes it newsworthy; to capitalize on the public's interest, the company provides the news media with a continuous stream of information on the development's features and progress. In addition, Sun City at Huntley is striving to become known locally as a "good neighbor." For example, project staff have contributed toys and food to area shelters during holidays, and they conduct one of the area's most successful United Way fundraising drives.

The scale and duration of Sun City developments make referrals an especially important marketing vehicle. The company schedules appointments "to bring priority customers through the buying process" and has developed a sophisticated system of communicating with prospects who request information about its products.

As part of its marketing program, the firm also plans to offer vacation getaway packages that are similar to those offered at its other active adult developments. Vacation getaways provide sales prospects with the opportunity to experience the lifestyle on site, during a short stay. For a very reasonable price, visitors can stay overnight in a furnished vacation villa or home, tour the model homes, sample the other community amenities, and talk to community residents and staff. This program will be in full operation by the summer of 2001.

A short walk from the lodge is the model park that showcases the developer's offerings. The homes in the model park, which are named after popular vacation destinations in the Midwest, are designed to eventually be part of the project. As new models are needed, they can be built on the land that remains in the model park, and the first group of models can be sold.

The model homes' garages are filled with displays of various options. For example, the garage of one model might feature cabinet, sink, and countertop options; another might showcase the various storage systems that could be incorporated into a home. Each model is decorated with an imaginary, profiled couple in mind, and that couple's taste, lifestyle, and family are reflected in the home's furnishings, option selections, and even in details such as knickknacks and photographs.

The model park is open from 9 A.M. to 5 P.M., seven days a week. Because no sales personnel are stationed in the models, prospects can take their time and not feel pressured. At one end of the model park is a staffed café, which offers free coffee, cookies, and a place for sales prospects to relax. Community residents out for a stroll often stop by for a cup of coffee as well, and talk with the sales prospects. According to Harriet Ford, Sun City's director of public relations, "Our residents are our best salespeople."

Schreiner notes that the project has no real competition in the Chicago area for people who prefer a community of this scale with these kinds of amenities. At the same time, the company recognizes that moving to a place like Sun City at Huntley is a discretionary, life-changing decision for the people who are considering purchase. "The toughest customer," Schreiner points out, "is the non-mover."

For people who are seeking a lifestyle retirement community, Sun City at Huntley's design, quality, and attention to detail sell the homes. The biggest marketing challenge has been to manage the large volume of prospects who have come through the project.

The typical purchaser of a Sun City home nationwide is 60 to 65 years of age and has an income of at least $40,000 yearly. The residents of Sun City at Huntley have come from throughout the Chicago region—from northwest Indiana to the Wisconsin border, from the city of Chicago, from the west to Rockford, and from downstate Illinois. Some had lived in traditional retirement states and wanted to return to the Chicago area.

The community is operated and managed by a community association, and all residents are members of the association. Each homeowner pays a monthly fee for use of all recreational facilities (except the golf course), for the services of the management staff, and for maintenance of

A landscaped bridge connects the sales center at Prairie Lodge to the model-home park.

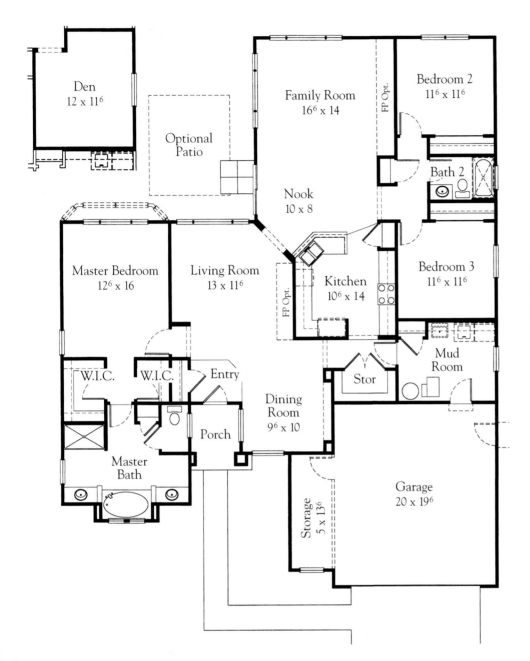

Den
12 x 11^6

Optional
Patio

Family Room
16^6 x 14

FP Opt.

Bedroom 2
11^6 x 11^6

Bath 2

Nook
10 x 8

Master Bedroom
12^6 x 16

Living Room
13 x 11^6

Bedroom 3
11^6 x 11^6

FP Opt.

Kitchen
10^6 x 14

W.I.C.   W.I.C.   Entry

Mud
Room

Dining
Room
9^6 x 10

Stor

Master
Bath

Porch

Storage
5 x 13^6

Garage
20 x 19^6

The 2,126-square-foot Traverse Bay Shoreline Premier home has three bedrooms and two baths.

common areas and facilities. (Because the community is not gated, its streets are publicly owned and maintained—a cost savings for residents.) Additional services, such as lawn care, snow removal, and exterior home maintenance, are available for a fee. Certain neighborhoods, such as The Clovers, enjoy all the maintenance services and therefore pay a proportionally higher assessment to cover those benefits.

The community association is governed by a board of directors. During the project development period, a majority of the board is controlled by the developer. As development nears completion, control of the board will transfer to the homeowners. A management company owned by the Del Webb Corporation oversees the day-to-day operation of the community.

Though the community does not restrict public access, the recreational building is for the

Labels within the map image:
Bocci Courts
To Tennis Center
To Lake Pavilion, Lot & Amphitheatre
Recep
Design Studio
Health & Fitness
Aerobic & Dance
Sales Center
Wellness Center
Mens Lockers
Lobby & Lounge
Fitn
Womens Lockers
Sauna
Indoor Lap Pool
Spa
Leisure Pool
Model Park

0 25 50 100
Scale in Feet

Del Webb's Sun City reserves
the right to make changes to the plan
as the development progresses.

Prairie Lodge, the center of community life,

includes social and dining areas; health,

fitness, and golf-related facilities; and the

sales center and administrative offices.

Arts & Crafts

Sewing Computers

Business &
Administration Center

Drendle
Hall

Social, Dining &
the Whisper Creek
Golf Club

Lobby Recep

Reading
Room Social Lounge

& Art
rpose

Stage

Banquet, Catering
& Kitchen Services

To Gol
Practice F

Solarium

The Walleye
Grill

Sports Pub

Whisper Creek
Golf Club
Pro Shop

Whisper Creek Golf Course

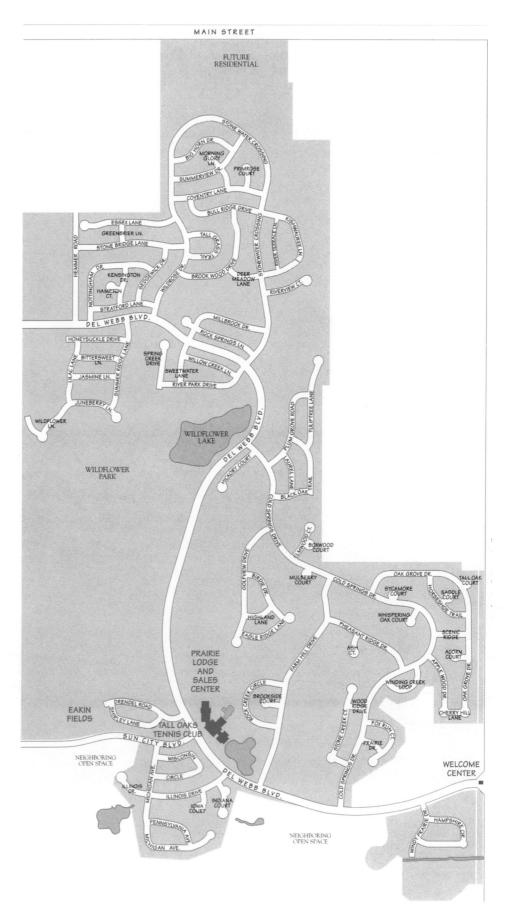

Site plan.

private use of the residents, who gain access with identification cards. The golf course is open to the public. Residents of Sun City at Huntley use the golf club at preferential rates and are offered priority tee times.

In addition, the community association offers a multitude of "soft" amenities—programs and activities designed to promote social life and a sense of community. At present, Del Webb Corporation maintains a staff of 270 employees to develop and manage the community. Of these, 100 are involved in creating "social infrastructure." With assistance as needed, residents are encouraged to form clubs and to initiate activities, classes, and programs that interest them.

Because it is an age-restricted community, there are limits on the length of time that a guest under the age of 19 may visit.

Schreiner cautioned that the risks in developing this type of project are enormous. As a result, Del Webb bases its development decisions and product offerings on extensive and regularly updated market research. Because of its longtime experience, its ongoing systems research and analysis, its referral base, and a successful track record that inspires the confidence of investors, Del Webb occupies a unique niche within the AARC development business. Only such resources would make possible the development of a community such as Sun City at Huntley, which required an upfront investment of over $125 million before the first home was closed.

Most industry experts agree that people come to communities like Sun City at Huntley in search of lifestyle rather than simply a new home; in a Del Webb community, lifestyle is heavily weighted to what is inside the community, rather than to its locational context. Lifestyle is created through amenities and activities that promote interaction, and the design of both recreational facilities and programs is driven by that goal.

For Del Webb Corporation, development of Sun City at Huntley was an extension—and adaptation—of a strategy that has worked well in nearly ten other markets. For a Sun City development, Huntley is somewhat smaller than most. Exterior materials—stone cladding, brick, siding—and exterior architecture were based on the preferences of the local market. Similarly, the design and finishes of the market-tested floor plans were adjusted to be consistent with local tastes. Street design had to incorporate room to store snow. Parkway sidewalks, which are typical for Chicago but not for Del Webb, were also included. Adapting the houses to a cold-weather climate also required a few adjustments. For example, options offered for the first time at Sun City at Huntley include mudrooms, three-season rooms (sun porches), and lower levels. Climate dictated the location of the homes' plumbing. The indoor recreational facilities were designed within a single structure rather than as a cluster of buildings in a campus setting, which is the norm for Del Webb's southern Sun City communities. And, for the first time, the company hired union trade contractors.

Del Webb prides itself on knowing its customers very, very well through extensive research and hard-won experience. Developing in a new region of the country was a challenge for the company because it had to plan and forecast without previous experience in this market. To date, its sales record demonstrates that it has met the challenge well. As Robert Eck, vice president for land development, pointed out, "We learn a lot from our customers. Over time, feedback from the community will teach us what we need to know."

PROJECT DATA

Land Use

Site area	2,150 acres
Clubhouse and other common buildings	94,000 square feet
Golf course	240 acres
Number of residential units planned	6,000
Gross density	2.79 units/acre

Residential Unit Information

Unit type	Lot size	Unit size (square feet)	Price range
Single-family units			
Northwood Classic	50' x 110'	1,130–1,520	$166,450–$189,950
Shoreline Premier	70' x 110'	1,624–2,126	$218,450–$252,450
Great Lake Estates	80' x 110'	2,176–2,635	$271,450–$302,450
Multifamily units			
The Clovers	–	1,014–1,559	$136,450–$179,950

Golf Course/Club Information

Number of holes	18
Course length	7,100 yards
Additional facilities	Two putting greens, chipping green, pro shop, driving range, teaching center

Development Schedule

Site purchased	December 1997
Planning started	August 1997

	Site work started	April 1998
	Project completion	2008 (estimated)

	Phase I	Phase II	Phase III
Number of units	900	800	500
Planning started	December 1997	December 1998	April 1999
Construction started	April 1998	April 1999	September 1999
Construction completed	December 1998	December 1999	July 2000
Sales started	September 1998	August 1999	–
First closing	April 1999	December 1999	–

Development Team

Developer
Del Webb Corporation
Post Office Box 20840
Phoenix, Arizona 85016
(602) 808-8000

Land Planner
Richardson/Verdoorn
Austin, Texas
(512) 480-0032

Golf Course Architect
Casper/Nash & Associates
Phoenix, Arizona
(602) 265-5612

Architect
PHN Architects
Wheaton, Illinois
(630) 665-8400

Landscaping
Hitchcock Design
Naperville, Illinois
(630) 961-1787

Project Address

12940 Del Webb Boulevard
Huntley, Illinois 60142

Contact Information

Harriet Ford, director, public and community relations
(847) 515-7735

Date of site visit: November 16, 1999

All project data are current as of November 30, 1999.

Report author: Diane R. Suchman

Village Walk

Naples, Florida

In a region dominated by golf-course developments, DiVosta and Company's Village Walk community represents a creative and highly successful alternative. Instead of being centered on a golf course, Village Walk is organized around a town center at the water's edge that includes not only recreational facilities but also a cluster of shops and services that create a village marketplace. The 850 waterfront homes are located on peninsulas that jut out into a man-made lake system. Walking paths and pedestrian bridges connect the peninsulas to the town center.

DiVosta and Company, Inc., of Palm Beach Gardens, Florida, has been building in south Florida for more than 30 years, primarily in Broward, Collier, Martin, Palm Beach, Martin, St. Lucie, and Collier Counties. The company, founded by Otto "Buz" DiVosta, was acquired by Pulte Corporation in 1998 (after Village Walk was built) and now operates as a separate, wholly owned subsidiary of that company. Pulte is the largest homebuilding company in the United

A clock tower readily identifies Village Walk's town center, which features retail shops and services as well as recreational facilities and gathering places.

A network of paths and bridges over the artificial lakes connects residential areas to one another and to the town center.

States, with operations in 27 states plus Chile, Mexico, and Puerto Rico. DiVosta and Company shares in Pulte's national purchasing, uses its financial services, and offers mortgage financing through Pulte's mortgage company. All profits go directly to Pulte Corporation.

Village Walk is the first DiVosta and Company development of this type. Development of a second, RiverWalk, began in West Palm Beach in 1994. A third community of similar design, Island Walk, is under construction nearby. The company is planning to build additional communities of this type in Florida and is currently considering a potential site in the Sarasota area.

Village Walk is located in North Naples, Florida, just five miles from the Gulf of Mexico. The site fronts on Vanderbilt Beach Road, which provides direct access to the gulf beaches. When DiVosta purchased the site in 1993, it was a flat, dry, rectangular tomato field with no distinctive features or development constraints. The property is surrounded by residential uses and is located close to Everglades National Park, three other state parks, a community hospital, and a plethora of golf courses.

Though Village Walk is not an age-restricted community, the community and the homes were designed to appeal to active adults. The Naples area attracts retirees, and a large segment of the housing market is composed of older people. According to Mike Rosen, vice president of DiVosta and Company, the company did not do extensive market studies before planning the project; instead, it simply observed the continuing high level of demand for retirement communities in the area and the kinds of developments that had been built to meet that demand.

To create a unique and exciting feature that would compete with the appeal of golf, DiVosta created a development concept based on a water amenity: an 80-acre man-made lake system that would enable almost every home to enjoy both direct water frontage and pedestrian access to the facilities and services of the town center (all but 14 homes are located directly on the water). In addition, the lakes are stocked with fish (including a species of carp that helps to eradicate undesirable vegetation and to maintain adequate levels of dissolved oxygen) and have attracted waterfowl to the community.

The lake system was designed to create peninsulas of land, each of which would accommodate one street of homes. Soil that was dredged from the site to create the lakes was used to fill residential lots. The peninsulas jut in from the perimeter of the site toward its center, creating a radial pattern of development. At the tip of each peninsula is a pedestrian bridge linking the land area to the town center site, which is located near the project's landscaped entryway. The lighted, 12-foot-wide walking paths that link the development accommodate a variety of uses—pedestrians, bicycles, and in-line skaters. A landscaped, illuminated ring road was constructed along the perimeter of the site to provide definition, to buffer the community from surrounding developments, and to give automobile access to each of the peninsulas' streets. The community is encircled by a fence and walls, and entrance is through a staffed guardhouse.

The 22,000-square-foot town center is the heart of the community and its primary amenity. As Rosen explained, the town center concept arose from the company's desire to provide an innovative vehicle for social interaction—one that was not based on golf. (The company had decided that though golf was a popular amenity in the area, it wanted to offer homes at prices that did not reflect the cost of including a golf course in the community.)

Three outdoor swimming pools are located at the town center. The free-form, heated, "resort pool" is for those who enjoy bathing and sunning. A second heated pool nearby, which is enclosed by screens, offers shade and protection from insects. A third pool, for swimming laps, is located adjacent to the fitness center and is also enclosed with screens. Six Har-Tru tennis courts with stadium-style viewing stands and an air-conditioned tennis lounge are a few steps away.

Though many communities in the area include clubhouses with recreational facilities, the Village Walk town center is unique because it includes shops and services as well. The town center is designed as a series of connected, low-rise, Mediterranean-style buildings that front on the hub of the lake system. The company's signature clock tower serves as the community's central point and identifying symbol. Within the town center, two multipurpose rooms, one on the first floor and one on the second floor of the "town hall" building, serve as gathering places for community events. The center also houses community offices, a number of smaller rooms that provide flexible space for uses such as card games, club meetings, and arts and crafts, and four residential apartments. Residents have 24-hour key access to the fitness center.

The town center also includes a convenience store with a café. Outdoor tables provide an inviting opportunity for coffee, culinary delights, and conversation overlooking the lake. A bank, beauty shop, and gift shop are also located within the town center. Just beyond the town center buildings, residents have access to an automated teller machine; two gasoline pumps; and, in a

The popular 2,681-square-foot Oakmont model (floor plan, facing page) includes three bedrooms, a den, and two baths.

small, separate, architecturally compatible structure, a car wash. Neither transportation nor health care services are offered on site.

By design, all mail is delivered to a U.S. postal facility within the town center, rather than to individual homes. Requiring residents to gather in one place to retrieve their mail makes it easy and natural for them to meet and chat with their neighbors.

The state regional planning council favored the inclusion of this array of activities within the town center complex because it would minimize the number of off-site automobile trips generated by residents of the development. The council was also pleased that the development consumes less water than the previous use—farming—and does not burden the ecosystem with pesticides. At the time the site was purchased, the property was zoned residential, so no rezoning was required. The only off-site improvements DiVosta needed to construct were deceleration and turning lanes on Vanderbilt Beach Road. As a result of its experience with Village Walk, Collier County changed its land development code to require developments over a certain size to include services within their clubhouses.

The homes consist of two-family (duplex) patio homes and single-family homes. Three models are offered. The smallest is the Capri, a patio (two-family) home with two bedrooms and two baths. The Oakmont model, with three bedrooms, two baths, and a den, is a single-family, zero-lot-line home. The largest home offered is the Windsor, which has four bedrooms and three baths. Originally, a larger and more luxurious fourth model was also available, but though it sold well, it was soon discontinued because its size and price were out of scale with those of the other homes in the development.

All homes include many standard features that would be sold as options in other developments, including two-car garages with remote openers, covered lanais, security systems, volume

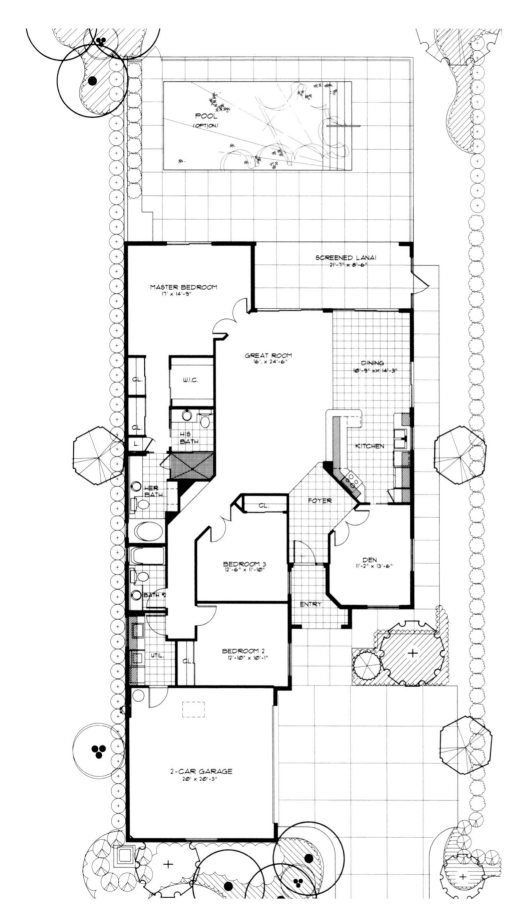

POOL
(OPTION)

MASTER BEDROOM
17' x 14'-9"

SCREENED LANAI
21'-7" x 8'-6"

GREAT ROOM
16'. x 24'-6"

DINING
10'-9" xx 14'-3"

CL.

W.I.C.

HIS
BATH

KITCHEN

L.

HER
BATH

CL.

FOYER

BATH 2

BEDROOM 3
12'-6" x 11'-10"

DEN
11'-2" x 13'-6"

ENTRY

UTIL.

BEDROOM 2
12'-10" x 10'-1"

CL.

2-CAR GARAGE
20' x 20'-3"

The interiors of the homes are light and open, with high ceilings and lots of windows.

ceilings, top-quality appliances, high-quality doors and trim, ceramic floor tiles, mirrored closet doors, closet organizers, central vacuum systems, and laundry-room cabinets. All homes are the same color and have tile roofs, which are available in three styles: gable, hip, and Boston hip. Among the few options offered are swimming pools, whirlpool tubs, a wall system/entertainment center in the living room, and an additional bedroom and den in the Windsor model. To maintain an efficient, more easily controlled construction process, the developer did not customize homes for individual buyers.

Architectural controls limit the kinds of changes that homeowners can make to their dwellings. One change that some have made is to replace cement driveways with pavers (cobblestones). In its Island Walk development, DiVosta and Company is constructing all the driveways with full pavers. Otherwise, the models are essentially the same.

In 1974, Buz DiVosta developed an efficient building system, called Moduplex, that makes it possible to construct a solid, high-quality home in just 47 working days. The homes are constructed of poured concrete walls reinforced with steel bars (or, in one model, concrete block exterior walls), and precut and preassembled roof trusses, air conditioning ducts, plumbing, cabinetry, and electrical systems. As a result, the homes are soundly built and offer excellent protection from wind and hurricanes. The company also builds the homes' optional swimming pools with solid, poured-concrete walls (rather than the more common gunnite) to ensure high-quality, long-lasting results.

The construction process is organized to enable the company to control quality and time. All homes on any given street are the same model, so that specialized work crews can proceed from one home to the next performing the same set of tasks with production-line efficiency. The company does all the major construction in house, including plumbing, electric, and air-conditioning installation. It has its own roof-trussing plant and millwork shop, and a facility for constructing the homes' cabinetry. In order to keep all components of its "production machine" busy, the company must (and does) sell at least one home per day. In its current project, Island Walk, DiVosta is selling two homes per day.

Development of the site proceeded in a counterclockwise direction from the town center, street by street, with street names following alphabetical order. To ensure that current residents would not need to pass a construction site to gain access to their homes, once all the foundations on a given street were prepared and the walls poured, construction activity proceeded from the outside perimeter road inward, toward the center of the site, on both sides of a street at once. During the construction period, DiVosta and Company issued residents regular letters to keep them informed about the community's progress.

The town center was built all at one time, when, as Rosen explained, "there were enough rooftops to support the retail uses." About 350 homes were occupied before the town center opened. At the time Village Walk was developed, DiVosta was a private company, and the project was self-financed.

Village Walk was marketed in local newspapers, on billboards on nearby Interstate 75, on the radio, and via direct mail. Referrals were also important. DiVosta trains its own sales staff and offered mortgage financing through its own title and mortgage company. Rosen estimates that about 40 percent of buyers paid cash for their homes. Most buyers came from out of state, especially from the Midwest and the Northeast. Typically, buyers had preselected the Naples area and were shopping for a home in that location. Many were "condo converts" who missed the privacy, convenience, and storage space of a single-family home. Approximately 80 percent of buyers were over age 52. The community's residents are largely full-time residents, and many work—part-time, as consultants, or as volunteers.

Rosen feels that within the Naples area, the development has no real competition that can offer attractions such as the lake system, the town center, and the quality and prices that Village Walk offers. Demand proved strong. Initially, prospective buyers lined up 21 hours in advance for the opportunity to purchase a home in Village Walk. As a result, as new phases of construction opened, the developer decided to conduct a lottery to determine priority rights to purchase. Village Walk sold out in 1998. Last year, the company sold 454 homes in its nearby Island Walk development.

The community is managed by a homeowners' association that has a representative form of government. Because homeowners' associations often have difficulty attracting a quorum, residents of each of the 21 streets in the community elect a representative to cast that street's vote at homeowners' association meetings. This process ensures that interested parties will show up and participate at meetings.

Management of the community was transferred to the homeowners in October of 1998 (at which time the homeowners gave DiVosta and Company a standing ovation). The developer (and now the community) retained a paid, on-site town manager to handle the day-to-day operations of the community, as well as a full-time activities director to schedule activities and the use of the town center facilities.

According to Rosen, there are two keys to the development's success: the town center, which affords buyers both opportunities for social interaction and convenient access to services; and the good value buyers receive when they purchase one of the community's high-quality homes.

As a result of its experience in Village Walk, DiVosta and Company has made some changes in the design of the town centers in its subsequent developments. For example, after observing the way that gathering spaces were used at Village Walk, DiVosta and Company designed the town center in the Island Walk development to include flexible, multipurpose space all on one floor. Observing that residents converted what had been designated as a planned card room into a library, by filling wall after wall with bookshelves, DiVosta plans to include a library in future town centers. The lap pool at Village Walk was 50 feet long; in response to buyers' feedback, the lap pool in future developments will be regulation size: 75 feet (plus one inch, for a touch pad). The screened pool has not proved particularly popular and will not be included in future developments. The company also learned to include a full catering kitchen.

Village Walk's town center was envisioned as a town hall. In Island Walk, the approach is more clublike, with a formal entrance—complete with furniture and a fireplace—where people can gather. Similarly, the Village Walk convenience store/café has evolved into a full-service restaurant at Island Walk.

Residents can refuel their cars at the town center's gasoline pumps. A car wash occupies a separate site within the community.

Originally, the developer leased space in the town center to a dry cleaner, but found that in this location, demand for this service was not great. The space was later leased to a beauty salon, which has proved to be quite popular. The residential apartments were originally intended for occupancy by the community manager (as a way to help lower the amount of salary that the community would need to pay) and by the operator of the convenience store (to encourage a store owner to set up shop in the community), as well as to be a source of rental income for the community. However, two of the four apartments did not serve their expected purpose, and their use for rental income raised legal and permit issues. At times, residents have used the apartments for card games. On the basis of this experience, DiVosta and Company does not plan to include rental apartments in the town centers of future developments.

Rosen explained that it is important for the developer to educate residents about the financial philosophy underpinning the concept of the town center. The shops and services are a convenience and an amenity open only to community residents. Because they serve a limited market, owners of these businesses can pay only minimal rents. (For example, when the developer controlled the community association, the beauty shop paid only $150 per month in rent.)

Site plan.

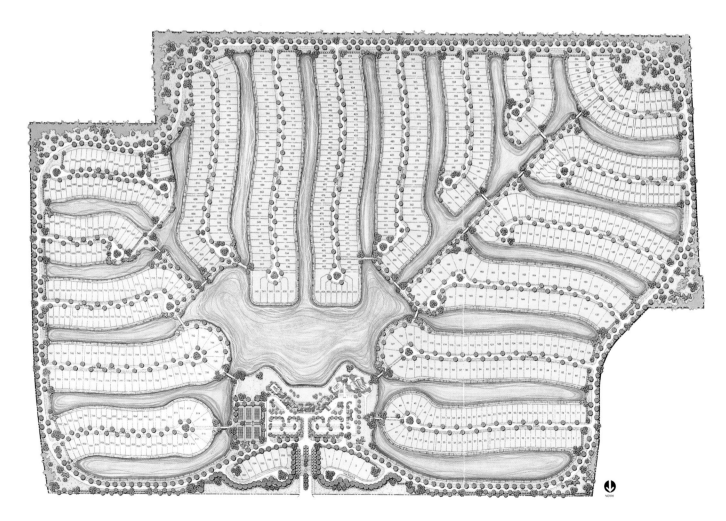

If they wish to retain the businesses in the town center, residents need to understand that they should not consider the leases a potential source of profit for the community.

Important keys to DiVosta's success in Village Walk were the company's keep-it-simple philosophy, which minimizes confusion and opportunities for mistakes at every stage of the process, and management systems that are designed for maximum efficiency and quality control. According to Rosen, "homes are finished properly at the base price," which makes it less confusing for the buyer and less complicated for the construction people. A standardized product and the strict and systematic control of all aspects of the building process are the hallmarks of DiVosta's highly successful approach.

PROJECT DATA

Land Use

Site area	335 acres
Town center (including retail space)	22,000 square feet
Number of single-family units	850
Gross density	2.5 units/acre

Residential Unit Information

Unit type	Lot size	Unit size (square feet)	Price range
Single-family units			
Glenwood	50' x 130'	2,000	$150,000–$200,000
Oakmont	60' x 130'	2,500	$200,000–$250,000
Windsor	60' x 130'	3,300	$200,000–$250,000
Two-family units			
Capri	38' x 130'	1,500	$119,000–$150,000

Development Schedule

Site purchased	September 1993
Site work started	June 1994
Project completed	September 1998

Developer

DiVosta and Company, Inc.

4500 PGA Boulevard, Suite 400

Palm Beach Gardens, Florida 33418

(516) 627-2112

Project Address

Vanderbilt Beach Road at Interstate 75

Naples, Florida 34119

Contact Information

Tom Harvey, regional president, Pulte Home Corporation

(561) 622-7516

Date of site visit: December 20, 1999

All project data are current as of January 2000.

Report author: Diane R. Suchma

141 – 158

Dee Why Gardens Retirement Village

Dee Why, New South Wales, Australia

Located on nine level acres in Dee Why, a suburb of Sydney, New South Wales, Australia, near beaches, shops, and public transportation, Dee Why Gardens Retirement Village is a leasehold development of 202 attached residences offering a leisure-oriented lifestyle to people over age 55. Like other retirement villages in Australia, the development also includes fully serviced units, which correspond to what in the United States is called "assisted living"—so that, if needed, residents can move to a more care-oriented environment within the development. Dee Why Gardens also includes a clubhouse, a swimming pool and other outdoor recreational facilities, extensive walkways, and numerous activities and services.

Dee Why Gardens was initially developed by Balino Constructions, a family company. The partly completed village was acquired in 1996 by Dee Why Gardens Partnership (DWGP). DWGP is a group of 20 investors whose goals in undertaking the project were to meet the identified housing needs of the older population

Richly landscaped walkways and roof-shaded pavilions mark the entrances to the apartments at Dee Why Gardens. Benches provide opportunities to gather and talk.

Water features, decorative pavers, and land-scaping enhance the walkways within the community and complement the brick-and-wood construction.

and, at the same time, to achieve an attractive long-term financial return. This community is the partnership's first active adult real estate development. With its architect, the partnership worked jointly to handle the design and construction of the continuing stages of Dee Why Gardens. Twibill Architects, which merged with dem design pty ltd. in 1996, specializes in residential design for older people.

Dee Why Gardens is located in the state of New South Wales, on the northern beaches of the state capital, Sydney. The site, in a residential neighborhood just a short distance from Dee Why Beach, is also near Warringah Mall, a major suburban shopping center. The village is located on a major public transportation route that leads both to a local ferry wharf at Manly and to Sydney's central business district. A 30-acre landscaped public nature preserve adjoins one side of the property. The development is across the street from Cromer Community Center and just down the road from the Dee Why Bowling Club and Cromer Golf Course.

The partly completed village purchased by DWGP consisted of 112 units, 37 fully serviced apartments, a village center, and an approved development application for 78 new units. When it purchased the development in 1996, DWGP maintained the original approach for the external design of the village but modified the unit mix and adopted minor internal layout changes in response to market demand. New residents were absorbed into the existing village structure.

The partners provided cash and bank guarantees to obtain a bank loan to fund the initial acquisition and complete the construction that was in process at the time of purchase. The remaining phases of construction were funded internally, with profits from the sales of residential units. Working capital was provided from the resale of leases when existing units became vacant. (On resale, the lease contract entitled the partnership to a deferred management fee and an equal share, with the homeowner who resold the lease, of the capital gain.)

The overall village design features clusters of residential units distributed throughout the site. To encourage residents to socialize informally, the residential clusters open onto courtyards that are connected by pedestrian walkways leading to the village center. A ring road defines the site's perimeter and provides automobile access to the homes. Parking is provided in clusters of garages, carports, and open spaces throughout the village. Garages are an additional cost and the subject of a separate lease, independent of the lease of the unit.

Clustering the units not only created intimate groupings of homes but also enabled the developer to stage construction over a number of years. DWGP is building the community in seven stages, with between 22 and 46 units in each stage. The clubhouse was built during Phase II. As of December 1999, construction had begun on Phase VII. The staged construction has enabled DWGP to adjust the unit mix, size, and design, as well as the timing of construction, to respond to changes in market demand.

The project required two development applications and seven building applications, one for each stage of construction. State laws encouraging the provision of housing for the elderly were used to determine design criteria such as building heights and unit densities. There were no environmental, infrastructure, or utility issues. However, because construction occurred over a long period of time, changes in building regulations—especially with respect to fire protection—created challenges. Fire-grade window screens (rather external sprinklers) were used to address new fire protection requirements.

To avoid the appearance of economic hierarchy among residents, all the units' exteriors are visually consistent and of the same quality. All units have concrete floors, double brick walls with timber panels and windows, and balconies or ground-level terraces. Roofs are concrete tile on timber trusses.

The residential units are grouped in clusters of 12 to 14 units. These clusters consist of groups of hexagonal forms joined around a common courtyard. The grouping of hexagons allows a variety of internal plan designs within the exterior envelope. For instance, two hexagons joined together can provide a range of units—either four two-bedroom apartments or two two-bedroom apartments plus one three-bedroom apartment. Because it creates splayed walls, the

unique hexagonal plan allows a greater variety of orientations and opens living areas out to a wider view than would be possible with a conventional rectangular design.

The hexagonal modules are joined in an irregular pattern to create buildings that vary in height from one to two stories. Generally, however, the buildings are two stories high, with staircase access to each group of two upper-level apartments. Single-story modules are used to vary scale, admit light into courtyards, and provide more variety in the mix of floor plans (one hexagonal module can be divided into three one-bedroom apartments).

Units consist of a combined lounge and dining room, a separate kitchen, a bathroom connected to the main bedroom, an additional bedroom or bedrooms, and a balcony or terrace. Units range in size from 585 square feet for one-bedroom units to 1,032 square feet for units with two bedrooms plus a den. Units are designed so that the second or third bedroom is a multipurpose room adjoining the lounge area. Moving a sliding wall combines these two areas into one larger space.

Because the clubhouse design is based on a series of interconnected hexagons, a series of separate spaces off the main lounge area are available for a variety of uses. For special events

Abundant natural light, exposed wood, and plants bring the outside in and give an open, airy feel to the community center.

such as Christmas, sliding walls allow these separate areas to be joined with the main lounge to create one large space. Large timber joists, high ceilings, and glassed-in roof areas bring light and space into the central area as well as into adjoining rooms.

Within the clubhouse, residents can enjoy sunrooms, tea and coffee facilities, billiards, a crafts room, and a library with a fireplace. A kiosk operated by community residents sells convenience items. On-site services include catering (meals), laundry, dry cleaning, and security. The community is partly fenced but is not gated. In the evening, security guards are present on site.

Outdoor amenities include a heated pool, a spa, barbecue facilities, walkways, a putting green, lawn bowling, and croquet. Tennis courts are located adjacent to the site. Because cars are restricted to the perimeter of the site, the development is interlaced with walkways, gardens, and sunny courtyards.

Various service providers visit the community on a regular basis, including a hairdresser, a podiatrist, and a beautician. Doctors and other medical specialists come to the community as needed, and the community offers a variety of personal services—such as cleaning, laundry, and repair services—on a fee basis. For short-term assistance when they are ill, residents have access

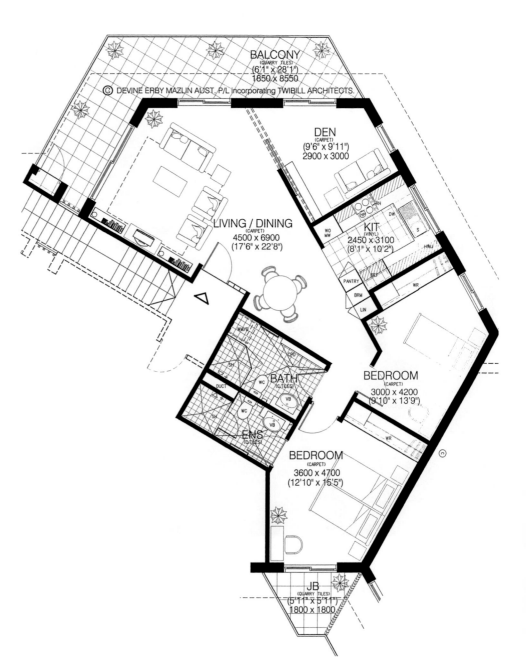

BALCONY
(QUARRY TILES)
(6'1" x 28'1")
1850 x 8550

© DEVINE ERBY MAZLIN AUST. P/L incorporating TWIBILL ARCHITECTS.

DEN
(CARPET)
(9'6" x 9'11")
2900 x 3000

LIVING / DINING
(CARPET)
4500 x 6900
(17'6" x 22'8")

KIT
(VINYL)
2450 x 3100
(8'1" x 10'2")

PANTRY

BATH
(C.TILES)

BEDROOM
(CARPET)
3000 x 4200
(9'10" x 13'9")

ENS
(C.TILES)

BEDROOM
(CARPET)
3600 x 4700
(12'10" x 15'5")

JB
(QUARRY TILES)
(5'11" x 5'11")
1800 x 1800

The unusual building configuration creates opportunities for both large and small apartments.

to fully serviced respite apartments for an additional rate, subject to availability. A village bus as well as a local public bus transports residents to nearby destinations.

The current owners have continued the leasehold method of the original developer, and no changes were made to existing lease agreements. Because Dee Why is a leasehold community, the sale of residential units (and the management structure) must meet the legal requirements of the New South Wales Retirement Villages Act. Buyers purchase the leasehold title for 99 years, beginning on the day of possession of the unit. The lease is registered in the purchaser's name at the State Government Land Titles Office, and the resident is free to resell the lease at any time. The leasehold title is terminated upon the sale of the unit, and the incoming buyer obtains a new, 99-year lease. The conditions of the lease are binding on the residents and the

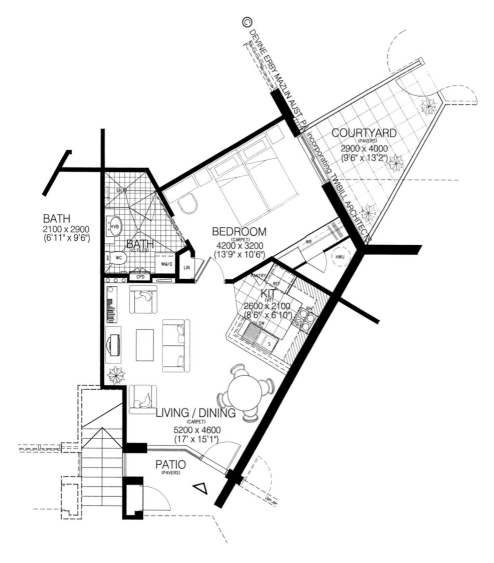

new owner of the development. At the time that they sell their units, sellers pay a deferred entry fee of 2.5 percent per year for the first ten years and 1 percent per year thereafter on the purchase price of the unit.

The land and buildings are owned by the partnership. Council and water rates are levied on the site by the local government authorities, and the management company passes on the charges to residents on a pro-rata basis.

Unit sales began in 1986. The partnership maintains a permanent sales staff, which averages two resales per month. As of December 1999, 166 units had been sold. (Because of a downturn in the general residential market in the mid-1990s, houses were difficult to sell. Demand fell for units in the village and there were no new sales in this period. This was a contributing factor in the decision of the original developer to sell the village.) Current prices average A$275,000. (A$ denotes Australian dollars.)

DWGP does its own marketing. Leads are generally obtained via word of mouth and from responses to advertisements in local newspapers and other media. The project is marketed to residents of the local community, where the partnership has identified a likely market of aging middle-class people. The primary marketing challenge is to match the timing of product delivery with demand—a challenge that is met, in part, through the staging of development.

The development's main competition is a village located on a hill, further inland, which has focused on providing larger two- and three-bedroom units. By contrast, DWGP offers a wider range of units; a location closer to shops, transportation, and beaches; and a level site.

The management structure for Dee Why Gardens consists of two companies, a development company and a management company. The development company is the project owner—DWGP— which is headed by a managing partner and a general manager. DWGP is responsible for the new (unsold) portions of the development, for refurbishing the existing buildings (including units at the time of resale), and for marketing the village. The management company is appointed by the project owner. Because the owner is responsible for ensuring that the village is operated in accordance with state law, the general manager of DWGP has direct supervision of the management company. At this point, the general manager of Dee Why Gardens is also the general manager of DWGP.

The day-to-day administration and operation of the village is handled by the management company and funded by the residents' monthly fees. Monthly levies are based on the size of the unit and average A$310. The levies cover all unit maintenance and repairs, landscaping, and community administration. Homeowners are responsible for the upkeep of the units' interiors and must maintain a comprehensive householder's insurance policy that includes a minimum A$5 million public liability.

The community retains an activities director who publishes a monthly newsletter and organizes social functions and tours, theater trips, and other outings. Residents play an advisory role in the governance of the community through a residents' committee; they also organize social clubs and activities. A great many social activities are available to suit a variety of tastes

The community's design is distinctive but blends well with its surroundings. This design, coupled with walkways that weave among the buildings, creates a dense but intimate effect.

dem design pty ltd

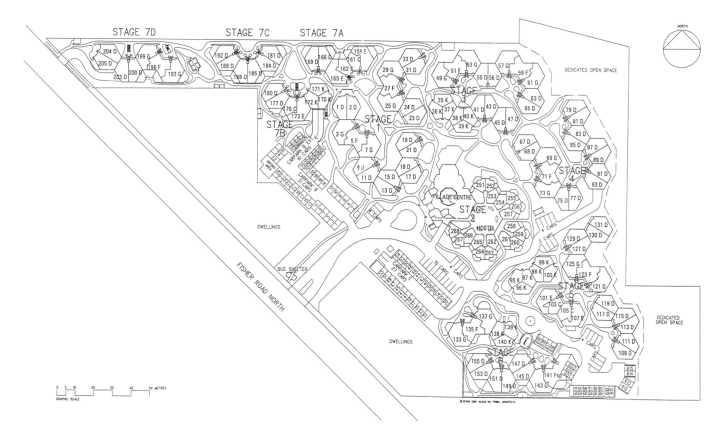

Site plan.

and interests—including, for example, participation in the Dee Why Gardens Choir, "aquarobics" classes, bingo, lectures, and special events.

Both fully serviced apartments and self-care units have the same standard lease, with similar conditions. For fully serviced apartments, the standard lease is extended to provide services such as catering, cleaning, and laundry. There is no formal structure in place to give current residents of self-care units preference in obtaining serviced apartments.

According to the developer, Dee Why Gardens differs from a non-age-restricted community in that both the community and the homes are designed to accommodate older people through a number of means, such as wheelchair-friendly site gradients and entrances, more stringent fire-safety standards, monitoring and emergency call systems, the village bus, the clustering of homes within the community, and the inclusion of elevators and of units designed for disabled persons.

Over time, DWGP has observed changes in market demand for finishes and technology, such as bathrooms connected to main bedrooms and granite countertops and European appliances in kitchens. In general, recent buyers prefer larger apartments, and demand for covered parking spaces and additional parking spaces has increased. DWGP expects the demand for retirement housing to grow as the population ages and the supply of developable land on Sydney's northern beaches diminishes.

As a result of its experience with Dee Why Gardens, DWGP has learned that it is essential to understand the long-term nature of the industry. The owner receives financial returns from two sources: (1) development profits and (2) lease entitlements (such as the deferred management fee) on resales. Because resales occur over time, the returns they generate require an ongoing commitment to the project on the part of the owner. Thus, it is important to assemble a top-notch management team and to identify clearly the targeted segment of the market, in order to ensure that the buildings and units are designed to suit that group.

The partnership plans to develop other active adult retirement communities because market demand is strong and the projects are financially attractive. However, future developments will not include fully serviced apartments or on-site meal services. The actual demand for these services is diminishing; and in recent years, the advent of off-site care and service providers makes possible more flexible and less expensive arrangements that allow any of the units to obtain the desired level of services.

PROJECT DATA

Land Use

Site area	9 acres
Residential buildings	3.5 acres
Open space and outdoor amenities	4.7 acres
Streets and parking	0.8 acres
Number of attached multifamily units	202
Gross density	22.4 units/acre
Number of off-street parking spaces	174

Multifamily Unit Information

Unit type	Unit size (square feet)	Number of units (planned/built)	Price range
1 bedroom	585	18/18	A$220,000–A$235,000
1 bedroom + den	775	124/104	A$260,000–A$275,000
2 bedroom	971	25/16	A$350,000–A$375,000
2 bedroom + den	1,032	35/28	A$350,000–A$375,000

Development Cost Information

Site acquisition cost	A$ 4,200,000
Hard costs (the insured value of the development)	A$24,200,000
Soft costs (estimated)	A$ 2,500,000
Total development costs (estimated)	A$30,900,000

Development Schedule

Site purchased	1986							
Planning started	January 1985							
Site work started	May 1986							
Project completion	2001 (estimated)							

Phase	I	II	III	IV	V	VI	VII-a	VII-b
Number of units	34	7	25	27	36	26	11	36 (planned)
Planning started	1984	1984	1984	1984	1984	1997	1998	1998
Construction started	1986	1987	11/87	7/88	5/89	12/96	3/99	
Construction completed	5/87	6/88	11/88	6/89	12/95	11/97	11/99	
Sales started	5/87	6/88	11/88	6/89	10/89	5/96	1/99	
Sales completed	6/88	6/89	1/89	3/91	5/97	4/98	11/99	

Development Team

Developer

Dee Why Gardens
  Partnership
155 Fisher Road North,
Dee Why, New South Wales
Australia
02 9971 8255

**Land Planner
and Architect**

Twibill Architects/dem
  design pty ltd.
Sydney
New South Wales 2603
Australia
02 8966 6000

Project Address

155 Fisher Road North
Dee Why, New South Wales 2099
Australia

Contact Information

Peter Reid
02 9971 8255

All project data are current as of December 1999.
Report authors: Ian Buckberry and Diane R. Suchman

Heritage in the Hills

Detroit, Michigan

Heritage in the Hills is US Home Corporation's premier effort to tap the growing market for smaller active adult communities in non-traditional retirement locations by building in partnership with local builders. A gated, amenity-rich community of 281 homes, the development offers active adults a secure, sociable, maintenance-free lifestyle in a location near family, friends, and other longtime ties.

Heritage in the Hills, the first age-restricted community in the state of Michigan, is a 50-50 joint venture between US Home Corporation and The Silverman Companies, of Farmington Hills, Michigan. US Home, based in Houston, Texas, is a publicly traded homebuilding company active in more than 190 communities in 31 metropolitan areas. Founded in 1954, it is one of the country's largest homebuilders and developers of active adult communities. The company has built more than 45,000 homes in active adult and second-home communities, primarily in traditional retirement areas. The Silverman Companies, founded in 1919, builds fine residential

Designed as a welcoming gathering place, the Heritage Hills Country Club includes an entrance lobby, a large, warmly furnished multipurpose room that can accommodate either large or small gatherings, a kitchen, a fitness facility, a room for billiards and cards, a library, offices, and space for arts and crafts.

homes, apartments, and condominiums throughout the Midwest. At the time the companies entered into the joint venture, The Silverman Companies was a family-owned company; it has since been acquired by Toll Brothers.

Responsibilities divide generally as follows: US Home provides the project concept; undertakes general management of the development; does the land planning; develops the marketing concept and provides marketing expertise; designs the product, including the floor plans for homes and the copyrighted clubhouse design; and devises the structure and management of the homeowners' association. Silverman handles land development, construction, sales, and customer service. Each partner shares equally in fees, profits, equity participation, and risk.

US Home initiated its Builders' Joint Venture Program for Active Adult Communities in 1998 to develop small (meaning approximately 250 to 300 units) active adult communities in metropolitan areas that were not traditionally considered retirement destinations. The focus on close-to-home locations arose from the company's extensive surveys and focus group research, which found that only 4.5 percent of retirees move to another city, while 11.5 percent move to a different home within their local area.

Investment considerations helped determine the size (and, to some extent, the location) of the joint-venture prototype community. A golf course was not included because research had also shown that only 15 percent of prospective buyers will reject a community that does not offer golf. According to Jim Migliore, president of US Home's Special Projects Division, "The equity investment in a large golf course community is many millions of dollars, and with a small prototype, we could enter a new market at a lower level of investment and of risk."

Once it had determined the development's approximate size and selected its amenities, the company decided where to locate joint-venture communities on the basis of three factors: the size of the area's qualified population, the existence of an interested and qualified local partner, and land availability and cost. The company decided to partner with local builders because they have the necessary knowledge of and reputation in the local market, an existing organizational structure, existing relationships with public entities, and subcontractor bases.

Though US Home has been developing active adult communities of various sizes for more than 30 years, Heritage in the Hills is the first development created under the national joint-venture program. A second US Home joint-venture development, Heritage Pines, is underway in Cary, North Carolina. The company is exploring possibilities for expanding this prototype in the Detroit market as well as other markets, including Atlanta, Pittsburgh, Raleigh, and St. Louis.

The Detroit metropolitan area was selected for the initial joint-venture development because it contains more than 5 million people, of whom 1.5 million are over age 50. Within the Detroit area, the developer looked at ten sites before selecting the project location. The chosen site is in Auburn Hills, a rapidly growing residential area that enjoys convenient access to major roads, including Interstate 75. The property is near existing middle- and upper-income communi-

As can be seen in this streetscape, the features of the exterior home design, such as roof and porch treatments, reflect local design traditions.

ties, shopping, health care facilities, dining, entertainment, and cultural attractions. Downtown Rochester, which has a traditional "Main Street" with upscale boutiques and restaurants, is a short drive away. Nearby Meadowbrook Hall, the Pine Knob Music Theater, and the Palace of Auburn Hills Civic Center and Park offer performing arts and sports events. Outdoor recreational facilities—golf courses, ski resorts, parks, and lakes—are all close at hand.

Although the selected site was attractively wooded and of appropriate size, the property had been passed over by other residential developers because, despite its otherwise excellent location, it fell within the boundaries of an undesirable school district. Because schools are not an issue for older adults, the site represented an excellent opportunity for the development of an age-restricted community.

The development consists of a spine road that winds through the property and connects a series of "villages" of approximately 35 homes each. Near the center of the site, easily accessibly from all the homes, is the recreation complex. Nestled among the villages is a stormwater drainage pond that also serves as an attractive visual amenity. Seventy-five of the site's 154 acres will be preserved for trails, trees, and other natural common areas.

Because demand analysis indicated that sales would likely total 60 to 75 per year, the community is being built in five phases. The project is now in the third phase of development. Comerica provided acquisition, development, and construction financing.

Six models are offered, ranging from a 1,417-square-foot two-bedroom ranch home to a 2,240-square-foot four-bedroom, two-story model. Most are ranch homes with three bedrooms. Lots are 52 to 55 feet wide and 120 to 160 feet deep.

The most popular model, the Hartwick, features 1,676 square feet of living space with three bedrooms and two baths. The largest and next-most-popular model, the Mackinaw, is 2,240 square feet: on the first floor are an owners' suite, a "leisure room," a living room, a dining room, and two and one-half baths; upstairs are two bedrooms, a bath, a hobby (or storage) room, and a loft area that could be used, for example, as an office.

All homes include front porches, two-car garages with remote openers, nine-foot ceilings, carpeting, a range, a dishwasher, a garbage disposal, and air conditioning. Because buyers' preferences in washers, dryers, and refrigerators differ so widely, these appliances are not included. The developer offers a number of options but discourages customization because, as Deborah Bokano, Silverman/US Home marketing representative, explained, "that would require too much manpower." Among the options offered are a "retreat," or sitting room, in the owners' suite as an alternative to an additional bedroom; a spa bath in the owners' suite; bay windows; hardwood or ceramic tile flooring; a deck; laundry-room cabinets; and, the most popular option, a fireplace. Basements were initially offered as an option, but demand for that option was so great that all homes built in designated sections of the development site now include lower levels in their base price. Homes without basements offer extra storage areas. Base home prices in December 1999 ranged from $203,990–$250,990. Construction costs average $60 per square foot.

To meet the needs of older purchasers, homes feature large windows to maximize natural light; lower light switches; raised electrical outlets; wheelchair-accessible, 30-inch-wide doors; grab bars in showers and tubs; and lever handles on faucets.

The community is gated (but not fenced), secure, and private. Recreational facilities include a 7,000 square-foot clubhouse (the Heritage Hills Country Club), a heated outdoor swimming pool and whirlpool, two tennis courts, and bocce courts. Indoors, the clubhouse features a large, multi-purpose social hall furnished with a fireplace and comfortable, homelike seating arrangements; an arts and crafts room; a fitness center; a cards and billiards room; a library and computer room; and a catering kitchen. The fitness center is the most popular amenity. Residents can use the clubhouse 24 hours a day, entering with a magnetic passkey that records their identity on a computer.

Though the development opened for lot reservations in June of 1998 and the clubhouse was completed in October, it was not difficult to sell homes before the clubhouse was in place. The first 25 residents bought from plans at preconstruction prices. Model homes were opened in February of 1999 on a parcel adjacent to the recreation complex. Since the first homes were sold, prices have risen by between $30,000 and $40,000 per home. As of December 1999, the developer had sold a total of 105 homes.

As noted earlier, US Home handles the overall project marketing theme and programs. The primary marketing vehicles include direct mail (which relies on purchased lists); print advertisements in newspapers and magazines targeted to older adults; the company's Web site; and radio ads. Emphasizing the new-found freedom that can be associated with child-free and retirement living, US Home's advertising theme for all its active adult communities is "Now the fun begins!"

The developer also sponsors events to attract people to the community. One such event was the project's opening celebration for people who had responded to a marketing survey. As a result of the celebration, which was held under a huge tent and included entertainment and prizes, 44 homes were reserved. When the clubhouse opened, the developer hosted another party, inviting not only residents of Heritage in the Hills but everyone who had ever visited the community.

Many residents have come from the Rochester Hills and Bloomfield Hills areas of suburban Detroit. A number have also come from Troy. According to Bokano, between 40 and 50 percent of the buyers at Heritage in the Hills are seasonal residents who spend part of the year in warm-weather locations such as Florida, although a number have moved back to the area from Florida. Seasonal buyers are especially attracted to the community's maintenance and security features.

Half the buyers pay cash; those who do not obtain very small mortgages. Bokano estimates that buyers' gross annual incomes range between $75,000 and $100,000.

The community is age-restricted, and approximately 60 percent of the residents are between 55 and 65 years of age. The Fair Housing Act requires that 80 percent of the units be

The two-level Mackinac model (floor plan, facing page) offers flexible living space, ample storage space, a front porch, and a two-car garage.

occupied by at least one person who is age 55 or over. The developer allows 10 percent of the units in any given phase to be occupied by persons who are between 50 and 55 years of age. Most buyers, however, have tended to come from the younger end of the allowable age range. According to Bokano, a number of people in the 45-to-50 age range have also expressed interest in the community. About 10 percent of the buyers are single women.

The primary reason that people move to Heritage in the Hills is for the lifestyle it offers rather than for a specific home design or product. However, most buyers are downsizing from a larger single-family home. The developers have found that prospective buyers will accept a second floor or half-floor, but the owners' suite must be on the first floor. Though Michigan homes typically include a basement, it has not been difficult to sell homes without lower levels.

Community management is effected through a two-tiered set of homeowners' associations. At the time of closing, buyers pay a one-time, $500 capital contribution to the homeowners' association. Homeowners' current monthly fee is $132 per month. Of the $132, $55 is for the neighborhood association, which handles lawn-mowing on individual lots, snow removal from driveways and lots, and trash pick-up. The remaining $77 is for the master association, which pays for the maintenance of the clubhouse, recreational amenities, and common areas; the salary of the social director; and community security. The developer now controls and contributes to the master association. Control of the homeowners' association will revert to the homeowners at a future date.

A full-time social director facilitates residents' clubs and activities. The director schedules activities in the clubhouse, organizes monthly lunches, publishes the community newsletter, surveys buyers regarding their interests, organizes shopping and theater outings, and, for now, plans social activities and programs. As more residents move into the community, it is anticipated that they will take more initiative in creating social programs. The community maintains a private bus to transport residents to nearby destinations. In the near future, Lisa Wilkes, the

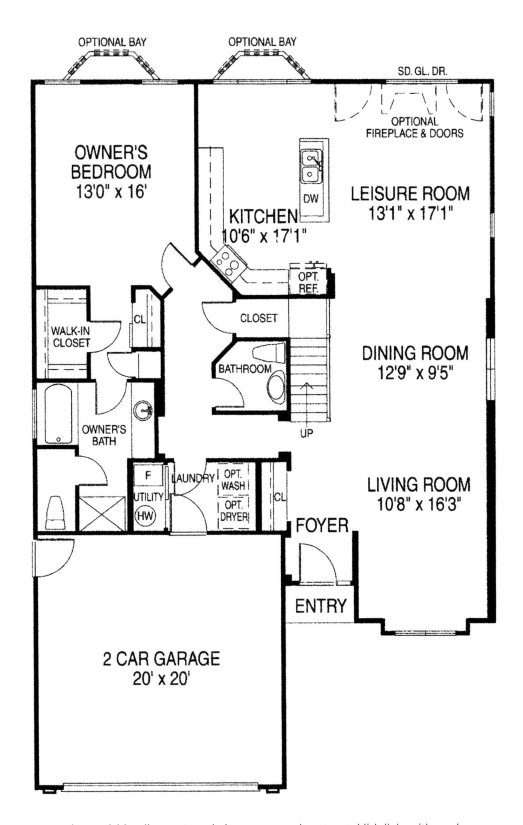

OPTIONAL BAY

OPTIONAL BAY

SD. GL. DR.

OPTIONAL
FIREPLACE & DOORS

OWNER'S
BEDROOM
13'0" x 16'

KITCHEN
10'6" x 17'1"

DW

LEISURE ROOM
13'1" x 17'1"

OPT.
REF.

CLOSET

CL

WALK-IN
CLOSET

BATHROOM

DINING ROOM
12'9" x 9'5"

OWNER'S
BATH

UP

F

UTILITY

HW

LAUNDRY

OPT.
WASH

OPT.
DRYER

CL

LIVING ROOM
10'8" x 16'3"

FOYER

ENTRY

2 CAR GARAGE
20' x 20'

community's activities director/association manager, plans to establish links with nearby

Oakland Community College and to hire a part-time physical trainer to conduct aerobics classes.

Heritage in the Hills successfully tapped the local pent-up demand for an adult lifestyle

community. According to Migliore, the project has no real competition in the Detroit area because no other development offers a similar lifestyle—with security, recreational facilities, and opportunities to socialize. "We were right on target with the concept," he commented, noting that market research was crucial to achieving the appropriate product design. No radical changes in the development concept are planned for future joint-venture communities, though there will be minor adjustments to accommodate differences in regional tastes and living patterns.

PROJECT DATA

Land Use

Site area	154 acres
Clubhouse and other common buildings	7,000 square feet
Open space and outdoor amenities	75 acres
Number of single-family detached units	281
Gross density	1.8 units/acre

Single-Family Unit Information

Unit type	Lot size (acres)	Unit size (square feet)	Price range
Charlevoix	1/6	1,417	$203,990–$223,990
Greenfield	1/6	1,513	$210,990–$230,990
Leelanau	1/6	1,525	$230,990–$263,990
Hartwick	1/6	1,676	$223,990–$243,990
Huron	1/6	1,798	$230,990–$250,990

Development Schedule

Site purchased	January 1998	Site work started	June 1998
Planning started	February 1997	Project completion	2001 (estimated)

	Phase I	Phase II	Phase III
Number of units	87	52	33
Planning started	6/97	6/97	6/97
Construction started	6/98	8/99	9/99
Construction completed	1/99	11/99	12/99
Sales started	7/98	10/99	10/99
First closing	5/99	–	–
Sales completed (estimated)	3/00	6/00	6/00

Future phases (expected dates)	Phase IV	Phase V
Number of units	56	53
Planning started	June 1997	June 1997
Construction started	September 2000	May 2001
Construction completed	December 2000	September 2001
Sales started	July 2000	March 2001
Sales completed	December 2000	December 2001

Development Team

Developer
Heritage of Auburn Hills,
   LLC
30840 Northwestern Hwy.
Farmington Hills, Michigan
(248) 932-4300

Land Planner
Robert Leighton Associates
Ann Arbor, Michigan
(313) 996-9600

Architect
Timothy D. Ollano
Chagrin Falls, Ontario
Canada
(440) 247-3675

Project Address

3837 Springwood Court
Auburn Hills, Michigan 48326

Contact Information

Lynn Philips, sales manager, or Deborah Bokano, marketing representative
(248) 375-1100

Date of site visit: December 13, 1999
All project data are current as of December 13, 1999.

Report author: Diane R. Suchman

8

Trends

William E. Becker, Managing Director/President,

The William E. Becker Organization, Teaneck, New Jersey

Through most of the first decade of the 21st century, developers of active adult retirement communities (AARCs) will experience continuous changes in buyers' desires, preferences, and choice of living environments. While the majority of the buyers in the active adult market will still be in their early to mid-60s, they will have an increasingly youthful outlook and will be seeking a fully active lifestyle. This shift will put greater emphasis on more participatory outdoor activities; on education; and on cultural, social, and volunteer interests. In addition, it will affect technology for the home, including intranet communication.

A number of factors will affect trends in the design of AARC developments. The average life span of an American is now close to 80 years, and the attitudes of active adults stem from what they have been doing for the past ten to 20 years—not when they were growing up, but during the years that they were working and raising their families. They want most of the "adult toys" (such as

Group exercises in the swimming pool are popular.

boats and computers) that they "grew up with" in their working years. Many of these buyers will not retire as their parents did but will continue working from their new home in an AARC. The rapid rise of home offices, flexible working conditions, and computer technology—as well as changes in clubhouse activities, on-site amenities, and land planning—will force a shift in the interior layouts of home design for mature households.

Preservation of the natural environment is a priority at Bonita Bay, in Florida, where carefully orchestrated and scientifically sound water-flows provide scenic views and support thriving populations of birds, fish, otters, and other native fauna for all residents to enjoy.

The concept of an age-restricted community development has completely changed. Even *retirement*—the "R" word—is rarely used because it does not reflect the developer's real focus in creating communities for active adults. Given the findings of market research on the needs and preferences of mature consumers, developers must seek to create a community of substance that will meet the demands and desires of active adults for at least ten to 20 years. Today's active adults and tomorrow's aging baby boomers will not sacrifice quality in the home, change their lifestyles, or revert to the way that their parents or former generations lived.

The pool of prospective purchasers of homes in AARCs has become virtually multigenerational: the average age at purchase decreases each year. And, as purchasers get younger, the 1990s clubhouse that emphasized more "passive" activities such as arts and crafts, card rooms, and libraries will be replaced by luxury amenities: full-service health clubs with spa facilities, cafés and restaurants, "Wall Street" rooms, conference and business centers, and concierge services—in addition to the obligatory fitness centers and swimming pools.

MASTER-PLANNED COMMUNITIES AND NICHE DEVELOPMENT

Many existing master-planned communities include large-scale recreational facilities that cater to all ages, including active adults. Beginning in the 1980s, developers began to create "small niche" communities of between 200 and 300 dwelling units for active adults within multigenerational master-planned communities. Because the recreational facilities and a lifestyle environment are already in place in these communities, this is a smart way for AARC developers to broaden their market share without having to make a heavy initial investment in community facilities.

Furthermore, because mature buyers pay cash for their homes, purchase custom options, and have high net worth, this strategy gives builders and developers the opportunity to upgrade their housing products. At the same time, they can tap into the increasing market demand for active adult environments close to where children and grandchildren live—especially if those children and grandchildren now live within the same master-planned communities.

Within large master-planned communities, AARCs will feature an increasing array of product types. Previously, most AARC housing products were detached, single-family homes; a few were attached products, typically duplexes. In the coming years, however, three to four product lines will become the norm, and choices will include not only ranch-style homes but also multi-family homes in low-rise and mid-rise buildings. In addition, more than one builder will likely be active in an AARC as developers expand their offerings to include a variety of lifestyles.

AMENITIES

As prices escalate above $200,000 in many of the resort, Sunbelt, and metropolitan marketplaces, the amenity package will also grow. Country-club amenities—golf and tennis facilities, fitness centers, and indoor-outdoor pools—are now becoming standard in AARCs; in addition, developers are starting to include other facilities in their clubhouses and community centers—indoor, elevated walking tracks in two-story buildings; concierge services; spas; conference and business centers; airport limousine service; and tie-ins with hospitals or health facilities. LeRoy Hanneman Jr., president and chief executive officer of Del Webb Corporation, points out that his firm's clubhouses will feature "a pure health spa environment," with massage therapy, mud baths, facials, and hair salons, as well as services such as wellness programs.

In smaller communities, a few developers are working with outside providers to operate and manage specific recreational facilities such as fitness centers. The days of using a property management or an association management company to manage community activities are fast disappearing as developers turn to professionals to run more efficient recreational, cultural, and educational programs for residents.

The design of clubhouses is also changing. As Art Danielian, president of Danielian Associates, in Irvine, California, explains, developers used to build several small clubhouses, phasing them in as they built successive neighborhoods of homes. Now the trend is to build one large clubhouse, which enables developers to provide a critical mass of activity. "In a phased development, the 'one large clubhouse' might be actually built in phases or consist of a number of small buildings, clustered together or constructed on either side of a 'Main Street' to tap into buyers' nostalgia for small-town life."

NATIONAL BRAND NAMES

In the years 2007 through 2009 and beyond, as the active adult and early retirement market broadens and starts to cater to the aging baby boomers, both public and private companies that undertake AARC development will continue to establish brand names along the lines of Del Webb's Sun City, US Home's Greenbriar and Heritage products, Pulte's Traditions, and—soon—Sunrise Colony's Siena communities. In addition, the recent merger of US Home and Lennar Homes reflects and reinforces a growing trend toward consolidation, as the developers of large, master-planned communities attempt to capture a share of the 21st century's largest residential market. Acquisitions are also likely to become more common as a means of increasing market share. For example, Pulte recently expanded its presence in the California housing market through the purchase of the Blackhawk/Nunn Communities and Presley's Sun Lakes.

EXPANSION INTO NEW MARKETS

Large private developers, whether or not they now confine their operations to one state or market, will compete with major public corporations by expanding into other areas where there is growth in demand. (For example, Robson Communities is extending operations from Arizona into Dallas, Texas, and Shea Communities, into California.) Increasingly, developers will move AARC operations beyond the Sunbelt states and will begin to develop communities in metropolitan areas where there are large concentrations of people in the targeted age cohort, such as Chicago, New York, Washington, D.C., and other large cities in the Southeast, Midwest, and Northwest. Small and mid-size markets will also share in the opportunity for growth. Examples of this phenomenon can be seen in builder-to-builder joint ventures, such as the US Home Joint Venture Program, and in the work of large public builders and developers who have undertaken similar programs, as Slenker Land Corporation and Centex Homes have in Ocean Pines, Maryland.

GROWTH IN DEMAND

With demand for AARCs currently outstripping supply, by 2005, active adult communities may be built not only in the largest 25 to 50 metropolitan statistical areas but also in many other locations—for example, in second-home and vacation areas, on large infill parcels, and in downtown redevelopment areas. Several developers have mentioned that younger baby boomers (those aged 45 to 54) are looking to purchase "initial second homes" in age-targeted AARCs for

use on weekends, with an eye toward using them as permanent retirement or semiretirement residences as they grow older. In the near future, the number of two-home households will increase as aging baby boomers with large discretionary incomes seek a year-round resort community to live in during the week and another home to escape to for weekends and vacations.

Del Webb and other developers who have ventured outside the Sunbelt into northern markets have done so in response to market surveys indicating that active adults prefer to spend their mature years in regions where they have established large social and professional infrastructures. This "staying put" trend affects community design, largely because AARCs in metropolitan markets tend to be smaller than those with a national draw.

Investors can check their stocks in the "Wall Street" room, in Prairie Lodge, the clubhouse of Sun City at Huntley, outside of Chicago.

CHANGES IN PRODUCT DEVELOPMENT

During the past four decades, as the target market for AARCs has shifted from fully retired households to a younger, semiretired market, the housing products have grown from small, cottage-type homes of 800 to 1,600 square feet to full-blown homes ranging in size from 1,200 to 3,500 square feet. Downsizing from the family home, which was common among active adults in the previous decade, is no longer occurring. Moreover, whereas a home of 1,600 square

Design centers such as this one, at SaddleBrooke, outside Tucson, offer active adult buyers an array of choices for the design and finish of their homes.

feet was once considered large, the average home is now 2,000 square feet or more, and many dwellings have lofts and basements.

Before 1997, few developers offered more than the standard two-bedroom, two-bath design with a two-car garage on a homesite of 4,500 to 6,000 square feet. Today, the standard lot size in many metropolitan markets (as well as in the Sunbelt) is approaching 5,500 to 7,000 square feet, with some new communities offering lots of 8,000 to 10,000 square feet.

Although conventional wisdom holds that most active adults prefer homes with all rooms on one level, a portion of the market will accept—or prefer—two-story homes or one-story homes with basements, largely because of the need to accommodate weekend guests (especially children and grandchildren), the increasing popularity of home offices, and the desire for hobby rooms or storage. Developers in major metropolitan markets outside the Sunbelt (such as Chicago or New Jersey) as well as in the southern states of Arizona, California, Florida, and Nevada, are adding space to homes by creating a "casita," or guest house, that is separate from the main home structure.

The trend toward entertaining at home and enjoying extended visits from family and friends has changed the layout of most homes and required increased living space. Formal dining rooms are giving way to great-rooms. Second bedrooms are not as important as larger kitchens, family rooms, master suites, solariums, and screened-in rear patios.

AARC buyers of today can be described as "healthy, wealthy, and financially stable households." They have reached a point in their lives where they want to live in relative luxury. More want to customize their homes today, and this trend will likely continue into the future—a circumstance that offers opportunities to add to builders' profits. While price sensitivity continues to exist in many areas, in other areas, where there is a particularly strong economy, many buyers

will "trade up," obtaining options, extras, and premium locations. In the higher price strata—above the $150,000 to $200,000 range—purchasers commonly add between $30,000 and $100,000 in options and premium locations to the base price of homes.

The architectural styles of AARC homes are also becoming more diverse. Not only are developers continuing to offer traditional home designs, but the current general interest in European design is being carried over to active adult communities. Today, French Country and Italian Renaissance themes can be seen in both neighborhood streetscapes and individual home designs.

In a new trend, some of the larger developers—including US Home and The Kokes Organization—are branching out into areas normally reserved for retail stores: they have attached to or included in the sales information center a design center where buyers can not only add optional or upgraded items to their homes but can also purchase furniture from national manufacturers based on what is in the model homes.

Active adult retirement communities are offering more sophisticated fitness facilities to appeal to their health-conscious market. The exercise room shown is in Winfield, in Scottsdale, Arizona.

TECHNOLOGY

Technology will have an increasing effect on the activities that AARC residents undertake in their community. The 25 to 35 percent of all buyers in AARCs who have computers or computer knowledge are creating a core group of computer-literate residents. In response to the needs and preferences of this group, many AARCs will offer an "intranet on-line" communication channel where residents can pull up information from a wide variety of sources as well as communicate with all types of service providers or organizations without leaving their home.

AARC clubhouses are also changing with the times. For example, as Bill Feinberg, president of Feinberg Associates, in Gibbsboro, New Jersey, explains, "A big feature in clubhouses today is

the 'Wall Street' room, where residents can do transactions on a fast-access computer with a tie-in to a broker. It's also a business center with a copier and other business machines. Five years ago, this was rare."

This age group's computer literacy and increasing interest in computers have made computer classes and computer clubs popular at AARCs. In fact, several companies—including Apple Computer, with its MAC 50 Club, and SHA-NAH, an intranet provider—are now looking seriously at expanding into providing technology services for active adult developments.

Technology is also creating new ways to market and sell homes. Already, most active adult communities have Web sites, and virtual walk-throughs of communities will become the norm. E-mail will make it easier for buyers to select, reserve, and purchase a home—including options, extras, and premium items—on the Internet. The future will bring a complete change in media as the Internet grows. Linkages among different Web service providers will provide access to new prospects through active adult databases.

Where technology will eventually lead the AARC industry is anyone's guess. "We are into a most exciting time, because we have no clue where the industry is going in technology and lifestyle changes that will result from technology," comments Ehud Mouchly, chief executive officer of READI, LLC, and REProjectCapital.com, in Santa Monica, California. "The production cycle is so long, we cannot react fast enough. Housing is a more certain element, because everyone will need a place to live, but everything else—how we will work, where we will shop, is all very fluid."

Clubhouse West at Leisure World of Virginia, in Lansdowne, Virginia, includes a convenience store with a take-out deli counter.

CHANGING MARKETING AND SALES PRACTICES

Because qualified prospects commonly take three to six visits—or more—to decide to move to an AARC, builders and developers who enter the active adult marketplace will need to look for a new breed of sales counselor. The members of this new breed will understand that making a sale to mature adults involves not only getting the order but also building the kind of relationship that will lead to heavy referrals.

The cost of creating an atmosphere that will encourage prospects to say "This is where I want to live" has gone up. Marketing and sales budgets that at one time were in the range of 5 to 6 percent of costs now often require upfront expense ratios of 8 to 10 percent in the first year.

The media mix—the types of communications media selected by advertising agencies and marketing professionals to market an AARC—needs to change. It must be more carefully targeted to appeal to the specific segments of the active adult market that a community seeks to attract. Active adult buyers are not homogeneous but highly segmented and diverse. Because different groups of active adults have different attitudes, needs, and preferences, different groups within this age cohort require different media approaches. Database management, a valuable marketing tool, can be used to segment the audiences and customize the media strategy. Adapting new, nontraditional media to buyers whose leisure time is valuable and who want a "lifestyle change" will separate successful communities from the "also-rans."

The sales information center will become more than a place to display the product. Borrowing from the worlds of retailing and entertainment, large communities will use theatrical presentation techniques designed to provoke a "Wow!" response—and to make prospects want to buy into the lifestyle immediately.

CONCLUSION

Observers expect the AARC business to account for between 20 and 30 percent of all housing by the year 2020. Builders and developers need to recognize that as the active adult marketplace grows from an embryonic market to a full-blown development industry, more and more firms will be attracted to this profitable area. As Michael Rubin, president of Avatar Retirement Communities, in Coral Gables, Florida, puts it, "Everyone wants to be in the business because of the compelling numbers." To stay successful, developers need to stay on the cutting edge by introducing new, consumer-tested "lifestyle living" to target audiences who want to see the lifestyle today—*now*—when they visit the community. Only those developers who create value and credibility will become and stay successful, attracting this new breed of buyers who are at a stage in their lives when they are more interested in a new and exciting lifestyle than in a new house. As Norman Dreyfuss, executive vice president of The IDI Group Companies, cautions, "Having a checklist just isn't sufficient: you have to have the sizzle."